THROUGH THE EYES OF REBEL WOMEN

THE YOUNG LORDS
1969-1976

Documentaries about the Young Lords

El Pueblo Se Levanta /The People Are Rising (Film 1970)
Produced by Newsreel

¡Palante, Siempre Palante! The Young Lords (Film 1996)
Iris Morales, Producer, Writer, and Codirector

Film Distributor: Third World Newsreel
www.twn.org

Palante: Voices and Photographs of the Young Lords, 1969-1971
Published by Haymarket Books

THROUGH THE EYES OF REBEL WOMEN

THE YOUNG LORDS
1969-1976

IRIS MORALES

Red Sugarcane Press, Inc.
New York, New York

Through the Eyes of Rebel Women: The Young Lords
Copyright © 2016 Iris Morales

Red Sugarcane Press, Inc.
534 West 112th Street #250404
New York, New York 10025
www.RedSugarcanePress.com

Interior Book Design: Iris Morales
Book Cover Design: Somos Arte, LLC
Art Director: Edgardo Miranda-Rodriguez
www.SomosArte.com

ISBN: 978-0-9968276-1-4
Library of Congress Control Number: 2016931163

First Edition
Printed in the United States of America

DEDICATION

For Almida Roldán Reices,
my mother and first teacher

DEDICACIÓN

Para Almida Roldán Reices,
mi mamá y primera maestra

CONTENTS

PREFACE

IN THE FALL OF 1969, the Young Lords, a group of young Puerto Rican activists, approached the pastor of the First Spanish Methodist Church located on 111th Street and Lexington Avenue to request use of its space to provide free breakfast to children in East Harlem, then one of New York City's poorest neighborhoods. He adamantly refused. The Young Lords returned, determined to speak directly to the congregation, but the reverend called the police to stop them. Eight men and five women were beaten and arrested. Three weeks later, a few days after Christmas, the activists returned. This time, they occupied the church and named it "the People's Church" igniting a public debate about the responsibility of institutions to their surrounding communities. For the next eleven days, thousands of people from all walks of life arrived at the church. They came to offer support, feed children a hot breakfast, receive free health checkups, and attend Puerto Rican history workshops. They arrived to enjoy communal dinners and poetry readings and to hear fiery speeches about justice and freedom. It was a moment of rebellion that sparked a generation.

Forty-five years later on July 26, 2014, people gathered in front of the People's Church for New York City's official street naming of "Young Lords Way." Former Young Lords from New York, Chicago, Philadelphia, Bridgeport, Newark, and Boston as well as hundreds of young and veteran activists, neighborhood residents, artists, poets, reporters, educators, politicians, and clergy assembled to acknowledge the contributions of the Young Lords and the Puerto Rican community. The street naming celebrated a peoples' history and honored the struggles of the Puerto Rican people for social, economic, and racial justice.

The tribute to the Young Lords also renewed interest in the women members. Women joined determined to fight poverty, racism, and inequality. About one-third of the members were women, although most accounts of the organization to date have focused on a few spokesmen ignoring the fact that this was a people's movement profoundly affected by feminist ideals, activism, and contributions. The diverse and powerful roles that women played have generally been ignored, marginalized, or presented in one-dimensional terms. Women's visibility in the historical record has been repeatedly diminished—or erased—not only in the Young Lords, but also in all the great social movements, even to the present day.

The first article about women in the Young Lords appeared in the *New York Times* a year after the occupation of the People's Church. "Young Women Find a Place in the High Command of Young Lords" reads the sensationalized title appearing in the "Food, Fashions, Family, and Furnishings" section on November 11, 1970, then reserved for special interest stories about women. The interviewees, Martha Duarte, Denise Oliver, Olguie Robles, and myself, were then sixteen to twenty-two years old. When asked about our role as women, I said, "We do everything that the brothers do," emphasizing our equality in commitment and action.

In 1971, Newsreel, a group of independent filmmakers, produced *El Pueblo Se Levanta/The People Are Rising,* a cinema verité documentary that highlighted women's activities in the Young Lords, specifically as community organizers. More than two decades later, I produced *¡Palante, Siempre Palante! The Young Lords* revisiting the story of the New York chapter and the struggles that successfully introduced feminist campaigns to the organization. The documentary was broadcast on national public television in 1996 and continues to be screened in classrooms and community venues across the country.

For the fortieth anniversary of the founding of the Young Lords in New York, Erica González, a journalist with *El Diario la Prensa,* wrote the article "Mujeres of the Young Lords" for the newspaper's Puerto Rican Day Parade 2009 edition. The story circulated widely on the Internet and revived interest. Urged on by the renewed attention, I reached out to former members. "This might be the last chance for a first-hand women's account," I said, "an opportunity to expand the historical narrative about the Young Lords." Our experiences varied depending on when, where, and why we joined, and the particular work we did. Only a few women had written about their involvement, and memories were rapidly fading. I wanted to document the story as we had lived it, through its ups and downs from the early formative days in New York City through its demise. I began to contact publishers and received several letters expressing interest, but none made a firm commitment, and the project came to a dead end.

Still, my interest persisted. Notwithstanding the political and social achievements of people of color in the United States since the 1960s, poverty, racism, policing, and countless other problems have remained unaddressed or gotten worse. Likewise, in working with young people over the years, I have heard the superficial information passing for Latino/Latina and African American history with no reference to the critical role of activists in transforming society. Now another generation in the streets was insisting that "Black Lives Matter," protesting the murders by police of innocent people and battling other realities of racial injustice. Latino/Latina activists were organizing to stop the mass deportations of immigrants and demanding just immigration reform. Women of color—still the most exploited, marginalized, and erased demographic in the world—were fighting escalating violence, and class, race, and gender oppression. Low-wage workers rallied for a living wage and better working conditions. Students demanded tuition-free colleges and cancellation of student debt. Activists of color battled gentrification and environmental racism while educating the public about the urgency of climate justice. Thousands mobilized to bring attention to the grave financial and humanitarian crisis in Puerto Rico caused by more than a hundred years of US colonialism and the corruption of local politicians, which had forced large numbers of people to emigrate so that today more Puerto Ricans live in the United States than on the island. Puerto Ricans also marched calling for the release of Oscar López Rivera who as of this writing has been incarcerated in a US prison for thirty-five years for advocating the independence of Puerto Rico. Another generation was on the move—organizing and demanding far-reaching societal transformation just as we had done in the Young Lords.

I joined the Young Lords Organization in 1969. My political awakening had begun several years earlier at a New York City all-girls public high school. I was the oldest of four daughters raised in a working class family with many *tías* and *primas* (aunts and female cousins) who taught me all the traditional expectations for a Puerto Rican woman concerning family and children, but I also wanted a life outside the home. My mother encouraged me to get an education; she believed it was the key to a women's independence. Born and raised in the United States, I hungered to learn Puerto Rican history. I found one book in the school library, *A Puerto Rican in New York and Other Sketches*, a collection of stories by Jesús Colón published in 1961 that I read and reread. I related to his accounts of Puerto Rican working people making their way in the city. A classmate and friend introduced me to the writings and philosophy of Malcolm X. When he was assassinated during our senior year, we cried together. From another fellow student, I learned about the imprisonment of Japanese Americans in US concentration camps during World War II. I learned about US military aggression in Vietnam, and I participated in marches to end the war.

After high school graduation, I went to work as a tenant organizer, knocking on doors, forming block associations, serving as an English/Spanish language translator, making court appearances, and coordinating rent strikes. Fighting greedy landlords and corrupt city building inspectors, I witnessed the injustices and racism of the legal system and how it was stacked against the poor. Shortly after, I entered the City College of New York in a pilot program designed for "underprivileged" African American and Puerto Rican students, as we were called then. Students of color comprised less than 5 percent of all undergraduates in the public university system. On campus, there were no Puerto Rican organizations, classes, or faculty, and very few Puerto Rican students. We felt invisible, but we connected to one another through our similar experiences with poverty and racism. I joined ONYX, the African American student organization, and together with other Puerto Rican students formed Puerto Ricans Involved in Student Action (PRISA), the first Puerto Rican student organization at the college. ONYX and PRISA united to demand that the college expand the admission of Puerto Rican and African American students, offer black and Latino/Latina studies courses, and hire faculty of color.

By then I was living on my own and working as an instructor at the Academy for Black and Latin Education (ABLE), a storefront program that prepared young people for a high school equivalency diploma. Many of our students were strung out on heroin, caught in the drug epidemic that was killing our generation. ABLE's director, David Walker, approached the local hospital seeking medical care, but was turned down. "Sorry, it's not our problem," the officials said. Nevertheless, Walker was determined and led a takeover of the hospital's administrative offices, advocating for services to meet the urgent health needs of our young students. Negotiations eventually resulted in the allocation of thirteen hospital beds to treat adolescents suffering with heroin addiction, one of the first such programs in New York City. Afterward, I taught my classes at the hospital as my students received treatment. From this experience, I learned that education is action that extends beyond the four walls of a classroom. I saw how local institutions could use their resources to save lives.

In the winter of 1968, I was offered an opportunity to travel with a group of Puerto Rican students to the tenth anniversary celebration of the Cuban Revolution, and I took a leave of absence from City College. Our delegation met with public officials, militants from the Women's Federation, workers, teachers, farmers, health practitioners, engineers, and artists from Havana to Santiago de Cuba. Seeing the society that the Cuban people were attempting to build inspired me to believe it was possible to arrange a nation's priorities to meet the needs of the majority of its people instead of just those of its corporations and super rich.

The following spring, I traveled with another group of activists of color to the National Chicano Youth Conference in Denver, Colorado. There, I met the Chicago Young Lords, and their ideas and direct action strategies appealed to me. I too wanted to take part in organizing for a just society. When I returned to New York, City College was on lockdown as African American and Puerto Rican students occupied the buildings on the south campus. They made five demands; foremost was an increase in the admission of students of color so that entering college classes reflected the racial composition of the New York City public high schools. The historic City College takeover led to the Open Admissions program in 1970 and to the formation of African American and Puerto Rican Studies departments.

Joining the Young Lords was a natural next step for me. I became a member in the fall of 1969 and remained with the organization for more than five years. Decades later, stored away in closets, I still kept several boxes labeled "Young Lords" that contained a variety of materials documenting the organization's history and the activism of its women members. I was impressed by the dedication, rebel spirit, and farsighted ideas—even for today. At its best, the Young Lords offered revolutionary ideals and examples of movement-building strategies and tactics, and tough, hard-hitting, and painful lessons from its setbacks and failures. As Audre Lorde wrote in *Sister Outsider: Essays and Speeches,* "We do not have to romanticize our past in order to be aware of how it seeds our present."

"Why not publish the book myself?" I thought. Acutely aware of the limitations of memory, I began to construct a timeline and sequence of events by reading newspaper articles and Young Lords' documents. I engaged in long discussions with former members and other activists gathering remembrances, including my own. I read more broadly about the Puerto Rican diaspora, feminism, and social protest movements. Immersed in this research, rediscovering and uncovering memories, and reliving those times, both joyfully and with pain, an outline emerged.

Through the Eyes of Rebel Women is an introductory history about the Young Lords and the first book describing the experiences of its women members—an untold *herstory* as seen from the inside out. We believed that the women's struggle for equality was the "revolution within the revolution." Similarly, this account offers "a story within a story" weaving together historical context, personal memories, new writings, interviews, research, and analysis. The voices are collective and individual, my recollections and those of others. It is a survey of a rich, complex, and layered history, and it is my hope that by setting a wide lens, future writers and researchers will delve further into these topics and themes.

The opening section, "Herstory of the Young Lords," consists of three chapters that describe the New York organization from its launch in 1969 though its demise in 1976. While each chapter has a particular focus, timelines and events overlap. "The Young Lords' Early Years, 1969 to 1971: An Overview" chronicles the group's revolutionary rise and its most impactful and best-known period. "Women Organizing Women" zooms in on the rise and fall of feminist ideals and campaigns. "New Directions to Shattered Dreams" reflects on the opening of Young Lords Party branches in Puerto Rico, and the group's decline and demise, about which little has been written. The entire history affords lessons about building a people's movement but also about how it was torn down.

The second part, "Palante Siempre Reflections" presents edited transcripts of the on-camera interviews that I conducted with former women members for the documentary ¡Palante, Siempre Palante! The Young Lords in 1995. Also included in this section is an essay by Martha Arguello (Duarte), an early member of the Young Lords in the East Harlem branch. In these testimonios, the women describe the conditions that propelled them into activism and affirm that social movements do not develop in a vacuum but arise to spearhead the necessary solutions to injustice occurring in society.

The closing part, "From the Frontlines (1969-1976)," presents articles and documents, most of them originally published in Palante, the Young Lords' newspaper. Written in the political language of the times, the writers reveal strong convictions and loving hearts on a mix of issues not a linear narrative. The rebel writers reflect what feminist Gloria Anzaldúa in Borderlines/La Frontera described as "the part of me that refuses to take orders from outside authorities" and "hates constraints of any kind."

Through the Eyes of Rebel Women speaks to all people who seek justice and who believe that a society free of systemic exploitation and barriers is possible. The demands of the Young Lords could have been written today. We believed in the power of the people and in community and personal transformation. We demanded the redistribution of economic and social resources. We fought for racial justice and the equality of women. As internationalists, we condemned all political, economic, and military intervention by one nation against another. We battled proudly against exploitation, social injustice, and colonial domination. It was a call for revolution!

Iris Morales
New York City
2016

INTRODUCTION

Unveiling and Preserving a Puerto Rican Historical Memory

Edna Acosta-Belén

HOW THE PAST IS unveiled and represented by an oppressed group or community is an essential component of constructing a collective historical memory that inspires their present and future spheres of activism and resistance. Building a historical memory, however, is always a rugged and convoluted terrain of contesting claims, but more so for those populations that have endured the coloniality of being silenced and are seeking to voice their untold stories and, in this way, contribute to the production of new decolonial knowledge.[1] Thus it is gratifying to have been invited to write this introduction and address the significance of Iris Morales's latest contribution to decolonial knowledge about Puerto Ricans and to the reconstruction of their collective historical memory—especially when the central subject of *Through the Eyes of Rebel Women: The Young Lords, 1969-1976* is feminist activism and experiences in one of the most memorable chapters of the Puerto Rican civil rights movement in the United States.[2]

As a baby boomer who started college student life in the mid-1960s at the University of Puerto Rico, I feel privileged to have witnessed some of the most progressive social, political, and cultural struggles both on the island and in the United States. Being a student during those years at what we fondly called "la UPI" inevitably meant being drawn into the anti-colonial struggles to free Puerto Rico, a US unincorporated territory since the Spanish-Cuban-American War of 1898. At the time, a radicalized independence movement on the island was entering one of its more effervescent and militant stages of protest and resistance.[3]

1

Reading the progressive literature of the past and present was essential for our generation's understanding of the structures and dynamics of power and oppression among different sectors of society, and to eventually develop the critical consciousness and understanding of power relations and the multiple levels of oppression that affect our societies, including the relationship between power and the construction of knowledge, and the need to unveil the suppressed histories of the "people without history"—colonized populations and those less privileged nonwhite sectors of society being belittled or rendered invisible in the official histories.[4] In other words, it was important to revisit and *decolonize* the dominant historical record, and envision new emancipating knowledge and decolonial imaginaries.

My 1967 arrival in New York City, where many of my island aunts, uncles, and cousins had been residing since the 1940s, allowed me the opportunity to live in the Puerto Rican neighborhoods of Manhattan, the Bronx, and Brooklyn for extended periods. Not long after my arrival, I was working with the Neighborhood Association for Puerto Rican Affairs (NAPRA) in the Bronx. Being in contact with primarily second generation Puerto Rican youth and their first generation working class families during those years was my best introduction to the real lives and concerns of the daughters and sons of the various Puerto Rican migrations to New York City, and to what it meant to be Nuyorican, a neologism coined to refer to New York Puerto Ricans. The use of the term was solidified in the 1970s by a generation of poets, writers, and artists born or raised in the city many of whom I had the privilege to come in contact with during subsequent years as a doctoral student at Columbia University. It was from these friendships and the multiple fronts of activism of what we now call the Puerto Rican Movement that I was able to solidify my own emerging research and teaching interests in the process of unveiling new decolonial knowledge about women and the Puerto Rican diaspora.[5]

The social and political movements that bourgeoned within the stateside Puerto Rican communities in the late 1960s and 1970s allowed many island Puerto Ricans who migrated to New York during those years to reach a better understanding of the conditions, hardships, and survival and liberation struggles afflicting the hundreds of thousands migrants who had settled in the city during the previous decades. In the frontlines of these struggles were the Young Lords Organization (later transformed into the Young Lords Party and the Puerto Rican Revolutionary Workers Organization), the Puerto Rican Student Union (PRSU), El Comité, and Resistencia Puertorriqueña, to name a few. Although their primary sphere of action was New York City, their fighting spirit and claims for social justice rapidly spread to other US cities with large concentrations of Puerto Ricans. These groups carried the banners of struggle and resistance on behalf of impoverished and disenfranchised stateside communities where Puerto Rican migrants had settled and for the liberation of Puerto Rico.

The nationalistic sentiments underlying the messages displayed in the Puerto Rican flag, the pinned buttons, T-shirts, and berets of Puerto Rican youth validated the roots and identities of those who had left the island but carried the island in their hearts. The slogans "Tengo Puerto Rico en mi corazón,"[6] "I'm Proud to be Puerto Rican," "Puerto Rican Power," "Qué Viva Puerto Rico Libre," "Free Puerto Rico Now," "Despierta Boricua, Defiende lo Tuyo" (Wake up, Boricua, and defend what is yours) and "¡Jíbaros Sí, Yanquis, No!" were proudly and defiantly flaunted throughout the Puerto Rican barrios of New York, Chicago, Philadelphia, and other cities where the Young Lords were making their presence felt.

During her post-Young Lords life, Iris Morales's indefatigable commitment and efforts to document the history of the Young Lords, and enrich the historical memory of both island and stateside Puerto Ricans, have yielded admirable results. *Palante: The Young Lords Party*, originally published by the Young Lords in 1971 (reprinted with a modified title in 2011), which relied on the testimonies of some of its members (including Morales), the party's thirteen-point platform and program, and the work of photojournalist Michael Abramson was the first major collective effort to introduce a full portrait of the origins of the movement, its far-reaching goals, and its initial successes. At the same time, *Palante: The Young Lords Party* represented an appealing and effective recruitment tool for an expanding inclusive movement, which attracted Puerto Ricans and youth from other groups of color and defined an agenda that embraced the spirit of proletarian revolution and anti-colonial/anti-imperialist liberation movements around the world. The word *palante* (a colloquial abbreviated version of the Spanish phrase *para adelante,* meaning moving forward) was a call to revolutionary action and the battle cry of the Young Lords. The rallying term was also adopted as the title of their bimonthly newspaper, which rapidly made its way to the streets of our communities, the offices of many agencies and organizations, and the halls of our schools and universities.

Over two decades later, Morales's revealing award-winning documentary *¡Palante, Siempre Palante! The Young Lords* (1996) offered a more substantive and multifaceted first-hand historical account of the organization's roots, the key aspects of its platform, and the internal and external reasons that contributed to its demise. The film also underscored some of the most laudable outcomes of the New York Young Lords' intensive community organizing and empowerment efforts. Introducing this compelling visual account, which included interviews with some of the best-known former men and women Young Lords, set the stage for engaging new generations of Puerto Ricans in recognizing their own potential to contribute to the advancement of their communities and become agents of social change. The *Palante* documentary is now regarded as a classic source for learning about the sparsely recognized participation of Puerto Ricans in the US civil rights movement, and a staple of many classrooms in secondary schools and colleges (including my own). In sum, *¡Palante, Siempre Palante!* opened the door to understanding the linkages between Puerto Rican migration and the dynamics of a long-standing US colonial domination over Puerto Rico, its control of the island's economy, and the oppressive nature of the internal colonialism Puerto Ricans face in US society. Developing consciousness about pervading class, racial, and gender inequalities inevitably leads to envisioning ways in which effective grassroots collective organizing and political engagement can bring about significant social transformations at the local and national levels, and also reaffirm the histories of oppression and resistance of marginalized peoples.

At a time when interest in the Young Lords has yielded a new stream of publications, exhibits, archival efforts, and numerous lectures and panels, Iris Morales's new mission is to give voice to the experiences of the *mujeres rebeldes* (women rebels) within the organization. Once again, Morales admirably accomplishes this worthy quest by selecting and compiling a series of essays, interviews, testimonies, poems, and photographs in *Through the Eyes of Rebel Women*. Reaching out, again, to several former members, Morales selects texts that place women at the center of the historical stage and allows them to relate in their own voices the views and ideals that guided their activism, their particular experiences and challenges as members of the Young Lords, and the expanding consciousness of their own oppression as women in what was then regarded as a revolutionary organization. As a whole, the stories told by these creative, dedicated, and courageous women activists render a candid and self-reflective individual and collective recollection of the gender- and nongender based internal divisions and conflicts that, combined with other external factors conscientiously described by each member, eventually contributed to the breakdown of the organization.

What we have here, as Morales clearly indicates, is "an untold *herstory*, as seen from the inside out;" the much too often suppressed or ignored feminist standpoint regarding women's contributions to and experiences in progressive and revolutionary movements. In other words, Morales unveils what was until now, an unaccounted counter-narrative of the Young Lords. Painstakingly, what is historically a common pattern within these movements reveals itself: there is a tendency for women members to be pressured into acquiescing to a male leadership that claims that discussion of any issues related to women's subordination must always be subsumed to the ostensibly "wider" or "more important" class-based liberation struggles of "oppressed peoples." (When referring to the masses, must men always be reminded that women represent slightly more than half of the world's population?) Predictably, the pattern of relegating women's issues to a secondary position or viewing them as "detracting" or "divisive" to a "greater" cause is by now a deeply rooted cliché. Just as achieving some degree of class and race consciousness is a prerequisite to understanding class and racial oppressions, developing a feminist consciousness is also a precondition for both progressive women and *men* to comprehend women's sources of oppression, unequal treatment, and diminished presence in historical narratives. Women's participation in revolutionary movements must not be exempt from a critique of the deleterious legacies of the patriarchy, male privilege, and ascribed gender relations and roles that perpetuate women's subaltern condition. The voices of the rebel women in the Young Lords openly address their gender oppression and underline their individual and collective coping and survival mechanisms, the strategies they de-

5

ployed in trying to "educate" (even if not always successfully) their male counterparts on the internalized and structurally entrenched sexism, prevailing gender hierarchies, and unequal relations, as well as their own "regressive" chauvinistic behavior. The fact that women represented about one-third of the Young Lords' membership only dramatizes these latter points.

And what is it that the intrepid women Young Lords are telling us through their forthright testimonies and interviews? That despite the condescending, patronizing, and clearly "machista" attitudes of the organization's male leadership, the humiliations and marginality they chose to endure were often overshadowed by their deep commitment to the *causa* (the cause); in this case, revolutionary social and political transformations that would lead to a more equitable and just society. There is no doubt that, at a young age, these gutsy women reached a clear understanding of and strong belief in what can be accomplished through grassroots organizing, collective action, and community empowerment even if the envisioned workers' revolution remains an elusive utopian goal. What separates these women from their male *compañeros en la lucha* (male comrades in the struggle) in the Young Lords, is that through their own activism they were able to achieve and share a collective consciousness of oppressive gender relations that privileged men and perpetuated women's subordinate status. As idealists, visionaries, and creative agents of revolutionary praxis, these women engaged in an organization with a male-centered name and, to a large degree, an authoritarian and undemocratic leadership style that privileged men and often curtailed discussions of women's issues, based on the women's convictions and belief in their capacity to challenge the capitalist structures and relations that benefited a few and exploited and oppressed the many, along with hierarchical gender relations that perpetuated their own subordination. These women activists are the Young Amazons of their time—the brave feminist warriors who battled for equality in intersecting (not isolated or separated) arenas of class, race, gender, ethnicity, and sexuality; part of that noble league of defenders of *universal human rights*.

The essays in part 1 of *Through the Eyes of Rebel Women* are intended to tell the story of the Young Lords from a feminist perspective and reaffirm the feminist adage that "the personal is political." Morales's opening essay is a valuable comprehensive historical account of the origins and evolution of the Young Lords, placing women as central participants in the numerous activities and key events that have come to define the organization. This particular essay also conveys the unrecognized leading role of women in advancing the daring and multifaceted local, national, and internationalist agenda of the Young Lords, the empowering effect of feminist collective consciousness; it relates how, in the end, the rewarding and conflicting past experiences and bittersweet lessons of being women members of the Young Lords transcended their involvement in the organization and still fuel these activists' dreams of social justice and human liberation. In the second essay, "Women Organizing Women," Morales articulates the feminist ideals that women members fought to insert into the Young Lords' political platform and grassroots activities. What women members named the "revolution within a revolution" involves a rich array of initiatives and multiple fronts of action: community organizing, collective consciousness raising and empowerment, coalition building and solidarity with other women of color in the United States and internationally, defining the status and needs of women of color, introducing a reproductive rights agenda, fostering a more inclusive environment for LGBT members at a time when sexuality issues were rarely addressed, creating a Women's Union, and demanding a leadership role within the Young Lords Party Central Committee. All of these remarkable endeavors were done, in addition to their active participation in advancing the goals of the Thirteen-Point Program and Platform of the Young Lords Party and performing the tedious office tasks that many men tend to relegate to the women around them. A third essay by Morales offers a more detailed account and assessment of the Young Lords' decision to open a branch in Puerto Rico and play an active role in the struggle to free the island from US colonial control—a tall order for an organization rooted in the realities of what it meant to be Puerto Rican living in *las entrañas* (the entrails or belly) of the colonial metropole, and a move that overextended the Young Lords' human and financial resources, exacerbated internal divisions, and severely weakened the organization.

In part 2, the inclusion of interview transcriptions with former women members, originally conducted in the mid-1990s for the *¡Palante, Siempre Palante!* documentary, deliver an insider's view of the different experiences of women, the numerous ways they contributed to the Young Lords, and their particular motives for eventually leaving the organization. What immediately stands out is the consistency of the issues these women raise, and the similarities in relating their stories and achieving a more sophisticated collective level of feminist consciousness—the shared beliefs, the empowering feelings of forging a unifying force, the constructive feedback in a supportive, non-hierarchical and equalizing space, the unwavering commitment to changing society and their hopes for a better future, the resourcefulness and creativity that come out of wanting to spread your transformative ideas to others, and the healing of wounds from the ordeals they individually and collectively faced and endured as women in a largely male-dominated organization. Diana Caballero underscores some of the most reprehensible moments in the history of the organization in its final days. But even those women members who experienced the degradation, violence, and fear in a period they would probably rather forget, choose to proudly remember that the activist work that engaged them in the past and the lessons learned from both the gratifying endeavors and hostile skirmishes still guide the work they do in the present.

On the whole, the original essays written for part 1 and the interviews in part 2 of the volume represent a comprehensive account of the most admirable and uplifting moments of Young Lords activism and the vital role of women in most of these endeavors, along with a balanced critique of the deplorable and distressing instances that these women went through as members of the organization. It is worth noting that they engage in this constructive critique without indulging in any personal recriminations or settling of scores.

The overall historical documentation process of this *herstory* of the Young Lords is further enriched in part 3. These papers reveal the issues and positions that women members conceived and introduced into the organization, some of which reflect the specific work of the Women's Union. The selected documents in part 3 are complemented by a series of reprinted articles authored by women that appeared in the Young Lords' newspaper *Palante* from 1970 to 1973. All of these valuable primary sources capture the young women's voices of a distant past as they raise the consciousness of their readers on issues related to colonialism, racism, and sexism; advocate for a free Puerto Rico and reveal the long legacies of nationalist militancy of the Puerto

Rican people; and denounce the FBI's domestic surveillance Counter Intelligence Program (COINTELPRO), aimed at infiltrating and destroying progressive movements of the civil rights era, including the Young Lords. In contrast to the essays and interviews that appear in the first two parts of *Through the Eyes of Rebel Women*, most of the views and perspectives expressed in the writings included in part 3— suitably entitled "From the Frontlines"—are those of their younger women selves in action, rather than those based on a retrospective look at a distant past from decades later, offered by former and older women members of the Young Lords in the previous sections.

Morales's afterword brings the volume back to more recent times. First, she includes the empowering poem "Berets and Barrettes," written in 2008 by Lenina Nadal, an activist of today's generation. This poem underscores the staggering capacity of women in "balancing magic with routine," to "reconcile their rebellions" and ultimately to achieve the signified unity of "locking arms in the streets together" (219). Second, faithful to the "looking back to look forward" (220) outlook that guides the whole creative effort behind *Through the Eyes of Rebel Women*, Morales closes the volume with a speech she gave in 2008 to commemorate the fortieth anniversary of the Young Lords in Chicago, the original birthplace of the organization that inspired the founding of the larger and better known New York branch. It should be noted that in the 2005-2015 period, former members of the Chicago Young Lords, along with the support of the city's Puerto Rican community and Grand Valley State and DePaul universities, also have engaged in oral histories and special collection documentation projects to reconstruct and preserve the trailblazing legacy of activism of what is in the present regarded as one of the most important organizations of the Puerto Rican Movement.

Over four decades after they joined the New York branch of the Young Lords, the rebel women contributing to this volume are now playing an important role in documenting the history of the Young Lords as a vibrant social and political movement in the long history of struggle and resistance of the Puerto Rican diaspora and the US civil rights movement. They are adding another equally important and, as stated before, largely overlooked chapter to this legacy. Today, they are not only narrators and guardians of history and historical memory but, once again, also active agents; they are inspiring teachers and admirable role models to new generations of Puerto Ricans and other youth of color. In their current occupations as filmmakers, writers, poets, community and union organizers, and academics, these remarkable women are still applying the experiences and skills they amassed from progressive literature, from collective discussions, from listening to the voices in the streets and homes of their working class communities, from building solidarity among women and men comrades, and from offering hope and envisioning the possibility of a better world.

The implicit lessons these committed activists offer from relating their successes, setbacks, and resilience chart new paths for other women and men to follow. After all, *la lucha continúa* (the struggle continues). It is hard to ignore the fact that the civil rights struggles that we were part of during our younger years to eradicate all kinds of inequalities, are being eroded in the present by unleashed backlashes in a US society still afflicted by a widening gap between the poor and the wealthy, and between the white population and rapidly growing populations of color. A swarm of right wing politicians and the corporate capital that controls their political campaigns want to turn back the clock on the most significant changes and accomplishments that came out of the US civil rights movement—whether by enacting legislation to limit or suppress the electoral power of Latinos/as and African Americans, gerrymandering districts to favor white voters, demonizing immigrants and fostering xenophobic, racist, and undemocratic discourses, infringing upon the reproductive rights of women, weakening unions, opposing increases in the minimum wage, curtailing all the government programs that benefit the most needy sectors of US society, diminishing opportunities to climb the socioeconomic ladder and thus shrinking the middle class, refusing to accept the catastrophic effects of climate change, and favoring laws that facilitate and perpetuate an insatiable accumulation of wealth by the white privileged elites and the corporate sector. A complicitous right-wing media only adds fuel to these ideological crusades by propagandizing similar positions, and fostering demagoguery and fearmongering against culturally and racially diverse populations and immigrants.

In the spirit of the rebel women making their voices heard in this volume, it is appropriate to indicate that despite the prevailing backlashes, progressive social and political movements and causes will continue engaging new generations and articulating new directions and strategies.[7] Oppression will always breed different forms of mobilization and organizing, protest and resistance. Building a historical memory of Puerto Rican struggles against different forms of subjugation is an indispensable component of envisioning those new paths and moving forward.

EDNA ACOSTA-BELÉN is a distinguished professor emerita in the Department of Latin American, Caribbean, and US Latino Studies, and the Department of Women's, Gender, and Sexuality Studies, at the University at Albany, SUNY. She is also an affiliate faculty at the University of Washington in Seattle. Among Dr. Acosta-Belén's book publications are the award-winning *Puerto Ricans in the United States: A Contemporary Portrait* (with Carlos E. Santiago); *"Adiós, Borinquen querida": The Puerto Rican Diaspora, Its History, and Contributions* (with Margarita Benítez et al.); *The Puerto Rican Woman: Perspectives on Culture, History, and Society*; *La mujer en la sociedad puertorriqueña*; *The Hispanic Experience in the United States* (with Barbara R. Sjostrom); *Researching Women in Latin America and the Caribbean* (with Christine E. Bose); *Women in the Latin American Development Process* (with Christine E. Bose); and *The Way It Was and Other Writings by Jesús Colón* (with Virginia Sánchez Korrol). In addition, she has published more than fifty articles in a variety of refereed journals and edited volumes.

PART 1.
HERSTORY OF THE YOUNG LORDS

I write to record what others erase when I speak, to rewrite the stories others have miswritten about me, about you. To become more intimate with myself and you.

Gloria Anzaldúa
(1942-2004)
This Bridge Called My Back

The Young Lords' Early Years,
1969-1971: An Overview

IRIS MORALES

THE YOUNG LORDS REPRESENTED a new awakening of Puerto Rican radicalism in the United States.[1] The slogans "All Power to the People" and *"Qué Viva Puerto Rico Libre"* (Long Live A Free Puerto Rico) most concisely expressed our hopes and dreams. We were mainly children of the Great Migration of Puerto Ricans who arrived in the United States after World War II as American citizens from a colony held hostage since the Spanish American War of 1898.

By the 1960s, Puerto Ricans lived in all fifty states, mostly concentrated in the Northeast and in New York City. The second-largest Puerto Rican population lived in Chicago where a street gang—the Young Lords—inspired by the Black Panther Party embraced revolutionary politics and emerged in 1968 as the Young Lords Organization (YLO). Under the leadership of José "Cha Cha" Jiménez, the YLO battled city officials and real estate developers who were pushing poor people out of their homes in order to gentrify the neighborhood where they lived. Like the Black Panther Party, the Young Lords ran "serve the people" programs that offered free food, clothing, and health services. They protested and mobilized against widespread police brutality and murders of innocent victims. The YLO also advocated for the end of the US colonial domination of Puerto Rico.

THE BEGINNINGS IN NEW YORK CITY

In 1969, the largest Puerto Rican population in the United States was in New York City. In East Harlem, one of the country's oldest and best-known Puerto Rican communities, the people lived in heart-wrenching poverty. The residents saw the garbage piled high in the streets as sending a clear message: "Puerto Ricans *are* garbage." A group of young men and women began sweeping the streets every weekend during the summer of 1969. Among them was a young Cuban mother and university student, Sonia Ivany, one of the first women to join the Young Lords. The nightly television news showed the young people sweeping and stacking up garbage, setting it on fire, and stopping traffic on Third Avenue. As they ran evading the police, the "garbage offensive" spread from East 110th Street to other blocks in the neighborhood. The community applauded; New York City officials in Mayor John Lindsay's administration took notice, and sanitation trucks cleaned the streets.

Hearing about the Young Lords Organization, several of the East Harlem activists traveled to Chicago to meet Cha Cha Jiménez and the other YLO members. Favorably impressed, the New Yorkers decided to form a chapter and selected a Central Committee of five men to lead the group, each with a "deputy" title indicating that they reported to the national organization in Chicago. They were Felipe Luciano as deputy chairman, Juan González as deputy minister of education and health, Pablo "Yoruba" Guzmán as deputy minister of information, David Pérez as deputy minister of defense, and Juan 'Fi' Ortiz as deputy minister of finance. Their combined talents, passions, and actions quickly moved the New York YLO into the public spotlight beginning with a rally at Tompkins Square Park on July 26, 1969. Well aware that the social justice movements were plagued with informants, the Central Committee members kept the details of planned actions and civil disobedience closely guarded among themselves, their spouses, and one or two trusted Defense Ministry officers.

Inspired by the Cuban Revolution, the Young Lords expressed the idea articulated by Che Guevara who said: "At the risk of seeming ridiculous, let me say that the true revolutionary is guided by a great feeling of love." This sentiment led members to live and organize in the poorest and most neglected areas of the city, and to open the first Young Lords' storefront office in East Harlem at Madison Avenue near 111th Street.

To articulate the Young Lords' vision for a new society, Central Committee members González and Guzmán drafted a Thirteen-Point Program and Platform. It was both a statement of beliefs and a call to action. The program spoke of liberation, self-determination, commu-

nity control, true education and culture, women's rights, racial equality, political prisoners, internationalism, self-defense, and socialism. As
the organization's most important document, every member not only
knew it but could recite it by heart. It began:

> We want self-determination for Puerto Ricans: libera-
> tion on the Island and inside the United States. We want
> self-determination for all Latinos, and liberation of all
> Third World people.

It ended with:

> We want a socialist society. We want a society where the
> needs of the people come first and where we give soli-
> darity and aid to the people of the world.

We considered ourselves "revolutionary nationalists" and believed that
Puerto Rican poor people would be best served by socialism. The reference to 'we' reflected a consensus among members to act for the
benefit of the poor and disenfranchised. Our commitment to "serve
the people" was a pledge to move beyond narrow self-interest, as explained in Chairman Mao's "Little Red Book":

> Our point of departure is to serve the people whole-
> heartedly and never for a moment divorce ourselves
> from the masses, to proceed in all cases from the interest
> of the people and not from one's self-interest or from
> the interests of a small group.[2]

We believed that our people's survival and well being depended on
collective, unified, and disciplined action to achieve a reordering of
society's priorities.

The Young Lords provided "serve the people" programs to respond to immediate needs and as examples of our beliefs in action.
Free breakfast programs, modeled after the Black Panther Party survival programs, did not yet exist in public schools. Young Lords would
solicit food donations from local merchants and by 6 a.m. were cooking breakfast in community centers throughout the neighborhood.
Women insisted that men also take part in preparing the meals, pick-

ing up children, and walking them to school. Similarly, the Young Lords offered free clothing, political education, and health testing.

The Young Lords ran programs voluntarily, without salaries, to serve and mobilize the community. We wanted the people to ask, "Why doesn't the government provide needed services?" The YLO was not a 501(c) 3 or a one-issue organization and did not receive government or foundation grants. Nor were the Young Lords social workers, government insiders, or an extension of the Democratic Party. We believed that the capitalist system would not meet working people's needs. We exposed what the government could and should do, and what it was not doing. Our grassroots organizing was a combination of revolution and reform.

The rebellious spirit and direct action tactics of the Young Lords attracted brilliant organizers, men and women, energetic, dedicated, and full of ideas. Activists joined from the civil rights, black liberation, antiwar, Puerto Rican pro-independence, and black cultural nationalist movements. Others united from labor organizations or from high school and college protests. Some had experience in the ongoing fights for quality education, health, housing, and other basic social services. Still others were Vietnam War veterans, mothers with young children, lesbians, former gang members, and recovering addicts or alcoholics. All of us were loyal to the Thirteen-Point Program and Platform, and we were determined to improve poor people's lives. After all, the richest nation on the planet had the resources to provide food, clothing, housing, and health care for everyone. It was unconscionable to have so few with so much, and so many with so little.

Given our range of experiences, we had to find ways to work together. The Young Lords followed the practice of "criticism and self-criticism" outlined in Mao's "Red Book." It said:

> The mistakes of the past must be exposed without sparing anyone's sensibilities; it is necessary to analyze and criticize what was bad in the past with a scientific attitude so that work in the future will be done more carefully and done better. This is what is meant by "learning from past mistakes to avoid future ones." But our aim in exposing errors and criticizing shortcomings, like that of a doctor curing a sickness, is solely to save the patient.

"Criticism and self-criticism" unlocked our minds and hearts to each other. It helped us to resolve and transcend political and personal differences. At weekly membership meetings, we discussed and evaluated our activities. Every member was encouraged to express an opinion, debate an idea, or disapprove of the offending behavior of another. The practice of "criticism and self-criticism" was an important tool that aided the political development of the Young Lords Organization and its members in the early years.

POISON ON THE WALLS

In the fall of 1969, several radical doctors informed the Young Lords about brain damage cases they were treating in young children living in East Harlem. To address the problem, the Central Committee arranged for groups of medical students and Young Lords to go into the neighborhood to test for lead—the metal responsible for brain injury, learning disabilities, attention deficit disorder, seizures, and even death. Even minuscule amounts of lead could poison a child. Every Saturday, the health teams went into the community building by building knocking on doors. At the time, landlords covered tenement walls with lead-based paint and the peeling paint chips fallen to the floor wound up in little children's hands and mouths. Working in pairs, the men and women collected urine samples from children in order to test it for lead content. The women in the Young Lords were especially effective in this outreach since mothers more readily opened their doors to other women. When the urine results were analyzed, they revealed unusually high levels of lead.

"Crimes against children!" declared the Young Lords as they educated the public about the profit-driven nature and corruption of the health system. The high lead results exposed the complicity of politicians, uncaring health officials, and greedy landlords. Recurring stories in the media about the hundreds of Puerto Rican and African American children poisoned inside their homes brought national attention to the alarming health crisis. As a result, New York State banned the use of lead-based paint in apartments, and New York City established the first lead poison prevention program. This fight was one of the "environmental racism" issues that the Young Lords addressed, although this term was not used at the time.

THE PEOPLE'S CHURCH (1969)

By October 1969, the YLO's free breakfast program had reached capacity and required additional space to expand. The Young Lords approached Reverend Humberto Carranza at the First Spanish Methodist Church on East 111th Street, thinking that he would welcome the opportunity to feed needy children since the church was largely unused during weekdays. However, the pastor, a Cuban refugee, was rabidly anticommunist, and when he met the Young Lords wearing purple berets and heard the request to use the space, he denied it.

Undeterred, a group of Young Lords returned to the church on December 7, a testimonial Sunday, intending to appeal directly to the largely Puerto Rican congregation, expecting a more compassionate response. However, when the deputy chairman, Felipe Luciano, stood up to speak, police were already inside the church at the pastor's invitation. The police grabbed Luciano and tackled and beat him to the ground, breaking his arm in the process. Women members in the church leapt to his defense and fought as hard as the men.[3] The policemen beat and arrested thirteen persons including a 15-year-old, Carlito Rovira, and five women: Elena González, Mirta González, Sonia Ivany, Denise Oliver, and Erika Sezonov, a reporter filming for Newsreel, a collective of filmmakers and photographers.

Oliver recalled her arrest:

When I was first placed under arrest, they put me in handcuffs and threw me into a police car. The handcuffs were large, and my wrists were quite skinny. I slipped them off, looked around to see if anyone was watching, and got out of the patrol car and ran. I made it about two blocks when I was apprehended. The police officer grabbed me, dragged me back to the car, and got ready to beat me in the street with his billy club. Two brothers from the community leaped out of the crowd that had gathered to stop him. They were arrested as well.

When we got to the precinct's holding pens, the Newsreel reporter was bleeding badly from wounds to her head, and Felipe had a broken arm. The brother from the neighborhood, Joe, was also injured. Our repeated requests to make a phone call to a lawyer were denied, as were our pleas for a doctor. Frustrated, I noticed a guy in plainclothes, outside the bars of the cell, who looked familiar. I knew his face from around the neighborhood. Suddenly, it dawned on me that he was the guy dating my cousin. I called out to him. Turns out he was an undercover detective. I whispered something in his ear that inspired him to let me use the phone to contact my parents, and he did get medical attention for those who were injured.

My dad called a family friend who was an attorney, and he showed up with him to our arraignment at 100 Centre Street in downtown Manhattan, where we were charged with thirteen felonies, including criminal trespassing, assault, and rioting. We were released on bail.[4]

The Sunday after Christmas as parishioners left the service, Young Lords reentered the church. This time they chained and nailed the doors shut. Most church members, angry or afraid, rushed out. The Young Lords hung a sign out of a second floor window announcing, "La Iglesia de la Gente, the People's Church." Central Committee leaders were already answering reporters' questions by the time the police arrived. "The Church is supposed to serve the people, help them and work with them. This is what it means to be Christian," one spokesman insisted. "This is also a public building, which does not pay taxes and just takes space in El Barrio," another emphasized.[5]

News of the church takeover spread like wildfire. "Young Puerto Ricans ask Church for Food Program for Children," read newspaper headlines. Thousands of people, women and men, young and old, arrived at the People's Church. At the entrance, a Young Lord greeted and welcomed each person, and conducted a search to make sure no one brought in weapons or drugs. All visitors signed a guest book. Inside, programs were in progress. Children ate hot breakfast before attending Puerto Rican history classes. Doctors and nurses from nearby hospitals tested children for lead poisoning and tuberculosis. In the church basement, Young Lords sorted piles of clothes preparing them for distribution.

Many distinguished and highly respected Puerto Rican community leaders arrived to offer support. Dr. Evelina López Antonetty, a Bronx community activist and educator, and José Chegüí' Torres, a world champion boxer, were among them. High profile celebrities and local politicians also made appearances. Women from the neighborhood arrived, many taking their first steps into the political arena. They came to the People's Church to have their children checked by a doctor or to eat dinner, and then stayed to enjoy cultural programs: poetry readings, and music and theater performances.

Among the church congregants was Pedro Pietri, a poet and Vietnam War veteran who allied with the Young Lords. He read his best-known poem, "Puerto Rican Obituary," now considered a seminal work of the late 1960s Latino/Latina experience in the United States. Fellow poet, playwright, and student activist José Angel Figueroa also recited at the church. His popular poem "A Conversation with Coca-Cola" condemned the exploitation and suffering imposed by US corporations on Puerto Ricans and other Latinos/Latinas. Pietri and Figueroa, both born in Puerto Rico, were raised in New York City. They were among the poets and artists forging a new literary direction that led to a Puerto Rican cultural awakening in the United States that become known as the "Nuyorican" arts movement. Their writings brought Puerto Ricans out of the margins, bridging their yesterday with the here and tomorrow. The themes of identity, language, poverty, migration, and survival resonated with young Puerto Ricans who had witnessed their parents struggle as low-wage workers and saw few opportunities for themselves. Many other artists arrived at the church; among the most popular were the Third World Revelationists, a performance theater group; the musicians Pepe y Flora; and Ana Marta Morales, who sang "La Borinqueña," the Puerto Rican national anthem, at many of the events. On December 31, a packed-house at the People's Church celebrated the coming year with a hopeful "revolutionary service" that confidently declared "the Decade of the People!"

The activities and media attention at the People's Church attracted more and more recruits wanting to join the Young Lords, and membership grew exponentially. Many women joined who went on to play long-term and leading roles. Young women were drawn by the radical political ideas but also because they saw women in charge, speaking on bullhorns, running programs, and getting arrested.

Among them, Connie Morales (Cruz), a young mother from the Bronx, arrived at the church with her five-year old daughter, Lisa, and joined the organization. Gloria Santiago (Rodríguez), a Brooklyn high school student, came to the church with her father, Willie Santiago, a District 65 union member and early supporter of the Young Lords. She recalled, "I walked in, and I felt like I was home." Deeply moved, she too joined the Young Lords.[6] Many others had similar experiences.

On January 8, 1970, the eleventh day of the occupation, the police entered and arrested 105 Young Lords and supporters. Occupiers filed out into waiting police vans and buses with fists raised, singing, *"Qué Bonita Bandera"* (What a beautiful flag). All were charged with trespassing. Among the lawyers who assisted those arrested were Daniel Meyers, Richard Ash, and Cesar Perales, and eventually all criminal charges were dropped. It was a defining moment signifying that a new generation and political movement had come of age.[7]

A YOUNG LORD: TWENTY-FIVE HOURS A DAY, EIGHT DAYS A WEEK

Like the Black Panther Party in its early years, the YLO was structured along paramilitary lines. At the top of the hierarchy, a Central Committee made all decisions and issued information to members on a "need to know" basis. The governing principle was called "democratic centralism." In theory, *democratic* referred to the freedom of members to discuss ideas and proposals in order to reach consensus about a policy or course of action; *centralism* required that members carry out directives of higher-ranking officers through a chain of command that went from minister to deputy minister, captain, lieutenant, cadre (member), and lord-in-training.

Though Young Lords were volunteers, not salaried workers of the organization, we were expected to be on call "twenty-five hours a day, eight days a week." Each member was assigned to a branch location and to one of the organization's ministries such as Defense, Education, Information, or Finance to carry out the daily work. Assignments were based on the individual's skills as well as the needs of the organization. For example, a member knowledgeable about Puerto Rican history might be assigned to the education ministry while someone with military experience would likely be assigned to defense.

Many members chose to live collectively to pool financial resources and for protection, to look out for each other's safety, to know if someone had gotten sick or been picked up by the police. Living arrangements were also experiments in creating new relationships and families in an attempt to bring revolutionary principles into every aspect of our lives. Many members entered into relationships, lived together, or got married. For full-time Young Lords who spent most of their time organizing, opportunities to meet potential mates were limited. Couples struggled to practice political principles in their personal relationships. Complications arose when the woman was in a higher leadership level; not many men at the time were willing to take orders from his significant other.

All Young Lords participated in weekly membership meetings and were required to be thoroughly conversant with the Thirteen-Point Program and Platform. Members also followed thirty rules of discipline that addressed issues such as arrests, drinking and drug use, weapons and criminal activity, public speaking, newspaper sales, and confidentiality. The consequences of violating a rule depended on the offense. Lateness might be disciplined by having the member run laps up and down the street while the most severe infractions could result in demotion, suspension, or expulsion from the organization. The unwritten rule was, "if you get busted for a jive tip, you swim alone!"

A person interested in joining the Young Lords entered as a "lord-in-training" or a "friend of the Lords." During a probationary period, he or she was required to attend weekly political education classes, learn the Thirteen-Point Program, and sell issues of *Palante,* the organization's newspaper. Upon successfully completing the probation, he or she became a Young Lord. Trainees who did not advance to cadre or member status were nonetheless welcomed to work with the YLO in other ways. The Young Lords had many such supporters who, though not members, participated with the organization.

Over time, it became clear that the time and financial commitment required of members was not a sustainable organizational model. People with full-time jobs or families could not readily devote "twenty-five hours, eight days a week." Thus the membership base of the Young Lords remained primarily youth, students, and the unemployed, even though the organization urged working people to join.

POLITICAL EDUCATION DEVELOPS A COMMON LANGUAGE

The Young Lords Organization placed a high value on political education, and all members participated in weekly classes. Under the direction of Juan González, the education ministry team prepared the curriculum, reading lists, and facilitated classes until 1972. Each session focused on a topic corresponding to a point in the Thirteen-Point Program. Through political study, the Young Lords developed a common language and became better organizers. Iris Benítez and myself were among the first women in the education ministry. Olguie Robles, a 16-year old community organizer from the Bronx and Gloria Colón, who had worked as a journalist in Puerto Rico, subsequently joined the ministry and also facilitated classes.

Seeking to understand the laws of history, the curriculum included the study of radical philosophies and economic theory. We read works by Marx, Lenin, and Engels, and the "Little Red Book" and other writings by Mao Zedong. Our list also included titles such as *Introduction to Socialism, Labor's Untold Story,* and Franz Fanon's *The Wretched of the Earth.* Since few members could read Spanish, we sought books in English about the history and contributions of Puerto Ricans, but these were scarce. We read *Puerto Rico: A Profile* by Kal Wagenheim and supplemented our study with essays and pamphlets about the Taínos/Taínas, African slavery in Puerto Rico, US colonialism, and the speeches of Nationalist Party leader, don Pedro Albizu Campos. The pioneering Center for Puerto Rican Studies in New York City did not exist yet (it was established in 1973 at Hunter College).

We also studied black history, including national and international movements, and biographies of leaders from the United States and Africa. Among the most popular readings were *The Autobiography of Malcolm X,* the Black Panther Party newspaper, and the writings of Amílcar Cabral, Patrice Lumumba, and Kwame Nkrumah. Though we had no books in English on the subject, we found articles about the history of slavery and racism in Puerto Rico. Well-versed in both the US and Puerto Rico brands of racism, the Young Lords were among the first activists in the United States to embrace the "Afro-Boricua" and "Afro-Puerto Rican" identity. "To study Black history is to complete the study of Puerto Rican history and vice versa," summarized minister of information, Pablo "Yoruba" Guzmán.[8]

Readings about women of color in social movements were also extremely difficult to find. Today's well-known feminist authors, Gloria Anzaldúa and bell hooks had not written their books yet. Women activists relied on each other to find and circulate women-centered essays with titles such as "Double Jeopardy: To Be Black and Female," "Women Hold Up Half the Sky," and "The Personal Is Political." We studied a booklet titled *Enter Fighting: Today's Woman, A Marxist-Leninist View* by Clara Colón. We read about past and contemporary Puerto Rican and African American revolutionary women, and any other materials we could find about women's struggles internationally. Often our sources were *Palante* and other movement newspapers.

The Young Lords also participated in martial arts self-defense classes in Korean tae kwon do. Defense Ministry cadres such as Mickey Meléndez and José "Pi" Díaz led the weekly training of forty to fifty men and women. The poet José Angel Figueroa also led some sessions, which were intended to build mental and physical discipline to prepare the Young Lords for demonstrations and confrontations with the police. Back then, just like today, many police officers used force and violence to exert control over Puerto Ricans and African Americans. Racist cops provoked confrontations with Young Lords in the streets or on subway platforms. Young Lords fought back on such occasions, sometimes with nunchucks (martial arts fighting sticks), and gained a reputation as street fighters.

THE WOMEN'S CAUCUS FORGES A COLLECTIVE VOICE

Through political education classes and community organizing activities, the women in the Young Lords become friends and comrades. As we shared experiences, an undeniable story of second-class status emerged. Several of us in the East Harlem branch talked about forming a Women's Caucus in late 1969 determined to change the situation. The caucus was the catalyst for radical changes in the organization described in the next chapter "Women Organizing Women." However, a few early struggles deserve mention here.

In one incident, Central Committee members arranged to meet with a black cultural nationalist group to discuss a potential alliance. The YLO leaders invited Denise Oliver to attend. In her position as Officer of the Day, Oliver was the highest-ranking woman although she was not on the Central Committee. Her responsibilities included making daily assignments, and she had discretion to hand out discipline for violations of the organization's rules, even to the top leaders. At the meeting with the black nationalists, Oliver witnessed the subservient role assigned to the women who were not permitted to speak or voice opinions; their role was to serve the men, cook meals, and take care of children. Denise returned and reported her observations to the Women's Caucus. Alarmed with what we heard, we were determined to stop a formal alliance between the Young Lords and the nationalist group. Fortunately, several Central Committee members also opposed the alliance, and it did not occur.

Nonetheless, the episode put us on alert. The idea that such an association had even been considered, and the inferior role for women it represented, increased our vigilance. We questioned why some Central Committee members had thought it was a good idea to partner with a group that diminished women. We realized that we had been naïve to assume that men who called themselves revolutionary would automatically support the equality of women. It became clear that to eliminate male supremacy and the inequality of women in the organization, just as in society, we would have to fight for structural changes.

The Women's Caucus put together a list of demands that we presented to the Central Committee. These included the promotion of women to leadership positions, the end of discriminatory policies and practices, and the organizing of campaigns focused on issues directly affecting women of color. (The demands are detailed in the next chapter.) Among our grievances, one of the most troubling was the treatment of women as sexual objects. Many male members eyeballed every woman who entered through the door making comments about her body and physical characteristics. We objected to this behavior, which led to conversations about sexism and male chauvinism and its impact on both male and female members. Through these discussions, some men in the Young Lords joined us in developing a general consensus that male chauvinist conduct was unacceptable and that those who engaged in it should be subjected to discipline. Since men were in the majority, without them, the Women's Caucus could not have won this victory. As a result, all the Central Committee leaders, except Juan "Fi" Ortiz, the youngest member, and other top leaders were suspended for male chauvinism and violations of the rules of discipline during 1970.

FROM YLO TO YLP (THE YOUNG LORDS PARTY)

In May 1970, the Central Committee leaders went into retreat to reflect on the organization's rapid growth and discuss strategies for sustainability. They concluded that the Chicago YLO was not providing satisfactory guidance or consistently producing a newspaper, which was essential to educating the community. A few Central Committee members headed west to discuss the issues, but it became clear that the Chicago group was struggling with its own problems and not equipped to extend leadership or resources. However, the Chicagoans viewed the New Yorkers as trying "to wrest control of the national organization."[9] Differences unresolved, the New York group broke off and formed the "Young Lords Party" (YLP) as a separate, national organization with the same all-male leadership: Luciano as chairman, González as minister of education, Guzmán as minster of information, Pérez as field marshal, and Ortiz as chief of staff. However, the next month, Denise Oliver was appointed to the position of minister of finance in a resounding victory for the Women's Caucus.

Shortly after Oliver's promotion, the Central Committee published the "YLP Position Paper on Women" analyzing the oppression of women of color and supporting the struggle for women's rights as "the revolution within the revolution." The next chapter further examines this document, which was so critical to advancing feminist ideas in the organization and the broader community. The challenges by the Women's Caucus to traditional ideas also made it possible for lesbian, gay, and bisexual people to participate as members in the Young Lords Party. Generally, this was not the case in other left organizations at the time, which had prompted the group Third World Gay Revolution to issue a call for "immediate nondiscriminatory open admission and membership for radical homosexuals into all left-wing revolutionary groups and organizations, and the right to caucus."[10]

REBEL IMAGINATION SPARKS PEOPLE'S CULTURE

The radical ideas of the Young Lords Party offered a framework and stimulated a rebel culture that opened minds to a different narrative about Puerto Ricans in the United States. The Thirteen-Point Program and Platform linked learning our true history with creating revolutionary culture. It said:

> We must learn our long history of fighting against cul-
> tural, as well as economic genocide by the Spaniards and
> now the *Yanqui*. Revolutionary culture, culture of our
> people, is the only true teaching.

Education ministry cadres conducted Community Political Education classes in thirteen-week cycles engaging the public in lively exchanges about history, culture, and political philosophy. Some sessions featured guest speakers or screened films not otherwise readily available about Vietnam, Cuba, and Palestine, or about peoples' struggles in the United States such as "Salt of the Earth," about a Mexican miners' strike, and many Newsreel-produced films about the Black Panther Party. During the hot summer months, we projected films against the side of tenement walls. One of the most popular was "The Battle of Algiers" about the struggle against French colonialists with riveting scenes of Algerian women activists. Community Political Education stimulated new ways of looking at the world and at ourselves, and it attracted a cross section of participants, many who joined the Young Lords after attending these classes. A people's culture emerged "out of the hopes and agonies, the strivings and dreams of people in barrios and ghettoes, in fields and mines, and shops, and on our city streets . . . also in our schools and campuses and professions."[11]

The Young Lords Party also emphasized media as essential to building peoples' movements. Under the direction of Pablo "Yoruba" Guzmán, the information ministry coordinated relationships with the press and the public, and produced a radio show on WBAI, a listener-supported station in New York City. Most significantly, the information team published *Palante*, a bimonthly, bilingual newspaper, a prime mover of ideas, and a main source of revenue. Every Young Lord sold the newspaper, which featured provocative headlines, and in-depth political analysis and historical writings in English and Spanish, illustrated with black and white photographs and colorful graphics. For example, an early issue included a drawing of Jesus Christ with the headline, "Jesus was a Young Lord." *Palante* was read widely, and its pages were often adapted into posters and flyers to be viewed on office doors and on walls along city streets.

Demands for justice and artistic vision converged. Puerto Rican artists organized resistance to the status quo and formed activists' organizations. Visual and literary artists such as painters, poets, play-wrights, writers, performers, and musicians birthed a cultural renais-sance that was fiercely rebelling, demanding an end to class, racial, and gender exploitation, and the liberation of Puerto Rico. A proud new Boricua identity emerged in the United States embracing Afro-Taíno/Taina ancestry and culture, and bilingualism in Spanish and English. While the rich history of Puerto Rican cultural activism is be-yond the scope of this chapter, scholars, artists, and activists credit the Young Lords as a powerful influence on the evolution of the Nuyori-can literary and artistic movement, and on the development of im-portant cultural institutions that had their genesis at this time, among them El Museo del Barrio (1969), the Taller Boricua (1970), the Asso-ciation of Hispanic Arts (1975), and the Caribbean Cultural Center (1976), the latter founded by scholar and cultural activist, Dr. Marta Moreno Vega.

VICTORIES FOR PEOPLE'S HEALTH

During the spring and summer of 1970, the Young Lords launched several major campaigns for health services. Concerned about the spread of tuberculosis in our communities, we began door-to-door testing every Saturday in East Harlem and the South Bronx. In three months, the Young Lords had tested eight hundred persons. One out of every three persons showed a positive reaction, but the only way to confirm that the disease was actually active was with a chest X-ray. The Young Lords approached the Tuberculosis Association asking to use one of their mobile testing trucks for this purpose; the association called the request "ridiculous."[12] But the Association was not testing in our neighborhoods, and so the Young Lords seized one of their mobile X-ray trucks, drove it to 111th Street and Madison Avenue near the Lords' branch office, and named it the Dr. Ramón Emeterio Betances Free X-Ray Truck. (Dr. Betances considered the father of the Puerto Rican nation was the leader of the 1868 El Grito de Lares uprising against Spanish colonial rule in Puerto Rico.) The technicians stayed in the mobile van and took X-rays, happy that it was being put to use. Within hours, a New York Health Department spokesman authorized the Young Lords to operate the truck and even agreed to pay the tech-nicians. The Young Lords tested 770 people in three days.[13]

In the South Bronx, Lincoln Hospital was the only medical facility available to the area's primarily Puerto Rican and black residents, and it exemplified everything that was wrong with New York City's public health system. The community named it the "butcher shop" because patients were subjected to such horrendous conditions and treatment, including experimentation with drugs and medical procedures. Under a multimillion-dollar contract with the Albert Einstein School of Medicine, Lincoln Hospital affiliated as a training and research site for medical students, interns, and residents, and hospital administrators prioritized the training objectives of students over the needs of the patients. In the summer of 1970, Lincoln Hospital officials announced cutbacks in services, and a coalition of Puerto Rican, black, white, workers, doctors, and community activists formed the "Think Lincoln Committee" to fight the rollbacks. They set up a patient-worker table in the emergency room to record complaints, and Cleo Silvers, a community mental health worker and the Committee's chairperson, reported handling fifty complaints a day. These were framed as demands and presented to hospital administrators. They included no cutbacks in medical services, a minimum weekly wage for workers, and the creation of a childcare center for workers and patients. They also called for door-to-door preventive services, a permanent 24-hour complaint table, and an oversight board made up of community residents and workers. The final demand: build a new Lincoln Hospital![14] At the heart of the struggle was the demand for community-worker control—the idea that the people who were most impacted and affected by hospital policies and practices should have a say in the running of the institution, setting its priorities, and arranging the day-to-day work with patients.

Looking to rally community support to fight the proposed cutbacks, members of the Young Lords Party, the Health Revolutionary Unity Movement (HRUM), and the Puerto Rican Student Union (PRSU) went to distribute flyers in the nearby neighborhood on 149th Street and Third Avenue. Police from the 41st, 42nd, and 43rd precincts approached and shouted at them to disperse immediately. The activists wanted to finish distributing the information, but the police began shoving, swinging clubs, and beating people. Ten activists were arrested; one suffered broken ribs and multiple head injuries requiring nineteen stitches. The community organizers denounced the attack insisting that the city administration had ordered it to quash demands for community control of medical services.[15]

By July 14, 1970, Lincoln Hospital had not responded to the community's demands. YLP leaders invited fifty men and women to a surprise party at an apartment on the Upper West Side of Manhattan. Once all the guests had arrived, the Central Committee revealed, "We're taking Lincoln Hospital!" No one could leave from that moment on. Each person was paired with someone else. "Do not let each other out of sight! No phone calls allowed!" These measures intended to prevent undercover informants likely sitting among us from disclosing the details of our plans to the police.

At 4:00 a.m., we loaded into the back of a truck going to Lincoln Hospital. The driver headed to the Nurses' Residence on 141st Street, and when he pulled in, we jumped out and ran into the building. The group met no resistance from staff, and patients cheered. Young Lords and supporters unfurled banners out of hospital windows announcing, "Welcome to the People's Hospital. *Bienvenidos al Hospital del Pueblo.*" We quickly set up TB and lead poisoning testing programs, and political education classes for patients. There was no disruption of patient care. Leaders of the "Think Lincoln Committee," the Young Lords, and the Black Panthers held a press conference for reporters and outlined the demands to the hospital administrators.

The takeover lasted approximately twelve hours, until the police surrounded the building. Young Lords left peacefully. Some members, wearing white lab coats and no purple berets, blended in and walked out with departing staff during the normal shift change. Five blocks from the hospital, police from the 40th precinct recognized Pablo "Yoruba" Guzmán, YLP minister of information, and arrested him along with Luis Pérez, a Young Lord who accompanied him. The police charged them with possession of karate sticks; but a judge threw out the case as absurd.[16] Once again, the Young Lords' takeover of Lincoln Hospital had exposed the city's neglect and blatant disregard for people of color living in poverty. Even those who disagreed with our tactics acknowledged that our cause was just. The *New York Times* reported, "Dr. Antonio Lecot, who has been the hospital administrator for only six weeks, said the Young Lords 'are trying to dramatize a situation which is critical.'"[17] Hospital officials later agreed that there would be no cutbacks in service and that a preventive health-screening clinic would be established.

However, another crisis exploded at Lincoln Hospital a few days later when Carmen Rodríguez, a 31-year-old mother, died from gross medical negligence. Her death sparked a new wave of community protests detailed in the next chapter.

THE FIRST ANNIVERSARY OF THE YOUNG LORDS

Within weeks of the Lincoln Hospital takeover, the Young Lords Party celebrated its one-year anniversary on July 26, 1970. A two-page centerfold in *Palante* recapped the action-packed year starting with the garbage offensive in the streets of East Harlem. Since then the YLP had gained a reputation for bold initiatives zooming in on critical, life-or-death issues affecting Puerto Ricans and other people living in poverty. Through grassroots community-based organizing and coalitions, the Young Lords had mobilized support from diverse sectors that put a spotlight on the city's neglect and failure to provide services to low-income neighborhoods. On several issues, such as garbage pickup, lead poisoning, tuberculosis testing, and public hospital services, the Young Lords had compelled an official response. The organization grew rapidly; recruits joined attracted by the People's Church activities, "serve the people" programs, clothing drives, and health campaigns, such as those at Lincoln Hospital and the TB truck takeover. A second branch opened in the Bronx and housed an information center to produce and coordinate all public communications. An affiliated branch, in Newark, New Jersey, working out of the Newark Christian Center, served a growing Puerto Rican population in that city. Other significant work that year focused on political prisoners, especially efforts to free the Black Panther 21 who were charged with several counts of conspiracy to bomb police stations and other public places in New York City and who were eventually acquitted of all charges. The police also targeted the Young Lords, and *Palante* documented the firebombing of the Newark and Bronx branch offices that year. (The FBI and police actions against the Young Lords are discussed in the chapter, "New Directions to Shattered Dreams.") Despite the intensifying government surveillance and police confrontations, the Young Lords expressed confidence in the rising people's movement.

CENTRAL COMMITTEE CHANGES (1970)

The Young Lords Party marked its first anniversary with no outward sign of any disagreement among the top leadership. Hence it came as a bombshell when Felipe Luciano was demoted from the position of chairman a month later. Certainly, the top leaders must have weighed carefully the impact that their decision would have on the membership, the community, and the social justice movement. Several principles were at stake. All Young Lords were required to obey the organization's thirty rules of discipline; no member was exempt. "In Felipe's case, the disciple was extended to an indefinite demotion from the Central Committee. We felt at the time that Felipe had started to consider himself above discipline, that he was increasingly taking on the mannerisms of an old-style Puerto Rican cacique," Juan González wrote years later.[18]

The first public mention of Luciano's demotion appeared in a *New York Times* article on September 5, 1970 stating that he had been charged with "male chauvinism, unclear politics, political individualism, and lack of development" as the reasons for his removal from leadership.[19] As previously explained, the general membership had reached consensus that male chauvinist behavior was unacceptable, and several top leaders had been disciplined and suspended for such conduct that year.

A week after the *New York Times* story, *Palante* published the Young Lords Party's official statement about the demotion.[20] The Central Committee wrote:

> We have seen historically that no party or organization should be built around one personality—because the strengths of that person become the strengths of the party, and the weaknesses of that person become the weaknesses of the party. . . .

> This happened to the Young Lords Party with Felipe Luciano . . . and Felipe's own inability to correct his weaknesses.[21]

The YLP press release also reported that Luciano would continue as a member of the Young Lords Party.[22] However, Luciano opted to resign, and several members loyal to him also left the organization.

The Central Committee regrouped. The position of chairman was discarded, and Juan González took on the responsibility of minister of defense as the highest rank in the organization. The other members kept their positions: Guzmán as minister of information, Oliver as minister of finance, Ortiz as chief of staff, and Pérez as field marshal. Gloria González (later using the surname Fontanez) was promoted to the top leadership as a second field marshal in September 1970.

One of the first acts of the new Central Committee was to call for a march to the United Nations to heighten international awareness about the colonial status of Puerto Rico. The plan included organizing networks of "Liberate Puerto Rico Now" committees in high schools and on college campuses. For this purpose, the Young Lords Party and the Puerto Rican Student Union (PRSU) jointly organized the first national Puerto Rican student conference in the United States coordinated by Hilda Ortiz of PRSU and myself representing the YLP. More than one thousand students attended the two-day conference held at Columbia University on September 23 and 24. Flavia Rivera from the Federación Universitaria Pro Independencia de Puerto Rico gave a keynote address expressing solidarity between the student movement on the island and Puerto Rican students in the United States. YLP Central Committee member, Denise Oliver, delivered an address highlighting the role of students to community empowerment and to the decolonization struggle of the island.

SECOND PEOPLE'S CHURCH AND PRISONERS' RIGHTS CAMPAIGNS

As the Young Lords Party prepared for the march to the United Nations, tragic events pulled the organization in another direction. On October 14, 1970, East Harlem residents, angry about the sanitation department's failure to make regular pickups, began burning garbage in the streets. As police and fire engine sirens were heard approaching, people scattered and ran in all directions. YLP members, Julio Roldán and Bobby Lemus were outside the building where they lived; and, in the ensuing melee, plain-clothes detectives grabbed and arrested them. The two men were charged with first-degree arson and thrown into the Tombs, the infamous city jail located in lower Manhattan, officially named the Manhattan Detention Complex. Roldán and Lemus were each held on $1,500 bail.

Two days later, Julio Roldán was found hung in his jail cell. Officials immediately disclaimed any responsibility: "He hanged himself with his belt," they reported. Guzmán, the Young Lords' minister of information, responded, "Murder! No Young Lord commits suicide."[23] On the same day that Roldán was found dead, another man, José Pérez, was found hung at the Rikers Island infirmary where he was held because he could not pay $500 bail. "Suicide" was the official answer to the many controversial deaths in prisons that year.

Horrific conditions in New York City jails were the cause of intense protests a few months earlier in August when African American and Puerto Rican prisoners had seized the eighth floor and later three other floors at the Tombs. They presented the public with evidence of delayed trials, overcrowded cells, excessive bail amounts, and vicious daily beatings by guards. "We rioted because of the stink and the stench and the roaches and ants and fleas. And the food, the slop food they gave us," wrote a prisoner from the Tombs.[24] Then on October 1, prisoners at five city jails held twenty-nine hostages for four days and demanded judicial and penal reforms. To present their grievances, they formed the Inmates Liberation Front (ILF), which later became an official section of the Young Lords Party fighting for prisoners' rights inside and outside prisons. The ILF demanded basic human treatment; affordable bail; speedy trials and access to counsel; inmates' committees to communicate with people outside of the prison; and jobs, housing, education, and other facilities and assistance for readjustment to the community upon release.[25]

Julio Roldán, 34 years old, was a quiet and gentle man; a Vietnam War veteran who proudly cooked Puerto Rican meals for members and took care of the Young Lords' mess hall. More than two thousand people attended his funeral procession through East Harlem. His pallbearers were Young Lords and Black Panthers as well as representatives from the PRSU, the Movement Pro Independence (MPI),[26] I Wor Kuen,[27] Justicia Latina, and Los Siete de la Raza[28] who carried his casket to the People's Church on East 111th Street. There the Young Lords and supporters reentered, this time to protest prisoner deaths, and this time with assault rifles and shotguns. Roldán's coffin was placed on the church altar; on either side stood a Young Lord, a man and a woman, each holding a rifle.

The Young Lords Party demanded that the city allow clergy to investigate prison conditions and the deaths of men who had died under suspicious circumstances such as Julio Roldán, José Pérez, and others that year. The YLP also demanded funding for a legal defense center whose work would be to document police brutality cases and to provide a community bail fund to assist cases in greatest need. Even Reverend Juan Antonio Velázquez, who had recently been appointed to the Second People's Church, supported the demands.[29]

After the viewing at the church, Roldán's body was flown to his home in Aguadilla, Puerto Rico, where he was buried. Young Lords, Aida Cruset and Jesús Villanueva, accompanied him to the island. In Aguadilla, they attended a rally of six hundred MPI militants who mobilized in support of Roldán and his family. Juan Mari Brás, the president of MPI, passionately condemned the widespread killings of Puerto Ricans at the hands of the US police. Cruset spoke about the conditions in New York jails and explained that the Young Lords Party had occupied the People's Church with guns.[30] Back in New York, the Central Committee had assembled a defense squad of Young Lords, mostly men, but also several women, to receive weapons training in the church's basement to prepare to defend against an anticipated police attack. A few men called the plan too reckless—a suicide mission—and they walked out. However, the majority of the squad participants continued their training, prepared to risk their lives.

On November 1, the police announced two more "suicides" in New York jails: Raymond Lavon Moore and Aníbal Dávila; both men were in the Tombs awaiting trial. Moore's autopsy showed that he had a fractured skull. Dávila's death was the eighth alleged suicide in city jails that year. Young Lords continued agitating, presenting letters, interviews, and autopsy reports to the Board of Corrections insisting that the two men had also been murdered.

Not surprisingly, the board issued a report stating: "Julio Roldán died by his own hand." Years later a few former Young Lords said that they believed that Roldán had committed suicide. However, we don't know what went on inside the prison with the police or in Roldán's mind and heart. What we know is that Roldán was alive when the police took him, and he wound up dead. The police were responsible for him. The many alleged "suicides" of Puerto Ricans and African Americans while in custody were not coincidences or isolated instances; they reflected a system-wide problem. Even a Board of Corrections report acknowledged the degrading and inhuman prison conditions:

> If we kept our animals in the Central Park Zoo in the way we cage our fellow human beings in the Tombs, a citizens' committee would be organized, and prominent community leaders would be protesting the inhumanity of our society.[31]

Months later the city accused four guards at the Tombs of beating Raymond Lavon Moore, and they were suspended.

Neither the Young Lords Party nor Mayor John Lindsey's administration wanted a violent confrontation at the Second People's Church. Last minute negotiations granted amnesty to the Young Lords on the condition that no weapons were found when the police entered the church.[32] With the assistance of East Harlem supporters, the church was cleared, and the anticipated bloodbath was averted.

The guns were unexpected. The Young Lords were known for taking over buildings, mass arrests, civil disobedience, press conferences, protests, and community mobilizations, but not guns. Nonetheless, as Young Lords, we believed this action was an appropriate response to the death of a member. Point 12 of the Thirteen-Point Program stated: "We believe armed self-defense and armed struggle are the only means to liberation." Then information captain, Richie Pérez, explained:

> We are armed because we have seen that the government won't hesitate to kill Puerto Ricans fighting for their rights. We are armed because we must defend ourselves, and we advise all Puerto Ricans and Third World people to begin preparing for their defense. The u.s. government is killing us, and now we must defend ourselves or die as a nation.[33]

The Young Lords Party made a distinction between self-defense and armed struggle. Central Committee leaders wrote extensively about the topic in the *Palante* newspaper, and members were familiar with these writings. In sum, when people could no longer achieve justice or social change by political tactics such as elections, petitions, demonstrations, court litigation, arrests, and civil disobedience, then armed struggle was compelled, as in the case of the African National Congress's struggle against apartheid in South Africa. Obviously, the Second People's Church incident was a political fight, not armed struggle, despite the show of guns. The church action intended to bring attention to the deadly conditions facing Latinos and African Americans in prison.

The prison rebellions, the deaths of Julio Roldán and other Puerto Ricans and African Americans in city jails, and the heightened media attention roused a public indictment against the criminal justice system that remains active and unresolved to the present day.

The Young Lords proceeded with the march to the United Nations, which had been planned prior to Roldán's death. October 30, 1970 marked the twentieth anniversary of the uprising in Jayuya and other towns in Puerto Rico when Nationalist Party militants engaged in armed insurrections intended to break the US colonial stranglehold. Thousands of people gathered at 125th Street and headed downtown on Lexington Avenue chanting: "*¡Despierta Boricua, Defiende Lo Tuyo!*" (Awake Puerto Ricans; Defend What is Yours!) Protesters carried huge Puerto Rican flags and large street-wide banners that read: "Self-Determination for Puerto Rico" and "US Out of Puerto Rico Now." From the hilltop on 100th Street and Lexington Avenue, we looked back and saw the long line of marchers, the bright purple berets of the Young Lords, and the black and maroon berets of the Black Panthers and members of the PRSU. We saw the placards carried by activists from the MPI, El Comité, Justicia Latina, Resistencia Puertorriqueña, the Black Panther Party, I Wor Kuen, Third World Women's Alliance, Gay Liberation Front, Third World Gay Liberation, and others. Chants of "Free Puerto Rico, Right Now!" filled the streets, and protesters stretched for blocks stopping traffic at major cross streets in midtown. Ten thousand people demanding an end to the colonial status of Puerto Rico, the release of Nationalist political prisoners: Oscar Collazo, Lolita Lebrón, Rafael Cancel, Andrés Figueroa, Irving Flores, and Carlos Feliciano, and an end police brutality in our communities. Supporters also joined in a show of solidarity with the Young Lords in the aftermath of Julio Roldán's death.

LINCOLN DETOX PROGRAM (1970)

During this time, New York City's low-income neighborhoods like the South Bronx were plagued with an influx of heroin readily available on the street. Activists blamed the CIA (Central Intelligence Agency) for bringing drugs into communities of color and launching the epidemic destroying young people's lives. The charge was considered extreme until the 1980s when a US Senate committee revealed that the CIA had indeed been complicit in the drug trade.

In New York City, an estimated forty thousand people suffered from drug addiction in the 1970s. Activists from the South Bronx Anti-Drug Coalition appealed to Lincoln Hospital for medical services, and when it received no response, the group united with the Young Lords, the Black Panthers, the Health Revolutionary Unity Movement, and ex-addicts on November 10, 1970 to occupy the sixth floor of the Nurses' Residence at the hospital. They set up "The People's Drug Program" and with the assistance of doctors, conducted physicals and administered detoxification treatment. As protesters negotiated with hospital representatives, forty police wearing helmets and riot gear got past the barricades, arrested fifteen persons, and the talks came to an end. Nonetheless, the protests and escalating drug epidemic compelled the hospital to respond. Within months, Lincoln Hospital funded the Lincoln Detox Program, hired community members as workers, and provided services to thousands of addicts. Initially, treatment used a ten-day methadone-to-abstinence cycle in combination with political education classes in which patients and counselors studied drug addition as a societal issue, not as an individual problem. Subsequently, the Lincoln Detox Program introduced acupuncture as a treatment modality and gained international acclaim for this work.

The second takeover of Lincoln Hospital brought the organizing work of the Young Lords Party to a close in 1970. Central Committee members—Juan González, Gloria González, Pablo "Yoruba" Guzmán, Denise Oliver, Juan "Fi" Ortiz, and David Pérez—went into a leadership retreat. At the conclusion, they issued a document titled "Report of the Central Committee Evaluation and Retreat," which announced that the Young Lords Party would open branches in Puerto Rico. This decision and its consequences are examined in the chapters that follow.

SUMMARY

The Young Lords represented a new generation of Puerto Rican activists in the United States. Identifying as "revolutionary nationalists," we believed that capitalism was a failed and declining system. Our ideas and direct action tactics rapidly attracted members, mainly young Puerto Ricans born or raised in US urban centers, other Latinos/Latinas, and African Americans. With a distinct vision and hope for society, the Young Lords organized the people most affected by institutional racism and exploitation. Our activities generated strong and fervent debate about poverty, governmental neglect of low-income communities of color, and the predatory role of big business and corporations—all issues still confronting us today.

In New York, the Young Lords' first storefront office in East Harlem was quickly followed by branch openings in the Bronx and the Lower East Side, and expansion throughout the Northeast with affiliated chapters in Newark, New Jersey; Philadelphia, Pennsylvania; and Bridgeport, Connecticut, and allied groupings in smaller cities and towns. Through door-to-door organizing, dramatic takeovers, and massive protests, the Young Lords mobilized at the grassroots demanding community control of public institutions and resources, quality health care, and police and prison reform. The Young Lords formed coalitions with other Puerto Rican, African American, Latino/Latina, Asian, and progressive white activists to fight poverty and racism, and also to end the war in Vietnam and free political prisoners. These collaborations also increased the public's awareness about the dire circumstances facing Puerto Ricans and brought thousands to the cause of the island's independence. The Young Lords believed in the power of the people to transform society with visionary goals, creative strategies, and collective action.

While the Young Lords Party continued to organize into the mid-1970s, the period from mid-1969 through the end of 1970 present its most significant accomplishments with the greatest impact on the Puerto Rican people and social justice movement in the United States. The next chapter documents the struggles and contributions of the women members. Feminists in the Young Lords transformed the organization and launched important campaigns, which fought for and advanced the rights and equality of women of color in society.

41

This planet belongs to all of us and is not the privilege of only a few. Why are there so many injustices? . . .

A final summing up: women are capable of everything and anything.

Luisa Capetillo
(1879-1922)
From *A Nation of Women*
An Early Feminist Speaks Out

Women Organizing Women

IRIS MORALES

WOMEN JOINED THE New York chapter of the Young Lords in 1969 as the organization was being formed. We enlisted to fight poverty and racism; to end gender discrimination; to free Puerto Rico; and to improve our lives and those of our families. Our struggle was for justice against powerful economic interests and institutions, and we believed that the equality of women was inseparable from society's progress as a whole. With an enthusiastic sense of possibilities, we embraced "the revolution within the revolution." This phrase, from a speech delivered by Fidel Castro in 1966, had credited Cuban women with furthering the revolutionary process of that nation. The women in the Young Lords pursued a similar idea, a story within a story that is barely known.

The women in the Young Lords were rebels, passionate about social justice, and young—most of us were between sixteen and twenty-six years old.[1] At the high point, approximately one-third of the members of the Young Lords were women. We were primarily Puerto Ricans, also African Americans, Cubans, and Dominicans, several from other Latin American backgrounds or mixed Puerto Rican and South Asian or Filipino descent. The majority of us had been born or raised in the United States in Spanish-speaking homes, but English was our primary, daily language. Arriving to the organization from different sectors of the community, we were wives, homemakers, and mothers with young children. Several of us had jobs in retail stores, offices, or hospitals, generally in clerical and administrative positions. Others were unemployed or were high school or college students. Several were lesbians. Some were survivors of domestic violence and drug addiction. We were also activists and community organizers.

The women in the Young Lords understood that to fight for social change, our organization had to mobilize the community and develop relationships with the people—with the politically, economically, and educationally disenfranchised. This meant living our political principles and working in coalition with other activists; it meant creating alliances with workers and students, and building new networks with artists and progressive policy makers. It also meant battling with city officials, self-serving politicians, and the New York City police.

The realities for Puerto Rican and other women of color at the time were extremely bleak with few prospects for a better future. Racist and sexist barriers dominated all facets of society. Educational opportunities were especially limited. The majority of workingwomen of color were steered into low-paying, unskilled, and semi-skilled jobs with few chances to advance. High numbers of Puerto Rican and African American single mothers with children survived on public assistance with no other options. Inevitably the early "survival programs" of the Young Lords responded to the needs of women. For example, the first Young Lords' clothing drive in East Harlem in 1969 reached out to 150 welfare mothers and distributed coats, sweaters, shoes, and other basic items to them. Successive free clothing programs aided similar families in need. The free breakfast programs fed the school-age children of single and working mothers. Door-to-door health testing in poor neighborhoods brought medical attention to children at risk for lead poisoning.

Convinced of the power of direct action, the women in the Young Lords became fighters, leaders, and political thinkers. We embraced three main principles in our organizing work: a belief in the right of poor people to economic, social, and political power; an emphasis on racial equality, self-determination, and human rights; and a feminist viewpoint that demanded a woman's right to control her reproduction and to share equally in all aspects of society. By imagining what society could be, we were energized to action.

Throughout New York City's poorest neighborhoods, young women in blue jeans proudly wearing the purple beret of the Young Lords were easily identifiable. We were out every day in Puerto Rican communities speaking with people who rarely received serious attention from anyone, listening to their opinions, and engaging them in discussions. Even in freezing cold weather, we sold *Palante*, the Young

Lords' newspaper, on street corners, in subways, bodegas, shopping centers, clinics, and beauty salons, wherever people gathered. During the summer months, we sold the paper at city beaches and parks, during festivals and parades. In the mornings, we cooked breakfast for children; and, in the evenings, we taught political education classes in community centers, housing projects, and other neighborhood venues. We helped fellow members who could not read or write to develop these skills and stayed up late into the night with recruits who wanted to kick the heroin habit, helping them to become drug-free. Women also participated in takeovers, organized protests, and got arrested. In many ways, women were the backbone of the Young Lords.

BE SEEN, NOT HEARD

In the early days of the Young Lords Organization (YLO), the women members were practically invisible. As outlined in the opening chapter, the YLO was a hierarchal paramilitary organization led by a Central Committee. The initial group in New York consisted of five men. Felipe Luciano, deputy chairman, was twenty-two years old, raised in East Harlem, a former Queens College student, and a member of the Last Poets[2] with ties to the Black Arts Movement. Juan González, deputy minister of education and health, was also twenty-two years old. Born in Ponce, Puerto Rico and raised in New York City, he was a former Columbia University student and activist with Students for a Democratic Society. Pablo "Yoruba" Guzmán, deputy minister of information, was nineteen years old, a second-generation Puerto Rican-Cuban, born and raised in the South Bronx, and a former student at the State University of New York at Old Westbury. David Pérez, deputy minister of defense, was nineteen years old. Born in Lares, Puerto Rico, he had arrived in New York from Chicago to attend Old Westbury, but joined the Young Lords Organization instead. Juan 'Fi' Ortiz, deputy minister of finance, was fifteen years old, a former student at Benjamin Franklin High School in East Harlem, an aspiring photographer, and a preacher's son. The men selected each other as the leaders. Although several women were already working with them, none was chosen for a leadership position. Women were not treated as equals in the Young Lords Organization, and the struggle for gender equality began then.

The second-class status of women was a problem not only in the YLO but also across society, and the men in the organization mirrored the prevailing patriarchal values and norms. Guzmán described the mindset of men in those days:

> The first time we heard about Women's Liberation, our *machismo* and our male chauvinism said, "Well, these chicks are all frustrated—that's their main problem. What they really need is a good—you know." That was the thing that we were coming from.[3]

The men in the YLO often repeated this infuriating and degrading commentary. Laughing in agreement, they conveyed their attitude of male supremacy and privilege, their hostility and sense of entitlement—their *right*—to treat us as sexual objects and mindless bodies.

Undoubtedly, YLO leaders were influenced by black nationalist[4] ideologies and Puerto Rican cultural values. Black nationalists at the time promoted male supremacy as a natural condition:

> We could never be equals . . . nature has not provided thus. . . . We will complement each other. . . . There is no house without a man and his wife. . . . When we say complement, completes, we mean that we have certain functions which are more natural to us, and you have certain graces that are yours alone.[5]

Machismo was highly compatible with these ideas. Traditional Puerto Rican society relegated women to the private sphere: taking care of men, children, siblings, and the elderly, and accomplishing all domestic chores, including cooking and cleaning. Machismo was a complex set of beliefs, attitudes, values, and behaviors passed down by families from one generation to the next. Men exercised total control over the family; verbal and physical violence to keep women "in their place" was condoned. Manliness, defined by sexual virility, fostered a double standard of sexual freedom for men and monogamy for women.

The ideas and practices of male dominance, and the subordinate status of women likewise characterized the social justice movement, as has been well documented:

> In every organization, women were responsible for keeping records, producing leaflets, telephoning, cleaning offices, cooking, organizing social events, and catering to the egos of male leaders, while the men wrote manifestos, talked to the press, negotiated with officials and made speeches.[6]

Similarly, women in the Young Lords were expected to be enthusiastic cheerleaders, clean offices, handle administrative tasks, and do the cooking, as well as perform as obedient sexual partners and wives. Women were expected to play supporting and submissive roles.

THE WOMEN'S CAUCUS: CATALYST FOR CHANGE

Facing this reality, several of us in the East Harlem branch discussed forming a Women's Caucus. By early 1970, we were meeting on Sundays, one of the few windows of free time in the relentless "twenty-five hours a day" organizing schedule. The meeting offered an opportunity to build sisterhood, to get to know each other, since we joined at different times and places. Several women had worked with the Young Lords as the organization was being formed; others arrived during the takeover of the Peoples' Church; still others entered when the Bronx branch opened in April 1970. Among the earliest caucus participants were Denise, Iris B., Cookie, Connie, Doleza, Emma, Lulu, Martha, Nydia, Olgita, Olguie, and myself.

The animated caucus meetings—with no formal agenda, hierarchy, or chain of command—were energizing. We talked, laughed, cried, shared hopes, and confided our fears and anxieties. We spoke freely about our families, and our relationships with men and with each other. Women joined at great personal sacrifice. Mothers with young children juggled a job and childcare in order to participate. A few women had been thrown out of their homes by parents who did not want them associating with the Young Lords. Several women revealed that a jealous boyfriend or husband had threatened to leave them if they continued on as members. Even the husbands and boyfriends who professed to understand women's oppression still expected women to take care of them, the children, and all household chores without any offer to share the work. Some wives and girlfriends of Young Lords took on all financial responsibilities as breadwinners to support their partners. Their contributions went unappreciated, although without this financial support their husbands or boyfriends could not have been full-time members. Within the organization and the community, women also had to fight the perception, that because we were activists, we were "loose women," sexually available to any man. Despite the problems, women joined the Young Lords Organization, eager to be part of a movement for social change.

Initially, some women were afraid to speak up in the caucus meetings because their husbands or boyfriends had warned them: "What happens at home between a man and a woman is private and personal, and not to be talked about with anyone." But we were learning that everything that affected women, inside and outside the home, was political, even housework. We read, "The Politics of Housework" by Pat Mainardi, which outlined men's exercise of power and excuses for not sharing in housework. The description mirrored our experience; and, several of us decided that we would no longer do all the housework and cooking or pick up after our companions even if it led to arguments or breakups. Motivated to take part in this mini-rebellion, we conspired with and prepared each other to accept the consequences. Admittedly, these were small steps, but defying the traditional roles emboldened us to take on bigger challenges later on.

We identified as revolutionary nationalists[7] committed to ending exploitation and colonialism. We were inspired by the herstories of women activists in Puerto Rico. We learned about Lola Rodríguez de Tió and Mariana Bracetti, early fighters for the abolition of slavery and the island's independence from Spain; Luisa Capetillo and Juana Colón, working class organizers and women's rights advocates; and Lolita Lebrón and Blanca Canales, Nationalist Party militants imprisoned for their actions to free Puerto Rico. We studied the lives of African American women such as Sojourner Truth, an abolitionist and women's rights activist, and Harriet Tubman, who freed slaves through the Underground Railroad. Our sisters in the Black Panther Party were diversifying the image of the revolutionary, and we joined the protests to demand the release of Angela Davis from a California prison, and of Afeni Shakur and Joan Bird in New York in the case of the Black Panther 21.[8] The long line of women activists, from past and contemporary social justice movements, became our role models and mentors.

In the Women's Caucus, we also studied the Young Lords' Thirteen-Point Program and Platform, especially Point 10, which stated: "We want equality for women. Machismo must be revolutionary . . . not oppressive." This passage included a few lines of explanation:

> Under capitalism, our women have been oppressed by both the society and our own men. The doctrine of machismo has been used by our men to take out their frustrations against their wives, sisters, mothers, and children. Our men must support their women in their fight for economic and social equality, and must recognize that our women are equals in every way within the revolutionary ranks.

"What is 'revolutionary machismo'?" a young woman asked hesitantly. After pausing to consider the question, a Puerto Rican woman answered. "I don't know." Shyly, one by one, we admitted that we didn't know. Finally, another woman said, "I'm not sure what it means either, because I've never known anything good to come out of machismo." She broke the ice, and we laughed. "How you gonna put 'revolutionary' and 'machismo' in the same sentence?" another woman added. "*¡Eso fue un hombre!* It had to be a man!" she joked. We laughed louder. "It's like saying revolutionary racism. It just doesn't make sense," an African American woman said. We agreed, this time more seriously.

Having been told that no other revolutionary nationalist organization even mentioned the status of women, we felt proud that the Young Lords did. We had not pushed back on this point because the inclusion of women in the platform was in and of itself a victory. Nonetheless, as we reviewed the section more carefully and scrutinized it, we realized that although Point 10 made reference to machismo's ills in daily gender relations, including domestic violence and spousal abuse, it simply amended the "machismo" concept by placing the "revolutionary" qualifier in front of it. We recognized that "revolutionary machismo" was an oxymoron, that it actually reflected an embedded ambivalence about the equality of women. It preserved a gendered hierarchy that kept men in power without any commitment to the radical societal and personal transformation needed to make the liberation of women a reality and not just flowery rhetoric. "Would we accept the notion of "revolutionary racism"? The unanimous response was an unequivocal, "No!"

While most of us did not refer to ourselves as feminists at the time, we were fighting patriarchy, sexism, and traditional gender roles. In the conflicts and struggles taking place in the Young Lords Organization, our feminist "awakening" deepened as the we began to question the inner workings of the group: "If women do the same work as men, why are there only men in the leadership?" As we challenged the double standard, tensions heightened and tempers flared within the broader organization. The Central Committee accused us of causing problems and ordered the Women's Caucus to stop meeting. "We can't let them stop us," we said, and the following Sunday, we held our meeting as usual. The Central Committee angrily charged us with disobeying a direct order.

During this time, all Young Lords participated in Korean tae kwon do martial arts self-defense training. At the next session, the all-male Defense Ministry leaders directed the members of the Women's Caucus to stay for workout beyond the customary routine. Denise Oliver, cofounder of the caucus, recalled what happened next. "Give me one hundred push-ups," one of them shouted. We complied, each of us glancing at the others in silent encouragement. We could do it. "Now give me one hundred sit-ups" was the next order. Winded and aching, but gritting our teeth, we complied yet again, silent, angry, but determined. I remember some men sitting on the side watched uncomfortably and sheepishly as we did what they knew would be difficult for them. We completed the workout, exhausted, but successfully. It was a test of wills and of women's unity, defiance, and resistance. We stood our ground, and the Women's Caucus continued to meet.

Eager to expand our knowledge about the activism of women of color, we read articles, pamphlets, and books on many subjects. As we did, we realized that the language of feminism was almost completely new to us, and we began to study it. "What does the word 'misogyny' mean?" a young Puerto Rican woman asked. "Misogyny is the hatred of women just because they are female," another member responded. "So then, what is machismo?" the youngest woman in the room asked. "It's an entire system of beliefs that maintains men are inherently superior to women and entitled to dominate and control them," an older woman explained. "Sexism" is also a system of oppression that privileges men, subordinates women, and discriminates against women based on gender. "Then what is patriarchy?" an African American woman probed. "Patriarchy is a system of society in which men hold the power, and women are largely excluded from it," another member answered. Although the word was new, we understood it; we lived it! Right there and then, we committed ourselves to fight patriarchy, and it didn't matter if we wore blue jeans or mini-skirts; or sneakers, combat boots, or platform shoes!

Excited to be part of a revolutionary movement, the Women's Caucus reached out to build solidarity with other women activists during 1970. We met with visionaries such as Yuri Kochiyama, a Japanese American living in Harlem whose family had been imprisoned in US concentration camps during World War II, a mother of six children, a friend of Malcolm X's, and a fighter for human rights. Through our coalition work, we met women in the Black Panther Party, the Brown Berets,[9] and I Wor Kuen[10] as well as members of other Puerto Rican organizations such as the New York chapter of the Movement Pro Independence (MPI)[11] and El Comité.[12] We quickly discovered the similarity of our experiences as women activists. Within the revolutionary ranks, we were all struggling to be treated as equals. Women in the Black Panther Party reported that when they voiced ideas, they were not respected and were generally ignored. Reflecting on those days, Kathleen Cleaver, Black Panther Party Communications Secretary, concluded, "The fact that the suggestion came from a women gave it some lesser value."[13] Ericka Huggins, the first woman to open a Black Panther Party chapter (in New Haven, Connecticut) recalled, "In every part of the movement, there were women doing all the organizational work, and all the programmatic work, and keeping offices running . . . and truth be told, in the Black Panther Party—keeping men happy. I don't mean happy in a 'wife-y' kind of way, but uplifting almost every situation."[14] In an interview conducted by scholar Mary Phillips in 2014, Huggins discussed her views on feminism in the Black Panther Party. She explained:

> We were feminists. We did all kinds of things to break down barriers within the Black Panther Party, gender barriers. . . . I would take issue with my own comrades and the women in the Black Panther Party. I would ask

them "what do you mean you are not a feminist? You absolutely are a feminist. You joined the Black Panther Party." You could not be in the Black Panther Party if you were not a feminist.[15]

The women in the Young Lords also met with members from the Black Women's Alliance (BWA) cofounded by Frances Beal.[16] Originating in the Student Nonviolent Coordinating Committee (SNCC), the BWA formed as a separate organization in disagreement with men who believed that the role of women was to support men and that women should devote themselves to having children for the people's army.[17] Beal's powerful essay, "Double Jeopardy: To Be Black and Female," critiqued the black liberation movement. She wrote:

> Since the advent of black power, the black male has exerted a more prominent leadership role in our struggle for justice in this country. He sees the system for what it really is, for the most part. But where he rejects its values and mores on many issues, when it comes to women, he seems to take his guidelines from the pages of the *Ladies Home Journal*.
>
> Certain black men are maintaining that they have been castrated by society but that black women somehow escaped this persecution and even contributed to this emasculation. Let me state here and now that the black woman in america can justly be described as a "slave of a slave."[18]

Beal also criticized the women's liberation movement, which consisted mostly of white, middle-class women, for not addressing issues relevant to black or other women of color. She wrote:

> Very few of these women suffer the extreme economic exploitation that most black women are subjected to day by day. . . . If the white groups do not realize that they are in fact, fighting capitalism and racism, we do not have common bonds.[19]

In 1970, BWA was in the process of creating a new feminist organization to bring African American, Puerto Rican, and other women of color under one banner; women in the Young Lords attended some of the early formation meetings. By the summer, the Third World Women's Alliance (TWWA) had organized in New York with the mission of ending racism, imperialism, and sexism. TWWA published *Triple Jeopardy,* a women-centered newspaper that provided information and analysis about human rights and social justice issues affecting women of color around the world. The women in the Young Lords were faithful and avid readers.

Members of the Women's Caucus also met with Chicana feminists, some of whom had been members of the Brown Berets in California. They explained that the largely male-led movement often sidelined or rejected what men called "women's issues" such as birth control, childcare, and equal rights for women. Hence Chicana feminists had also formed separate women's groups,[20] citing the failure of Chicano nationalist organizations to include women's concerns in their agendas. Similar to the experiences of Black feminists, Chicanas found that the second-wave feminist movement led by mostly Anglo-American women did not provide common ground for Chicanas to speak out about the unique oppressions they faced as workingwomen and members of "la Raza." However, not all Chicana activists agreed with forming separate women's organizations; some believed that racism was the most important issue facing the community and that gender inequality would best be resolved internally within the movement. Despite the differences, leading Chicana activists explained:

> When Chicano men talk about maintaining *La Familia* and the "cultural heritage" of *La Raza,* they are in fact talking about maintaining the age-old concept of keeping the woman barefoot, pregnant, and in the kitchen. On the basis of the subordination of women, there can be no real unity. . . . The only real unity between men and women is the unity forged in the course of struggle against their oppression. And it is by supporting, rather than opposing, the struggles of women, that Chicanos and Chicanas can genuinely unite.[21]

We agreed. There could be no unity without struggle. "Unity, struggle, unity," we said.

WHICH PATH FOR THE WOMEN'S CAUCUS IN THE YLO?

The exchanges with the African American and Chicana feminists gave the members of the Women's Caucus a lot to consider and underscored the problems that women of color faced in male-led organizations. The obvious question was: "Should we separate and form our own organization?" Standing at a crossroads, the Women's Caucus invited all female members in the Young Lords Organization to participate in this dialogue. The overwhelming majority joined enthusiastically; a few refused. During our discussions, the women expressed different ideas. Several were afraid of retaliation and advised that we ask the Central Committee leaders to clarify their views. Others, tired of talking, wanted action and suggested that we give the leaders an ultimatum instead.

With so many perspectives, we decided to focus on one question: Was it possible to change the Young Lords Organization? Although we were not all of one mind, we reached consensus to continue as members, but only on the condition that we attained equal rights. As revolutionary nationalists and feminists, we envisioned an organization of both men and women committed to fighting for women's rights as part of "the revolution within the revolution." We believed that men had to join us to end sexist oppression within the political movement, our communities, and US society. We proposed structural changes to the organization to unite all members in the struggle against the exploitation of women, both its practices and the ideas that justified it, to ensure that the future we were fighting for would benefit the entire community. Otherwise, why should women remain in the Young Lords Organization?

This early struggle for women's rights also reflected one of the first efforts to democratize the organization. Dissatisfied with the Central Committee's absolute and total control, the Women's Caucus sought to open up the decision-making process beyond a handful of men. Our demands intended to eliminate all barriers to women' equality. It was clear that this goal would involve a battle, but we were steadfast in our commitment to end the prevailing politics and culture in the Young Lords Organization that subjugated women, diminished our work, and placed obstacles to our activism.

THE DEMANDS OF THE WOMEN'S CAUCUS

The Women's Caucus drafted a list of demands to present to the Central Committee; essentially, it was an appeal for respect, equal treatment, and accountability. A basic demand was to end the sexual objectification of women by men in the Young Lords. We considered ourselves comrades in struggle not sexual pawns or mindless bodies. The objectification of women was a chief barrier to equality and progress in all areas. Although not all male members engaged in overt sexist behavior, the actions of those who did were generally overlooked or ignored. The caucus members demanded that such conduct stop and that men face organizational consequences for it.

Another main concern was the absence of women in leadership. The caucus insisted that women be promoted to all levels, including the Central Committee. We sought to end the existing male-leader model, which perpetuated lack of confidence in women's abilities. Even at the entry level, female recruits (lords-in-training) were not being promoted to full member status. The Central Committee claimed that they were not sufficiently "politically developed" but did not specify what criteria determined that a woman was less prepared than a man to join or advance in the organization. Likewise, we wanted to abolish the "no women" policy of the Defense Ministry, the all-male enclave considered the street fighting unit, which explicitly declared women were too weak and helpless to perform in this capacity.

Mothers with young children were at the greatest disadvantage. Dragging young children to meetings and protests at all hours of day and night was not a good situation for children or mothers. In spite of their great sacrifices to balance activism with parental responsibilities, the Central Committee members restricted the possibilities for mothers to advances in the organization. Fathers, on the other hand, were not limited because it was assumed that a woman (wife, girlfriend, mother, or grandmother) would take care of his children. The caucus demanded a childcare solution so that mothers could participate as fully as men.

The Women's Caucus also insisted that the political education program be expanded to include the study of feminist ideas and her-story, and the achievements of Puerto Rican, African American, and other women of color. Likewise, recognizing the important educational role of *Palante,* we advocated that the newspaper carry stories about women. Specifically, we pressed for half of all articles to be about issues affecting women of color and for 50 percent of the writers to be women. Lastly, we wanted the words "revolutionary machismo" removed from the Thirteen-Point Program and Platform. "*Machismo* is not revolutionary," we emphasized.

WOMEN'S RIGHTS GAIN MOMENTUM IN THE YOUNG LORDS

When the Women's Caucus presented the demands to the Central Committee, the men reacted angrily, "What do you mean, demands?" They accused us of divisiveness and causing conflict. "You're veering the Young Lords away from "real" political work and weakening the organization," they said. "This is not the place for personal complaints," a few remarked. "The personal is political," we responded. In general, they treated our concerns as an annoyance and tried to reassure us that women's issues would be handled *after* the revolution. "What happens between now and *after*? If you change nothing, then when we arrive at *after,* we'll still be in this same situation. There has to be a process of change, between now and then," I said. We aspired to be treated as equals and were unwilling to wait for some theoretical "*after*" to end the daily discrimination that we faced in the organization and society. The more the caucus members discussed it, the more we were convinced that waiting for "the revolution" to happen first was not a smart strategy for women. Ours was a grander vision. We wanted gender equality to be an essential and nonnegotiable part of the revolutionary process, not just a postrevolution promise.

Since the majority of Young Lords were men, the women in the caucus were acutely aware that we had to persuade them to our cause, and we discussed strategies to do so. During our daily community work and other organizational activities, we engaged in one-on-one exchanges with our male peers, speaking to convince them. "If we expect to fight oppression, we need to involve every man, woman, and child to win,"[22] we reasoned. "When men treat us as sex objects, we are not comrades," we insisted. We were relentless in challenging all expressions of male supremacy and privilege. We critiqued everything, including language. When a man referred to a woman as a "girl," we corrected him, pointing out that he would not want to be called a "boy." Some men got tired, annoyed, and exasperated with us. Arguments exploded as all Young Lords wrestled with deeply ingrained beliefs about gender roles.

The most open-minded men encouraged the others to engage with the Women's Caucus. Signs of progress began to materialize when the Central Committee members abolished the "no women" policy of the Defense Ministry. Among the first women assigned to the ministry were Connie Morales and Martha Duarte. Morales was a young mother who joined during the People's Church takeover despite being discouraged by her brother-in-law, who told her the organization was only for men.[23] Although it was Morales's first experience as a community activist, her unwavering commitment brought her to the organization with her daughter every day. Duarte, born in the Dominican Republic and raised in New York City, was a New York University student. She was appointed to the Defense Ministry in East Harlem and later was transferred to the Lower East Side when the branch opened in September 1970. Minerva Solla, a young woman from the Chelsea neighborhood in Manhattan, was also assigned to defense when she joined the Lower East Side branch. Myrna Martínez was one of the first women appointed to the defense ministry in the Bronx branch. More advances followed when the Central Committee introduced a childcare policy. Young Lords, both men and women, were assigned to take care of children during meetings and demonstrations, freeing mothers to engage in activities knowing that their children were safe. From then on, communal childcare became an important practice for gatherings across the social justice movement.

Tackling the issue of sexual objectification proved more difficult. The Women's Caucus continued to criticize the actions of men who used their Young Lords' membership as a calling card to pursue sex. Women in the community and rank-and-file members repeatedly complained, and this gross behavior resulted in women hesitating to join the organization. "Without consequences for this conduct, our principles are hollow, and the community will not take us seriously," women members insisted. At the weekly general meetings, we brought up our concerns and engaged in back-and-forth exchanges. We began to gain support, first among the very youngest cadres (members), and then others, who were learning about women's herstory and the particular exploitation of women of color in political education classes. A consensus began to evolve that male chauvinist conduct should have consequences, even for Central Committee leaders.

The commitment to fight sexism and male chauvinism was groundbreaking and transformative. The pledge to support women and combat the misogynist macho culture was a victory for the "revolution within the revolution." It put political principles into practice. The Women's Caucus made progress on this problem with the support of men in the Young Lords; without them, it would not have been possible because women were not the majority. Although not all members agreed, the general consensus prevailed and resulted in several leaders being suspended for male chauvinism. Among the men in the East Harlem branch who participated on either side of the debate were: Che JaJa, Américo Berríos, Benjamín Cruz, Esteban Ferrer, David "Pelu" Jacobs, Huey Jung, Larry Louzau, Frankie Maldonado, Ramón Morales, Robert "Muntu" Bunkley, Mark Ortiz, Carl Pastor, Luis Pérez, Richie Pérez, José "Pi" Díaz, Richie Rodríguez, Julio Roldán, Carlito Rovira, José Torres, Luis Torres, Félix Velásquez, Jesús Villanueva, the Central Committee members, and others.

As the debates with the Women's Caucus were taking place, the Central Committee was involved with another issue discussed in the last chapter. In sum, the New York Central Committee leaders, dissatisfied with the Chicago YLO leadership, decided to separate and formed the Young Lords Party (YLP)[24] as a distinct national organization in May 1970. Shortly after, Denise Oliver was appointed to the all-male Central Committee as minister of finance reflecting another advance for women's equality in the organization. Oliver was an excellent candidate, an activist with the Young Lords since the earliest days when the group was being formed, and one of the thirteen persons arrested at the First People's Church in 1969. She was a cofounder and leader of the Women's Caucus and had served as Officer of the Day and Communications Secretary. Oliver was twenty-three years old, African American, fluent in Spanish, familiar with Puerto Rican history and culture, and lived in East Harlem.

Other women also broke the gender barrier taking on key responsibilities and assignments. With the expanded national activities of the Young Lords Party, the Central Committee members formed a Central Staff, and later a National Staff, a second-level of leaders reporting directly to them. I was the first woman assigned to this collective, which was responsible for managing the New York City branches. Likewise, the Central Committee enlisted women into leading roles in the production, design, and distribution of *Palante* in order to boost its growth. The top leadership also assigned more women to represent the Young Lords Party as speakers at rallies, demonstrations, radio shows, and press conferences responding to growing requests for Young Lords to make public appearances. On all levels, women were changing the politics, practices, and image of the Young Lords.

LAST PUERTO RICANS ON THE PLANET!

Among the most important activities spearheaded by women in the Young Lords were reproductive rights campaigns. We demanded access to birth control options, safe and legal abortions; an end to sterilization and experimentation on our bodies; and access to affordable and quality health care. Puerto Rico had been a laboratory for US pharmaceutical companies carrying out contraceptive research from 1952 to 1960 and the testing of the birth control pill. The drug companies told women that the pill they were taking was medication to prevent pregnancy without informing them that it was experimental.[25] Women experienced side effects, including severe cramping, nausea, dizziness, headaches, stomach pain, and vomiting. Unaware of the pill's potential dangers, five women died. The deaths went unreported, and the Food and Drug Administration approved the pill.[26]

The Women's Caucus also learned about the mass sterilization policies implemented in Puerto Rico through a summary report of an island-wide study conducted by the Puerto Rican Department of Health in 1965. In examining the possible connection between uterine cancer and sterilization, the study found no link, but it revealed that 35.3 percent or more than one-third of Puerto Rican women aged twenty to forty-nine years had been sterilized. The practice dated back to the 1930s when the official discourse attributed overpopulation as the reason for the island's extreme poverty, arguing that the economy would improve by reducing the birth rate among poor and working class women.[27] A government marketing campaign declared that the procedure would free women to work without the worry of families.[28] Naming the procedure *"la operación"* or "getting the tubes tied" hid its irreversibility, and women were often unaware of this fact. Sterilization, made culturally acceptable, was more accessible than birth control, and so pervasive that all of us in the Young Lords had mothers, aunts, cousins, or sisters who had been sterilized. Some of us had even considered it a viable option for ourselves. Because the practice went on for decades, Puerto Rico attained the dubious distinction of having the world's highest sterilization rate.[29]

In reviewing the history of sterilization in Puerto Rico, we learned that Native American, African American, Chicana, and Puerto Rican women across the United States were also being sterilized in great numbers. In New York City, Puerto Rican women were sterilized at seven times the rate of white women and twice the rate of black women.[30] Policy makers and administrators looked away in tacit acceptance. Evidently, controlling the bodies of low-income women of color, stereotyped in the public eye as having too many babies, was deemed justified.

We called it genocide![31] We were very vocal on this issue and joined with other activists to bring attention to and protest the mass sterilization of women in Puerto Rico and of low-income women of color in New York hospitals. In our effort to build a movement around this problem, we organized forums about quality health care, spoke on radio shows, and attended many community meetings and conferences emphasizing the dire situation. We published our first article about Puerto Rico's sterilization policy in *Palante* in May 1970. "We may be the last Puerto Ricans on the planet!"[32] These words from a Puerto Rican Student Union pamphlet reflected our sentiment.[33]

In 1973, Dr. Helen Rodríguez-Trías, head of the pediatrics unit at Lincoln Hospital in the Bronx, founded the Committee to End Sterilization Abuse (CESA), determined to stop the genocidal practice of sterilizing women of color and poor white women. A CESA publication titled "Sterilization Abuse of Women: The Facts" explained that it was common practice to use elective hysterectomies to train medical residents. The article quoted the acting director of obstetrics and gynecology at a New York municipal hospital who confirmed: "At least 10% of gynecological surgery in New York City is done on this basis, and 99% of this is done on Black and Puerto Rican women."[34] CESA filed and won several lawsuits in the late 1970s; as a result, guidelines were adopted to stop sterilization abuse by the New York City's municipal government as well as by the federal government.[35]

The women in the Young Lords also advocated for the right to an abortion. Unlike other nationalist organizations that opposed abortion and other forms of reproductive control, even when voluntarily chosen, the Young Lords Party developed a more nuanced view that supported a women's right to choose safe and legal methods of fertility control, including abortion and birth control options. Restrictive laws had not prevented or reduced the incidence of abortions; instead they forced low-income women to resort to unsafe, clandestine, and fatal procedures. Thousands of women of color died through botched or self-induced "hanger" abortions.

When the New York state legislature legalized abortion in 1970, it was a victory for women. However, legalization alone did not respond to the concerns of low-income women of color as shown by the case of Carmen Rodríguez, the first to die under the new abortion law. Rodríguez, a 31-year-old Puerto Rican mother of two children, died at Lincoln Hospital, the only facility in the South Bronx available to approximately 300,000 residents and whose horrific conditions were described earlier.[36] The hospital's administrators immediately declared that Rodríguez died from a rare reaction to the saline solution injected into her uterus.[37] Unfortunately, the doctor who performed the abortion had failed to take into account her history of rheumatic heart disease. If he had, he would have known that she should not have received the injection. The saline got into her bloodstream causing fluid accumulation in her lungs, and she went into a deep coma from which she never recovered. A worker at the hospital reported that abortions were performed in a small room previously used as a storeroom, not in a well-equipped, sterile operating room.[38] Carmen Rodríguez died from negligence and medical malpractice.

An outraged community protested. Members of the Young Lords, Black Panthers, and the Health Revolutionary Unity Movement (HRUM) demanded the firing of the head of the Obstetrics and Gynecology Department, Dr. Joseph J. Smith.[39] In response, hospital administrators obtained an injunction to stop the demonstrations; the militants countered with more rallies. The Pediatric Collective, a group of thirty doctors and residents, went on strike in solidarity and closed down the OB/GYN Department. In turn, they were fired by the Albert Einstein College of Medicine Einstein, which assigned personnel to Lincoln Hospital through an affiliation contract. However, the activists were reinstated when the Health and Hospitals Corporation, the administrator of municipal hospitals, threatened to terminate a $28 million contract.[40] Under the community pressure, Dr. Smith resigned.

Rodríguez's death illustrated that hospitals could not be trusted with the lives of low-income women of color. It was clear that the quality of care a woman received depended entirely on her class status, race, and nationality. The Young Lords demanded community control and oversight of medical policies and hospital procedures affecting patients in order to prevent negligent deaths. Reproductive rights were an issue for the entire community, not just for women. Gloria Colón of the YLP's Education Ministry explained:

> We believe that abortions should be legal if they are community controlled, if they are safe, if our people are educated about the risks, and if doctors do not sterilize our sisters while performing abortions.[41]

The Young Lords Party defended a woman's right to an abortion and birth control choices understanding that raising large families posed financial and other hardships. Women of color in tough economic circumstances needed to have options. Emphasizing capitalism as the root of the problem, we said: "Change the system so that women can freely be allowed to have as many children as they want."[42]

YLP MEN'S CAUCUS

The Young Lords Party introduced a Men's Caucus intended to strengthen understanding about internalized sexism and women's oppression. Part study group and part consciousness-raising session, the men in the organization met to examine their views about male-female relationships and to study the connection between sexism and capitalism. Deputy Minister of Information Richie Pérez explained: "Male chauvinism is a problem that every man has by virtue of being raised in this society. . . . We recognize machismo is one of the biggest problems in making revolution."[43]

David "Pelu" Jacobs, a Young Lord in the Defense Ministry who worked in both the East Harlem and Bronx branches, remembered how men responded to the caucus: "There were guys who didn't like the idea." Jacobs explained: "It's tough for someone who has been dealing a certain way with women, whose father was dealing with women a certain way . . . and now they have to change."[44] Men in the Young Lords were expected to alter their interactions with women, treat women as equals, and those who could not, left the organization. Jacobs recalled: "Since the party had a military structure, orders from women leaders had to be followed, regardless of the attitude toward them, and when they weren't, it was brought up in the open criticism sessions, and insubordinates could face discipline."[45]

Recognizing the difficulties in putting new ideas about gender roles into practice, Pérez made a powerful appeal for change:

> [O]ne of the things that we understand is that because we're oppressed people we have a lot of neuroses to deal with. It's no use making revolution if after we make it and take state power we're as fucked-up as the people we replace. We not only have to change the political structure of this country, we've also got to change everything else. Revolution means change from the top to the bottom, and that includes the way we deal with each other as human beings.[46]

The willingness of Young Lords to take risks in order to practice their beliefs was a special quality of the organization and its members. Though the struggle to achieve equality between women and men was often angry and confrontational, big and small changes were seen as Young Lords began to transform their views. Men cooked breakfast for children. Women took up defense. Men reported to and took direction from women leaders. Women led rallies and spoke at press conferences. All members protested butcher-shop abortions, mass sterilization, and lack of quality health care. Nonetheless, the fight for the equality of men and women was a constant and everyday struggle.

LESBIAN, GAY, BISEXUAL, AND TRANSGENDER YOUNG LORDS

The challenges of the Women's Caucus to conservative notions of gender identity and roles also opened the door for gay, lesbian, bisexual, and transgender (LGBT) women and men to join and participate in the Young Lords Party. Certainly, the acceptance of LGBT members in a paramilitary organization led by a male chauvinist hierarchy would not have been possible without the presence of a strong cadre of women defying and redefining the boundaries of traditional societal roles and demanding gender equality and justice.

Several Young Lords met with Sylvia Rivera, a Puerto Rican-Venezuelan transgendered woman and leader of the June 1969 Stonewall riots in Greenwich Village. She was a cofounder of Street Transvestites Action Revolutionaries (STAR) and the Gay Liberation Front. Although Rivera was not a member of the Young Lords, she associated with the organization. In a 1998 interview, she reflected favorably on her experience.[47] "Any time they needed any help, I was always there for the Young Lords. It was just the respect they gave us as human beings. They gave us a lot of respect," she said. Her comments attested to a budding consciousness about gender identity and sexual orientation among some YLP members. In the same interview, Rivera recalled a protest organized by the Young Lords: "There was a mass demonstration that started in East Harlem in the fall of 1970. The protest was against police repression, and we decided to join the demonstration with our STAR banner." There were many protests that fall, but her reference could have been to the march to the United Nations that attracted 10,000 people demanding the decolonization of Puerto Rico, the release of political prisoners, and an end to police brutality.

At this time, the Young Lords held progressive views relative to other left-wing nationalist groups. LGBT men and women joined all branches and participated in all activities and ministries, including the Defense Ministry. They engaged in door-to-door health testing, represented the Young Lords at public events, managed *Palante* sales and distribution, assisted in establishing new branches, and coordinated community-organizing campaigns. Micky Agrait, a leading organizer with the Health and Field Ministry, described her work with East Harlem tenants in *El Pueblo Se Levanta/The People Are Rising,* a documentary produced by Newsreel. She also organized on Manhattan's West Side with two hundred Latino/Latina squatters who moved into abandoned and neglected buildings, fixed them up, and turned them into livable spaces.[48]

In September 1970, when the Young Lords Party opened a branch on the Lower East Side, several lesbian and bisexual members joined the organization. An informal Gay Caucus formed and a couple of the Central Committee leaders met with the women, collectively and individually, to discuss issues of sexual identity and orientation. However, these topics were not brought into the YLP's general political discourse. Members neither discussed nor hid their sexual orientation; it was an in-between space of coexistence.

The truth is that the idea of equality with gays was less acceptable to the community than women's equality. Although the Young Lords Party supported the participation of LGBT members in the organization, no self-identified LGBT member was ever appointed to the Central Committee or to other leadership collectives like the national or central staffs. Nor did the Young Lords Party organize specific LGBT-issue campaigns or publish a position paper on LGBT rights. Minister of information, Pablo "Yoruba" Guzmán acknowledged, "it's a lot quicker for people to accept the fact that sisters should be in the front of the struggle than saying that we're gonna have gay people in the organization." In discussing the deeply rooted prejudices against LGBT women and men, he wrote:

> I'm not gay, but maybe I should be. It would probably give me a better outlook on a whole lot of things. . . . Being gay is not a problem; the problem is that people do not understand what gay means. . . . [T]his society has created a false division based on a thing called gender. Gender is a false idea, because gender is merely traits that have been attributed through the years to a man or a woman.

> [T]he Gay Struggle really rounds out the individual. . . . Because certain traits have been assigned to people historically by society, we've actually developed as half-people, as half-real. . . . The Gay Liberation struggle has shown us how to complete ourselves."[49]

This stunning statement from a male Central Committee member was published in the *Palante* book of essays and photographs in 1971. Guzmán's essay seemed to express the Young Lords Party's point of view about Gay Liberation, not just his personal opinion. The *Palante* book gained enormous popularity, and the declaration about the gay struggle within its pages provoked debate and commentaries throughout the Puerto Rican community and social justice movement.

In this way, the Young Lords Party contributed to the fight against backward ideas about sexual identity and sexual orientation in the long struggle for LGBT rights that is still evolving today.

YLP POSITION PAPER ON WOMEN

The debates for feminist principles and campaigns culminated in the "YLP Position Paper on Women" published in *Palante* as a two-page centerfold in September 1970. It was a comprehensive statement synthesizing the struggles of the women in the Young Lords as well as the dialogue among feminists of color throughout the United States.[50] As background was our study of early communal, matriarchal social systems, preceding the rise of private property, class society, patriarchy, slavery, and the state, when women held primary roles as both mothers and producers of material necessities. Over time, an economic system had developed that divided society into classes, and a privileged class of men amassed property that they passed to their sons. Monogamy was introduced to give wealthy men legal heirs, and women were severely punished if they broke the marriage vows. Violence against women was institutionalized, and women—as a group—were left without power.[51]

The YLP position paper reflected a major advance and definitive break with the early view of women as "mindless bodies." Affirming the vital role of women of color in creating global social change and of the "revolution within the revolution," it declared:

> Third World Women have an integral role to play in the liberation of all oppressed people as well as in the struggle for the liberation of women.

> Puerto Rican and Black women make up over half of the revolutionary army, and in the struggle for national liberation, they must press for the equality of women; the women's struggle is the revolution within the revolution.

Summarizing the exploitation of women, the paper concluded:

> Third World women have always been used as a cheap source of labor and sexual objects. . . . Because this so-

ciety produces these conditions, our major enemy is capitalism rather than our own oppressed men.

The "YLP Position Paper on Women" also advanced ideas accepted by US feminists of color about "triple oppression," that women of color suffered multiple, intersecting, and interconnected oppressions based on nationality/race, class, and gender, which had to be addressed together; today recognized as the theory of intersectionality.

After the paper's release, the Central Committee published a revised version of the Thirteen-Point Program with a new section about women rights. It now read: "We want Equality for Women. Down with Machismo and Male Chauvinism!" The words "revolutionary machismo" were removed, and the rewritten section was moved up to Point 5 from the original Point 10. These amendments clearly signaled a greater importance given to women's rights. Shortly after, the Central Committee drafted a new document, "Ideology of the Young Lords Party," with a section devoted specifically to an analysis of the oppression of women of color.

As we battled to introduce feminist ideas to the Young Lords in 1970, we continued to organize in the community, run "serve the people" programs, and conduct political education classes. Women participated in setting up new branches in the Bronx and Lower East Side. Women played leading roles in preventative health campaigns and joined in commandeering a mobile TB truck, rerouting it to East Harlem where hundreds of residents were tested. When Lincoln Hospital announced staff and service cutbacks, women joined in the takeover of the facility demanding worker-community control and quality reproductive health services. Women helped to mobilize 10,000 people to the United Nations bringing international attention to the colonial status of Puerto Rico and coordinated a national conference where 1,000 college and high school students planned "Liberate Puerto Rico Now" committees and networks. After Young Lord Julio Roldán was found hung in his jail cell in the Tombs, women in the Young Lords took up guns alongside men in the Second People's Church ready to be locked up or die. From storefronts to schools, hospitals, churches and streets, women in the Young Lords were at the frontlines.

In the years that followed, feminist ideals and programs would rise and fall. However, the period from the summer of 1969 through the end of 1970 was exceptional. The struggles of the Women's Caucus successfully moved the Young Lords Party to adopt feminist principles as central to its political agenda. Women advanced into leadership and developed campaigns centered on issues of reproductive justice and raised awareness about the institutional oppression of women. Old ideas about the inferiority of women were discarded, and members committed to and attempted to practice "new ways of being."

CHANGING YLP LEADERSHIP AND DIRECTION

On July 26, 1970, the Young Lords Party proudly celebrated its first year anniversary. A few weeks later in an astounding announcement, the Central Committee members disclosed that Felipe Luciano had been indefinitely demoted from the position of chairman of the Young Lords citing the reasons as lack of political development and male chauvinism.[52] The top leaders initially indicated that Luciano would continue as a member in the organization, but he resigned.[53] (The events surrounding Luciano's removal from the leadership and the consequences were described in the previous chapter.) In the immediate and messy aftermath, the Young Lords were still recovering from the shock of Luciano's departure when a second woman, Gloria González, was appointed to the Central Committee joining Juan González, Pablo "Yoruba" Guzmán, Denise Oliver, Juan "Fi" Ortiz, and David Pérez.

Gloria González (who also used the surnames Cruz, Fontanez, and Wright) was twenty-six years old and a cofounder of the Health Revolutionary Unity Movement (HRUM), a leading hospital workers' group in New York City. As an HRUM activist, González first met the Young Lords in the fall of 1969 and had collaborated with members on several hospital worker organizing drives and community health testing initiatives. She joined the Young Lords Organization in February 1970 and aided in organizing the health campaign that culminated in the Lincoln Hospital takeover. She and Juan González, minister of defense, entered a revolutionary marriage that July.[54]

As a former hospital worker, Gloria González' background and experience made her a viable candidate for the Central Committee, and her promotion also responded to the demands of the Women's Caucus to advance women into leadership positions. Still, some caucus members, including myself, were unsure about her commitment to feminist ideals since she had refused to join or participate with the Women's Caucus and had given no reason for it.

The new Central Committee—Juan González, Guzmán, David Pérez, Ortiz, Oliver, and Gloria González—held their first leadership retreat to evaluate the work of the Young Lords Party in early December 1970. A substantial portion of their agenda was devoted to a review of the status of women in the organization, not surprising given the struggles with the Women's Caucus that year. As background, Oliver presented an analysis of "colonized mentality" surveying sexism and racism as systemic ideologies of oppression, which was subsequently published as part of the "The Ideology of the Young Lords Party." Central Committee members also summarized the reports received from the local branch leaders and concluded: "Every branch found that we're still a long way from rooting out chauvinism and passivity at all levels."[55] Among the examples cited was the low number of women officers, only three—Denise Oliver, Gloria González, and myself—out of twenty officers in the Young Lords Party at the time. The top leaders admitted in the report that several capable women had been passed over for promotions, but they gave no reason.[56] *Palante*, which had made some progress, was still criticized as being too male oriented and chauvinist in its reporting, editorial content, and writings: "*Palante* really is not geared toward the one half of our nation that is sisters," the leaders wrote.[57]

To remedy the deficiencies, the Central Committee leaders promised to make additional structural changes to "fight institutional chauvinism." Yet the only action that they approved immediately was to disband both the women's and men's caucuses, even though these gender-based groupings had been highly effective in educating members about sexism and male chauvinism, and had expanded gender equality within the organization and the broader community. However, there was no further discussion about the caucus closures as other issues emerged and took precedence when the Central Committee outlined the political objectives of the Young Lords Party for 1971. First was the opening of Young Lords Party branches in Puerto Rico. Second was the building of "people's organizations" in the United States.

The announcement about the opening of Young Lords Party branches in Puerto Rico was unexpected, and not all leaders and members supported the decision. Most notably, Denise Oliver, minister of finance and economic development, disagreed. Nonetheless, the Central Committee went ahead with the plan. The debate about the Puerto Rico decision and its consequences are fully examined in the next chapter. Suffice it to say that the Puerto Rico project represented a drastic and across-the-board move that changed the YLP forever, including the progression of the struggle for women's rights. Oliver resigned in February 1971. With her departure, the Young Lords Party lost the only feminist advocate it had on the Central Committee.

THE WOMEN'S UNION

In addition to opening branches in Puerto Rico, the Central Committee intended to develop "people's organizations" in the United States as a strategy to activate different sectors of the community and build a mass movement. Among the organizations proposed was a Women's Union, to which I was assigned. Eager to launch the project, I invited women into the planning process. We formed a steering committee composed of two Young Lords and two supporters including Elsie, a thirty-eight-year-old woman born and raised in Puerto Rico but living in East Harlem for years; Yvonne, a Puerto Rican college student from the Bronx; Gloria González, in absentia, since she was in Puerto Rico, and myself. Although González had refused to participate in the Women's Caucus, now, as the only female on the Central Committee, she was designated to oversee the Women's Union.

The steering committee reached out to Puerto Rican and third world women[58] around shared commonalities. High school and college students, homemakers, workers, mothers, and activists attended the meetings excited to participate in an organization that valued women of color. For the majority, it was the first-time they attended women-led meetings to build the collective power of women. As we discussed the realities facing women of color, we noted that even in social justice and national liberation struggles around the world, women had to fight for their own rights to be included in the vision of a new society. "This is the 'revolution within the revolution'," I explained.

70

The agenda of the Women's Union included planning a daycare center in East Harlem, recruiting women of color to social justice activities, and conducting political education. The all-women classes encouraged participants to imagine a society where we could fully develop all our capacities.[59] We studied the societal complexities of women's exploitation—the systems, policies, and barriers blocking the progress of women of color. We concluded that all institutions affecting women's societal roles and interpersonal relationships had to transform. "That's a protracted struggle," one of the members exclaimed loudly, and all of us agreed.

As a unifying document, the Women's Union developed a twelve-point program reflecting forward-thinking ideas and demands. Focused on the needs and interests of low-income women of color, the program called for full employment, equal pay, employer-provided childcare, and compensation for housework—all demands still not met today. It also advocated for the rights of sex workers and drug-addicted sisters, the most vulnerable and oppressed women of color in society—the women society treated as the most disposable.

The twelve-point program analyzed the multiple exploitations of women: the use of our bodies for cheap labor, prostitution, and experimentation, and as sex objects to sell products. It articulated a broad reproductive rights agenda with demands for safe and accessible methods of fertility control, and an end to sterilization, forced abortions, and unnecessary gynecological exams. Discussions about women's health and safety triggered recollections of widespread violence against women, and members felt safe to share their personal experiences. One woman described seeing her sister get shot and killed by a jealous boyfriend. Another told how her husband had knifed her; another how her father had beat her black and blue so that she had to be hospitalized. Others revealed unsettling tales of being raped by uncles and grandfathers. Still others talked about being grabbed, groped, touched, and ogled daily by men on the street. Women described brutal attacks by personnel in the US military, sexual assaults by the police, and rapes by prison officials. The accounts enraged and saddened us, but they also propelled us to action. We condemned all forms of violence against women and declared: "We believe in the right to defend ourselves against rapes, beatings, muggings, and general abuse."

The twelve-point program linked our demands for justice and equal rights as women to the collective right of self-determination of a people and nation. The Women's Union called for the liberation of Puerto Ricans on the island and inside the United States, and demanded freedom for all political prisoners. We envisioned a socialist society and self-determination for all nations. Lastly, we denounced political, economic, and military intervention by one nation against another.

The Women's Union produced a bilingual English/Spanish newspaper, *La Luchadora* (The Fighter), written entirely by women, which we sold for ten cents a copy. The first issue featured an article titled "Why a Women's Union?," which stated:

> Because as women we can best organize other women for the liberation of Puerto Rico and for the self-determination of all oppressed people. Because as women, we best understand our own oppression and can organize ourselves for our liberation, always remembering that we will not be free until all our people are free. We don't want to be cheap labor horses anymore. We don't want to be used as guinea pigs anymore. We want to be respected and treated as human beings by our men. We want all our people to be treated like human beings, and if not, we will fight till we are.[60]

La Luchadora's primary audience was Puerto Rican, Latinas, African Americans, and other women of color. The newspaper featured stories about women workers in factories and hospitals, and in other people's homes as domestics, as well as women who were homemakers or who received public assistance. Women wrote about governmental policies affecting women of color in the welfare and prison systems. Often, a writer related a personal situation that described a collectively shared experience. *La Luchadora* did not shy away from feminist or political language. "Machismo" was the title of one full-page article. Another article, "House Slave" described the drudgery of housework and the oppression of women in the home.

The Women's Union collaborated with women activists from other organizations including the Movement Pro Independence (MPI), which later became the Puerto Rican Socialist Party (PSP), El

Comité, the Puerto Rican Student Union, and others in New York City. Working together, we also realized how widespread sexism was across the Puerto Rican movement. Carmen Vivian Rivera, a leading MPI-PSP member, described the gender politics at the time:[61]

> The mystique and aura surrounding the revolutionary were built on the *male* figure. The woman as revolutionary and leader was rarely understood, accepted, validated, or promoted. Therefore her projection both at the time and in the recording of our history is woefully absent. We tried to change the definition of leader itself, but we weren't always successful.

Rivera further explained:

> The men in the states [the United States] seemed to display a more covert sexism, probably because they did not want to be ostracized by the women in the MPI-PSP or by other movement women. Publicly they [men] denounced sexism and the oppression of women, but they often used that rhetoric as a shield they could hide behind to project themselves as a more advanced *hombre nuevo* [new man]. When it came to their personal lives, many of them talked the talk but couldn't walk the walk.

As activists, we insisted on more than rhetoric or pretense. We had to change oppressive systems but also ourselves. We believed that transforming capitalist thinking and power dynamics required a conscious and intentional struggle to "a new way of being."[62] However, the process of transformation was not a straight path, and the exchanges between men and women about these issues were explosive. Yet the willingness to engage already indicated a positive change.

The commitment to personal transformation led us to look inward. We, too, consumed, and unconsciously accepted, the dominant stereotypes about societal and family roles reserved for women of color. Collectively, we scrutinized the prejudices embedded in the national psyche about our abilities, physical appearance, and skin color, drummed into our minds, hearts, and bodies since birth, passed down from generation to generation by families, media, and all other institutions. As women of color, we grappled with the attitudes of inferiority and feelings of inadequacy these caused. Our passivity often showed as timidity or fear of questioning authority. Facing deep-rooted self-negativity also meant challenging complicity with practices that placed a higher value on men. "Male-identified females" favored men and gave more credence to their views; they automatically accepted men as more adept leaders and thinkers, believing that women were less capable. As we deconstructed the negative narratives about women, we became more determined to fight for social change.

The members of the Women's Union understood that talk meant nothing without action. Both women and men had to act to achieve gender equality and justice. Not all women were sisters simply because we were of the same gender, and men could be allies. In the words of feminist scholar bell hooks, "While they [men] need not blame themselves in accepting sexism, they must assume responsibility for eliminating it."[63] In our struggles to achieve justice and equality for women, we never lost sight of the fact that men of color were our fathers, brothers, sons, friends, husbands, and lovers who were also oppressed by the same capitalist system and institutions as we were.

INDOCHINESE WOMEN'S CONFERENCE

The women in the Young Lords also participated in international exchanges with other women activists. In April 1971, the Young Lords Party attended the Indochinese Women's Conference to meet North and South Vietnamese, Cambodian, and Laotian women traveling to the West to build support for their national liberation struggles.[64] We were excited to meet them. It was a time when the Vietnamese and Cuban revolutions, the perceived progress of the People's Republic of China, and armed movements in Latin America, Asia, Africa, and the Middle East appeared unstoppable and victorious,[65] even though this was not the case. Gloria González and I represented the Young Lords in a New York contingent at the conference in Toronto, Canada, which included women from the Black Workers' Congress, El Comité, the Puerto Rican Student Union, and I Wor Kuen; a similar conference was held in Vancouver. Police surveillance was extremely high, and we were detained and questioned at the Canadian border by US authorities on the return trip home.

The Indochinese women had traveled through war-torn areas and under great hardship to arrive at the North American conferences that were important venues to expose the war's impact and mobilize actions to stop US bombings and end the war. Approximately one thousand women convened in Toronto to hear and exchange ideas with the Indochinese delegation, which included women from different sectors of society: a homemaker, several teachers, a literature professor, and a physician, ranging in ages from twenty-nine to fifty years old.[66] They were the featured speakers and presenters, and the reason everyone gathered. On the opening day, the Indochinese representatives addressed a general assembly of all the North American women in attendance. On the second day, the delegation met separately with North American women of color. This meeting responded to criticism of a prior women's conference where the conveners had failed to invite any women of color or workingwomen to attend. The Indochinese women described the horror caused by US bombers and the crippling effects of napalm and other chemicals. A representative from the South Vietnamese Women's Union, Madame Dinh Thi Huong, detailed her torture at the hands of US military personnel.[67] Moved by their accounts, we committed to continue mobilizing against US atrocities. As residents of the United States, we understood the importance of our support and solidarity.

The conference also afforded an opportunity for North American activists with diverse experiences—white women and women of color with various class backgrounds, sexual orientations, nationalities, ages, and political ideologies—to meet. However, differences among the women exploded into sharp disputes and angry arguments about racism and self-determination, the role of separatist women's organizations, and the inclusion of lesbian feminists. Many white women's groups were in attendance. Some were friends and allies; others were elitist only intent on taking the power that white men had for themselves. They were not interested in transforming society or improving the lives of women of color.

When we returned to New York, González and I reported the fiery clashes to the top leadership, and we evaluated the women's organizations attending the conference. Subsequently, the Central Committee published a critique titled "Position on Women's Liberation," which underscored the class and political differences. We considered our struggles part of a working class movement, while the white groups were predominantly middle class women with a different set of concerns. The article in *Palante* concluded:

> [O]ur major enemy is capitalism rather than men. But there ain't no doubt about it, there are a few rich men who control this planet. They are our enemies. Not because they are men, but because they are capitalists. Some of the rulers are women (and some of them are in the right wing women's movement). They are also our enemy, not because they are women, but because they are capitalists. [68]

Emphasizing that women in the Young Lords were not anti-men, the Young Lords insisted that women and men working together would transform capitalism.

FEMINISM AND NATIONALISM COLLIDE

Some months after the Indochinese Women's Conference, the Young Lords Party convened an organization-wide retreat in July 1971. It was an important gathering for all members in the New York, Philadelphia, Bridgeport (Connecticut), and Aguadilla and El Caño, Puerto Rico branches to reflect on the Young Lords' activities since the start of the year. At the end of the retreat, the Central Committee distributed a 49-page report to all members setting forth the political philosophy and direction to be followed. The focus was on building the Young Lords Party in Puerto Rico and a working class base in the United States. To ensure alignment with these goals, the report reviewed all aspects of the Young Lords' ideology.

Hence Central Committee members scrutinized the feminist ideals and practices, which had been adopted by the Young Lords Party as a result of the struggles with the Women's Caucus. In an unexpected about-face, they insisted that women's issues had received too much attention, and they wrote:

> Too much time has been given to this contradiction [women's oppression] more than any other. This was incorrect.[69]

They asserted that YLP members tended to discuss sexism and colonized mentality as "bigger problems" than those of nation and class, and that members were confused about the organization's "correct" priorities.[70] By way of clarification, the Central Committee declared:

> The biggest contradictions in our nation are the division of the nation and the division between classes. Then come the divisions of sex and race.[71]

The statement reframed the organizing priorities of the Young Lords Party: first was the national liberation of Puerto Rico and class struggle, then issues related to "divisions of sex and race." However, it contradicted principles already in place. Almost a year earlier, the Central Committee had published the "YLP Position Paper on Women" promoting "the revolution within the revolution"—the belief that the women's struggle for equality was integral to national liberation. The position paper had also embraced the idea of "triple oppression"—that women of color suffered multiple and intersecting oppressions based on class, nationality/race, and gender, which had to be addressed concurrently.[72] Now the introduction of a priorities framework put feminism and nationalism on a collision course.

The clash between feminism and nationalism was not new. In national liberation movements across the world, feminists were criticized for proposing that women's issues be part of these struggles. Nationalists fighting colonialism tended to view feminist agendas as subordinate, deferring their implementation until after the success of the anti-imperialist movements. In some nations, women were expected to frame their concerns within the parameters of nationalism or shelve them; while in others, feminists were portrayed as traitors.[73] Yet the study of nationalist movements worldwide revealed that, more often than not, the failure to combine a gender analysis with an anti-colonial one only increased the chance that colonized women's lives would not improve after national liberation, as the new male leaders were reluctant to give up any power they recently gained.[74]

Puerto Rico had its own examples. Historically, nationalist, socialist, and independence parties privileged the national liberation struggle and lowered feminist issues to secondary status.[75] In the early twentieth-century, island women fighting for the right to vote and

participate in the political and public sphere were accused by nationalist leaders of "failing to support Puerto Rican men in their struggle for
independence from US imperialism and putting personal concerns
before those of nation."[76] Into the 1970s, the independence movement
sidelined feminist activism. "The rhetoric of liberation and self-
determination rarely made reference to women or rarely addressed the
question of the nation from the perspective of women," concluded
scholar Maria I. Bryant after an extensive review of *Claridad*, the island's main pro-independence newspaper.[77] In a study of activism and
feminism, leading women's studies scholar Elizabeth Crespo-Kebler
confirmed that to mention women's rights and still be accepted by
men in Puerto Rico, it was necessary to affirm heterosexuality and
recognize class struggle as the primary social conflict.[78] Carmen Vivian
Rivera, a militant with the MPI-PSP during the 1970s, also observed:
"The men in Puerto Rico practiced a more overt sexism. They felt no
compulsion to appease the feminist movement, which they viewed as
"an aberration spawned by the *yanqui* radical Left."[79] With sexism and
male chauvinism so deeply rooted in Puerto Rican culture, the tendency was to construe demands for women's equality on the island as a
manifestation of the US white women's liberation movement and as a
divisive force in the pro-independence struggle. Feminism was viewed
as foreign and threatening to traditional values and roles.[80]

Evidently, the YLP Central Committee members also held these
views. Fixated on gaining a stronghold in Puerto Rico's pro-
independence movement, they were determined to prove that the
Young Lords Party was a viable alternative on the island. Apparently,
the Central Committee members assumed that the YLP feminist ideas
and activities accepted in the United States would not be well received
in Puerto Rico and would hamper recruiting efforts. Looking through
this lens, consciously or not, they made a U-turn back to the idea of
the revolution-in-stages—first national and then women's liberation—
which had dominated prior to the victories of the Women's Caucus,
and they implemented measures that suspended or diluted feminist
ideals and activities. The formation of the Women's Union in Puerto
Rico was put on hold,[81] and the Women's Union in New York was
criticized for its rapid growth citing this as an example of "incorrect
priorities." Additionally, the Central Committee leaders instructed

Young Lords not to speak publicly about "sexism," maintaining that it was too extreme and would turn people away from the YLP.[82]

Similarly, the Central Committee leaders avoided addressing the issue of homosexuality. During the July retreat, members in the Puerto Rico branches had described escalating homophobia, and the Central Committee issued a short statement in the retreat report denouncing "the oppression of homosexual cadres in the Party." However, no resolution or plan of action was offered. Instead the Central Committee abolished the homosexual caucuses stating: "Just like women's caucuses, they [homosexual caucuses] are not the solution for resolving this contradiction."[83] No further explanation was given. The top leadership abolished all gender-based groupings; they had disbanded the women's and men's caucuses six months earlier.

Clearly, the Central Committee ignored or disregarded the active movement for women's equality and gay rights in Puerto Rico that at the time was fighting against sex discrimination and for the right to abortion and maternity leave, and organizing around issues of domestic violence, sexual harassment, and sexist representation in the media. Puerto Rican feminists saw no contradiction between the struggle for gender equality and national liberation—the fight against US colonialism was to dismantle all systems of oppression. As a reminder to men in the movement that feminists also prioritized national liberation, the Federation of Puerto Rican Women wrote in 1975: *"Si los hombres no logran la independencia, la logrará la mujer."* "If men don't achieve the country's independence, then women will."[84]

The July 1971 retreat marked a turning point for the Young Lords Party. The unique balance that had been achieved between feminism and nationalism came to an abrupt end. The Central Committee abandoned the "revolution within the revolution" and feminist initiatives, once at the forefront, were relegated to the bottom rung of a hierarchy. The almost 50-page retreat report did not once mention the Thirteen-Point Program or the Position Paper on Women, the YLP's main documents addressing women's rights. From this point forward, feminist ideas and campaigns stagnated and advanced no further.

After the July retreat, the priority of the Young Lords Party in the United States focused on building worker organizations. However, the new directive deemphasizing gender-related organizing did not immediately affect the work of the Women's Union in New York, and we did not fully grasp its long-term ramifications. We continued to meet, conduct political education, and publish *La Luchadora*, as we had done. Women of color participated in our activities, and we recruited members to the organization. However, a confrontation between the Central Committee and the Women's Union was not far off.

RIGHTS AND WRONGS

By the fall of 1971, many Young Lords were vocalizing serious concerns about the move to Puerto Rico. When Pablo "Yoruba" Guzmán returned from a trip with a US delegation to the People's Republic of China, David Pérez and Juan "Fi" Ortiz reported to him that the Young Lords Party was in disarray and rapidly losing members. Determined to reenergize the organization, Guzmán, Pérez, and Ortiz developed a plan. (Juan González and Gloria González were out of New York at the time.) However, it was more than a little shocking when the Central Committee's proposal revealed the intention to "wither away" the Women's Union,[85] which was successfully recruiting Puerto Ricans, African Americans, and other Latinas into the social justice movement. The men gave two reasons. They argued that the Workers' Federation, another people's organization, should have been developed first, then its women members should have formed the Women's Union in turn. Second, they said that the members of the Women's Union were needed to staff the Puerto Rican Student Union, the Workers' Federation, and the Committee to Defend the Community,[86] clearly prioritizing the work of these organizations.

David Pérez called me to a meeting at the national headquarters to deliver the news. I was furious. The decision made no sense. "Why would the YLP close down an organization that is recruiting women into the movement?" I asked. Pérez responded that the Women's Union was supposed to be the last priority but had developed faster than the Workers' Federation, which was supposed to be first. "What? Organizing is not a competition or a race. Are you penalizing women for being good organizers?" I questioned. It sounded like he was making up things to rationalize the shutdown. "What is this really about?" I demanded. Then Pérez accused me and other members of the Women's Union of putting women's issues over those of workers, harking back to the "priorities hierarchy" introduced at the July retreat.

"Women are also workers," I said and suggested that he read *La Luchadora.* "Our struggle is a class struggle. The members of the Women's Union are workers, homemakers, students, and unemployed," I emphasized. In Puerto Rico, as in this country, women have a long history as both labor activists and feminists. Luisa Capetillo, Puerto Rico's best-known feminist and working class leader of the early twentieth-century, devoted her life to organizing workers, both men and women, as well as to the emancipation of women. As scholar Norma Valle-Ferrer wrote, Capetillo "revolutionized the role of women in Puerto Rican society,"[87] and her "concerns centered on the premise that women are complete human beings with almost no freedom."[88] Through her life's work, Capetillo demonstrated the necessity to fight all forms of class oppression.

"How will the YLP respond to the particular oppression of women?" I asked. "We don't have the resources," Pérez replied. It was clear; organizing women was deemed nonessential and unimportant. The decision to shutdown the Women's Union was final, even though the organization had successfully created a safe space for women of color to organize. Nonetheless, the Central Committee proposed to move the women around like chess pawns.

A few months later, I was transferred to the Young Lords Party branch in Philadelphia and was no longer a member of the Women's Union. My transfer was the result of yet another conflict with the Central Committee, which will be more fully explained in the next chapter. Briefly, I joined with several top YLP leaders seeking to refocus the organization, and we proposed that the Puerto Rico branches be closed. The chief proponents of the Puerto Rico project, Juan González, Gloria González, and David Pérez, disagreed, and we were demoted from our leadership positions and transferred to different branches.

A short time after the announced "withering away of the Women's Union," the Central Committee released another communiqué stating that the closure of the Women's Union had been an "error." The flip-flop appeared to originate from an internal struggle among the Central Committee members about who had the authority to make binding decisions for the organization. Several months later the Women's Union was reinstated in New York under direct and strict Central Committee control, but *La Luchadora* was never published again.

Other Latinas in New York continued to build on the work of the Women's Union. Carmen Lora, a leader of El Comité, invited me to a meeting of the newly formed Latin Women's Collective in 1975. Years later, Esperanza Martell, another leader of El Comité, wrote: "We believed that working class women historically had been the backbone of most political and community organizations, but they never took or got the credit for their hard work. To be leaders we had to develop writing, speaking, and analytical skills and the courage to take up the struggle against sexism within us and our community. We took the challenge."[89] The Latin Women's Collective continued the work begun by the Women's Union.

WOMEN LEADERS IN THE PHILADELPHIA BRANCH

It was early 1972 when I joined Pablo "Yoruba" Guzmán, Michael Rodríguez, and Gloria Rodríguez on the steering committee of the Philadelphia chapter, which had officially affiliated with the Young Lords Party about a year and a half earlier. Philadelphia was home to the third largest Puerto Rican population in the United States, mostly first-generation, working class people, primarily Spanish speaking, with strong ties to the island. The Young Lords Party office was located on Third and Diamond Streets in North Philadelphia, one of the city's largest and poorest Puerto Rican communities where we lived and worked.

Juan Ramos, a young Philadelphia activist, was the cofounder of the branch, which he led until 1972 when the Central Committee transferred him to the Aguadilla branch in Puerto Rico. By then, Guzmán was headed to federal prison sentenced to two years for refusing induction into the US Army at a time when most (white) anti-Vietnam War activists were receiving probation with no jail time for the same offense. Michael Rodríguez was also headed to federal prison on an arrest dating back to October 1971. Riding in a car with a Reverend Donald Murphy, who turned out to be an Alcohol, Tobacco and Firearms (AFT) agent, they were stopped by four carloads of AFT agents who pulled a fifty-caliber machine gun from the trunk of the car. Rodríguez was convicted of machine gun possession.

When Guzmán and Michael Rodríguez went to prison, Gloria Rodríguez and I assumed leadership of the chapter. We were both native New Yorkers in our mid-twenties when we accepted responsibility for the organization in the City of Brotherly Love with the notoriously brutal Frank Rizzo as mayor. It was a daunting task.

By mid-1972, the Young Lords Party had assumed a new name, the Puerto Rican Revolutionary Workers Organization (PRRWO), with a mission to organize workers directly at their workplaces. The YLP storefront had closed, and not many members remained from the early days of the Philadelphia branch, only a few unemployed men in their late teens and early twenties with an outspoken hostility to women in leadership. Rodríguez and I had to rebuild the chapter, almost from scratch, with few resources and no assistance from the New York headquarters.

Our earliest and most dedicated PRRWO members were Puerto Ricans, but also several African Americans and one Asian. They included Philadelphians and out-of-towners; young factory, hospital, and service workers; Vietnam War veterans, and university students. We worked closely with the Black Panther Party, the Black United Liberation Front, and the Yellow Seeds[90] collaborating on many issues, especially police brutality. We were under constant surveillance and harassment; our telephones were tapped. Whenever we stepped out of our homes, the police followed. We were stopped on the street, pulled out of our cars, and routinely searched. Mayor Rizzo, a former police commissioner, a right-wing conservative, and law-and-order proponent, condoned police brutality, beatings, and shootings. The police were vicious.[91] This was the same police department that raided the Black Panther Party office in 1971, lined up members against a wall in the street, had them undress, and then held them there butt-naked at gunpoint.

We frequently witnessed the police drive into the North Philadelphia community where we lived, round up black and Latino men, put them up against a wall, pick one, and throw him into a patrol car. The police would drop him off in an all-white area, so racists there could beat him on his walk back home. In one such neighborhood, a young newly wed Puerto Rican couple purchased a house, but before they could move in, it was totally vandalized. The newspapers reported comments from local residents who admitted destroying the home saying, "Spics bring dirt, and dirt brings niggers." Racial conflicts raged throughout the city that summer.

The PRRWO members dedicated themselves to organizing working people in factories, hospitals, and migrant farms. I got a job as a sewing machine operator in a large men's clothing factory for piecework wages with a half-hour break to eat a brown-bag lunch brought from home. The boss moved me daily from machine to machine, wherever I was needed as a "utility worker." He wandered throughout the facility, smiling at young women and inviting them to dinner as if it were a privilege to be in his company. It never crossed his mind that a woman might say "no" since refusing his advances would likely result in being fired. It was no use complaining to the shop steward or union delegate supposedly there to represent the workers, because they were enthusiastic agents and cover-ups for the boss. Many women lost their jobs for declining the boss's invitation and resisting his sexual advances.

After the factory job, I worked as a clerk in a health clinic at a large non-unionized hospital in North Philly for the purpose of organizing workers. Other PRRWO members also worked in hospitals and a few as day laborers alongside Puerto Rican and Mexican-American migrant workers on New Jersey farms picking fruit for two or three dollars an hour. With our limited resources, we wrote and distributed *Abuso*, a semimonthly newsletter dedicated to Philadelphia-area news. We conducted political education classes with Puerto Rican women, and we supported the efforts of Temple University activists to establish a Puerto Rican studies program and increase financial aid for low-income students. We made our presence known by marching in the city's Puerto Rican Day Parade, and supporting activities to decolonize Puerto Rico and free Puerto Rican political prisoners. We continued to mobilize and recruit members even as the PRRWO was in decline, and even without any financial support and infrequent communication from the national leadership.

After two years in Philadelphia, the Central Committee reassigned me to New York City in 1974. I was sad to leave my comrades and friends, but I was ready to return home. I hoped to continue my organizing activities back in the city, especially recruiting women and workers into the social justice movement. However, word was that PRRWO in New York was less involved in organizing and more engaged in the ideological debates discussed in the next chapter.

SUMMARY

Women joined the Young Lords Organization to make revolution, to fight poverty, racism, and the exploitation of women, and to free Puerto Rico from US colonialism. With visionary ideas, a warrior spirit, and loving hearts, women performed leading and significant roles. Our battle was against capitalism and imperialism, and the powerful forces in control of the world's resources. We pursued the "revolution within the revolution" uniting the struggles for women's liberation with demands for social, economic, and racial justice.

Women in the Young Lords led campaigns to achieve better living conditions and opportunities for the most vulnerable and exploited women in our communities—working poor, working class students, mothers on welfare, women in prison, drug addicted women, and prostitutes. Differences among women of color were acknowledged, and we believed that improving the circumstances of the poorest and most oppressed among us would transform society and benefit everyone. We found it necessary to form women's groups within and outside of the YLO/YLP in order to have our demands for equality and justice included on the social justice agenda. Working from within, the Women's Caucus introduced feminist ideals and activities to the organization. The Women's Union brought feminist ideas and campaigns to the community and recruited women of color into the social justice movement. We achieved important victories; we also suffered profound losses. When the Young Lords Party abandoned its commitment to "the revolution within the revolution," the social justice struggle went backward and lost its momentum.

The most powerful and effective organizing activities of women in the Young Lords were rooted in principles still relevant today. The struggle for human liberation must be both feminist and anti-racist. The multiple oppressions experienced by women of color—labor, gender, and racist exploitation tied together historically—are linked to the fight for racial, economic, and social justice. The women in the Young Lords understood that the inequities lived by women of color were never just solely the result of gender; rather, they were the outcome of intersecting social locations, class and economic interests, race and national origin, and the legacy of history.

YOUNG LORDS PARTY

13 POINT PROGRAM

AND PLATFORM

THE YOUNG LORDS PARTY IS A REVOLUTIONARY POLITICAL PARTY FIGHTING FOR THE LIBERATION OF ALL OPPRESSED PEOPLE

1. WE WANT SELF-DETERMINATION FOR PUERTO RICANS, LIBERATION ON THE ISLAND AND INSIDE THE UNITED STATES.

For 500 years, first spain and then the united states have colonized our country. Billions of dollars in profits leave our country for the united states every year. In every way we are slaves of the gringo. We want liberation and the Power in the hands of the People, not Puerto Rican exploiters. QUE VIVA PUERTO RICO LIBRE!

2. WE WANT SELF-DETERMINATION FOR ALL LATINOS.

Our Latin Brothers and Sisters, inside and outside the united states, are oppressed by amerikkkan business. The Chicano people built the Southwest, and we support their right to control their lives and their land. The people of Santo Domingo continue to fight against gringo domination and its puppet generals. The armed liberation struggles in Latin America are part of the war of Latinos against imperialism. QUE VIVA LA RAZA!

3. WE WANT LIBERATION OF ALL THIRD WORLD PEOPLE.

Just as Latins first slaved under spain and the yanquis, Black people, Indians, and Asians slaved to build the wealth of this country. For 400 years they have fought for freedom and dignity against racist Babylon. Third World people have led the fight for freedom. All the colored and oppressed peoples of the world are one nation under oppression. NO PUERTO RICAN IS FREE UNTIL ALL PEOPLE ARE FREE!

4. WE ARE REVOLUTIONARY NATIONALISTS AND OPPOSE RACISM

The Latin, Black, Indian and Asian people inside the u.s. are colonies fighting for liberation. We know that washington, wall street, and city hall will try to make our nationalism into racism; but Puerto Ricans are of all colors and we resist racism. Millions of poor white people are rising up to demand freedom and we support them. These are the ones in the u.s. that are stepped on by the rulers and the government. We each organize our people, but our fights are the same against oppression and we will defeat it together. POWER TO ALL OPPRESSED PEOPLE!

5. WE WANT EQUALITY FOR WOMEN. DOWN WITH MACHISMO AND MALE CHAUVANISM.

Under capitalism, women have been oppressed by both society and our men. The doctrine of machismo has been used by men to take out their frustrations on wives, sisters, mothers, and children. Men must fight along with sisters in the struggle for economic and social equality and must recognize that sisters make up over half of the revolutionary army: sisters and brothers are equals fighting for our people. FORWARD SISTERS IN THE STRUGGLE!

6. WE WANT COMMUNITY CONTROL OF OUR INSTITUTIONS AND LAND.

We want control of our communities by our people and programs to guarantee that all institutions serve the needs of our people. People's control of police, health services, churches, schools, housing, transportation and welfare are needed. We want an end to attacks on our land by urban renewal, highway destruction, and university corporations. LAND BELONGS TO ALL THE PEOPLE!

7. WE WANT A TRUE EDUCATION OF OUR AFRO-INDIO CULTURE AND SPANISH LANGUAGE.

We must learn our long history of fighting against cultural, as well as economic genocide by the spaniards and now the yanquis. Revolutionary culture, culture of our people, is the only true teaching. JIBARO SI, YANQUI NO!

8. WE OPPOSE CAPITALISTS AND ALLIANCES WITH TRAITORS.

Puerto Rican rulers, or puppets of the oppressor, do not help our people. They are paid by the system to lead our people down blind alleys, just like the thousands of poverty pimps who keep our communities peaceful for business, or the street workers who keep gangs divided and blowing each other away. We want a society where the people socialistically control their labor. VENCEREMOS!

9. WE OPPOSE THE AMERIKKKAN MILITARY.

We demand immediate withdrawal of all u.s. military forces and bases from Puerto Rico, VietNam, and all oppressed communities inside and outside the u.s.. No Puerto Rican should serve in the u.s. army against his Brothers and Sisters, for the only true army of oppressed people is the People's Liberation Army to fight all rulers. U.S. OUT OF VIETNAM, FREE PUERTO RICO NOW!

10.WE WANT FREEDOM FOR ALL POLITICAL PRISONERS AND PRISONERS OF WAR.

No Puerto Rican should be in jail or prison, first because we are a nation, and amerikkka has no claims on us; second, because we have not been tried by our own people (peers). We also want all freedom fighters out of jail, since they are prisoners of the war for liberation. FREE ALL POLITICAL PRISONERS AND PRISONERS OF WAR!

11.WE ARE INTERNATIONALISTS.

Our people are brainwashed by television, radio, newspapers, schools and books, to oppose people in other countries fighting for their freedom. No longer will we believe these lies, because we have learned who the real enemy is and who our real friends are. We will defend our sisters and brothers around the world who fight for justice and are against the rulers of this country. QUE VIVA CHE GUEVARA!

12.WE BELIEVE ARMED SELF-DEFENSE AND ARMED STRUGGLE ARE THE ONLY MEANS TO LIBERATION

We are oppose to violence - the violence of hungry children, illiterate adults, diseased old people, and the violence of poverty and profit. We have asked, petitioned, gone to courts, demonstrated peacefully, and voted for politicians full of empty promises. But we still ain't free. The time has come to defend the lives of our people against repression and for revolutionary war against the businessmen, politicians, and police. When a government oppresses the people, we have the right to abolish it and create a new one. ARM OURSELVES TO DEFEND OURSELVES!

13.WE WANT A SOCIALIST SOCIETY.

We want liberation, clothing, free food, education, health care, transportation, full employment and peace. We want a society where the needs of the people come first, and where we give solidarity and aid to the people of the world, not oppression and racism. HASTA LA VICTORIA SIEMPRE!

Thirteen-Point Program and Platform (1970)

New Directions to
Shattered Dreams

IRIS MORALES

THE 1960S WERE REVOLUTIONARY times. Across the world, people demanded national independence, racial equality, women's rights, and more humane societies. Their actions gave birth to radical changes in politics, culture, and social relations that influence our lives to the present day. Specific events and individuals moved the hearts of young Puerto Ricans living in the United States. The African American struggle for freedom and justice led the way. Malcolm X's powerful speeches about self-determination and self-defense taught us that revolutionary change was in our hands. When Malcolm was assassinated in 1965, we mourned the loss of a great spokesman and leader. Two months later, don Pedro Albizu Campos, Puerto Rican freedom fighter, died after being imprisoned for twenty-six years in the United States where he was subjected to radiation experiments.[1] Again, we cried and grieved a national hero.

The war in Vietnam dominated global attention. In 1968, the Tet Offensive—a series of attacks by North Vietnamese forces on South Vietnamese cities, including on the US Embassy grounds in Saigon—shocked the world.[2] The American command retaliated swiftly causing heavy casualties, and live television coverage brought the war's reality into our homes. Worldwide protests intensified.[3] A year earlier, Dr. Martin Luther King Jr. had spoken out against the war, calling it an enemy of the poor among other things.[4] Emphasizing the relation between the war machine and poverty, Dr. King organized the Poor People's Campaign urging black, white, brown, and Asian people to camp out in front of the Capitol Building in Washington D.C. until either a job or a living income was guaranteed for all.[5] When Dr. King was assassinated on April 4, 1968, thousands took to the streets in more than two hundred uprisings in 172 cities.[6] Many had lost faith, and no longer believed, that America could be reformed via elections or demonstrations. A new wave of grassroots militancy surged.

The Black Panther Party for Self-Defense, initially founded in Oakland, California in 1966, grew rapidly across the United States, as young people formed chapters in major cities. Among them, the Illinois chapter, organized in 1968 on Chicago's West Side, quickly recruited hundreds of members.[7] That same year in Chicago, as previously described, the Young Lords, a former street gang, became politicized and formed the Young Lords Organization (YLO) determined to achieve "human rights not just civil rights," thus making the distinction between revolutionary change and reform.[8] The Young Lords joined the Rainbow Coalition to fight racism and poverty alongside the Black Panther Party, the Brown Berets (Chicanos/Chicanas), the Young Patriots Organization (Appalachian migrants living in Chicago), Rising Up Angry (white working class youth), and several other organizations. Encouraged by the Chicago Young Lords, young Puerto Rican activists across the country were inspired to take action to change the dismal economic and social conditions facing the Puerto Rican people.

THE GREAT PUERTO RICAN MIGRATION

Most Young Lords were the children of the Great Puerto Rican Migration that arrived in the United States after World War II. Under US domination since 1898, Puerto Rico's agriculture had been destroyed when large-scale absentee corporations took ownership of the land, forcing displaced farmers into migrant labor and low wage jobs. A government program called "Operation Bootstrap" gave tax breaks and offered cheap labor to US companies further transforming the economy as islanders moved from rural to urban areas, where they faced extreme hardship. Officials blamed the island's glaring poverty on "overpopulation" and instituted population control policies. By 1965, roughly one third of Puerto Rican women had been sterilized, as detailed in the last chapter. The government also orchestrated the export of laborers. Approximately 470,000 Puerto Ricans migrated during a ten-year period enticed by the promise of economic opportunity in the United States.[9] Most found entry-level jobs in the service and manufacturing sectors working long hours for low wages;[10] but Puerto Ricans were nevertheless stereotyped as lazy welfare recipients, gangsters, drug addicts, and criminals.[11]

My parents arrived with this migration. In 1945, my mother, Almida Roldán, followed her sister to New York City from a rural area outside of Aguadilla in the northwestern part of the island. A day after her arrival, she was working as a sewing machine operator in a garment factory. As a child, she had been pulled out of school when her mother died of tuberculosis and her father of a heart attack shortly after to help raise her five siblings. My mother was nine years old then and in the third grade. As a teenager, she cleaned houses and did needlework for piecework wages. My father, Julio Morales, born in Sabana Grande, a town in the mountains of southwestern Puerto Rico, had been a sugarcane cutter and had attended school through the sixth grade. His first job in the city was as a dishwasher, and later he worked as an elevator operator until he retired from the Waldorf Astoria Hotel. He joked that everyday had ups and downs and proudly told stories about meeting every US president since Eisenhower and many celebrities on that elevator ride. He never missed a day or was late to his job. He worked the early shift so that he was home when his daughters arrived from school. Sometimes my younger sister and I accompanied him to pick up *mami* at her job. We stood quietly by her machine, watching in awe her swiftly moving hands under dim purple lights, sewing beautiful appliqués on fancy lingerie that she would never be able to afford.

Puerto Ricans wrote letters to family members back home, sent financial support, and helped bring relatives to the United States. Like so many people who migrate to another country, my parents' dream was to return home. For them, New York City was a temporary necessity, a stop before returning to the island. The words in "En Mi Viejo San Juan," the classic Puerto Rican song about migration, went deep into our souls: "Me voy pero un día volveré" (I'm leaving, but one day I'll return). My mother repeated stories about Puerto Rican soldiers arriving home after World War II, falling to their knees, crying tears of joy, and kissing the ground, happy to return safely to their beloved island of Borinquén. "We'll return to Puerto Rico," my father often promised.

By the late sixties, Puerto Ricans had settled across the United States with the vast majority living in the Northeast.[12] The passage of time, cold winters, and freezing snowstorms dimmed memories of the Caribbean sun. Puerto Ricans built new lives, established homes, raised families, and developed another language, "Spanglish." Growing up "in the belly of the beast,"[13] we witnessed the exploitation and suffering of our parents as they worked hard to survive and create opportunities for us. We also experienced poverty and racism as Puerto Ricans and as blacks. In school, we were reprimanded when our parents could not speak English and were met with contempt when we spoke Spanish. We faced societal disdain in neglected neighborhoods where government services were almost non-existent. We were a new generation living side by side with African Americans, developing internationalist perspectives, and we joined with others in similar circumstances to fight for human rights.

TENGO PUERTO RICO EN MI CORAZÓN

On July 27, 1969 a group of community activists in New York City affiliated with the Young Lords Organization in Chicago and, during the next year, established branches in East Harlem, the Bronx, and the Lower East Side, and a branch in Newark, New Jersey under the leadership of Ramón Rivera. Two additional branches opened in 1970, one in Philadelphia led by Juan Ramos, and another in Bridgeport (Connecticut) led by Willie Matos. (This early history is detailed in the opening chapter "The Young Lords' Early Years, 1969-1971: An Overview.") In 1971, a Young Lords' group formed in Boston led by Luis Garden Acosta and Josefina Vásquez. Following the Chicago example, the East Coast Young Lords wore purple berets on which they pinned the small, round button designed by the Chicago YLO with a drawing of the island and the words *"Tengo Puerto Rico en mi Corazón"* (I have Puerto Rico in my heart). The phrase sprang out of the migration experience and reflected our love for Puerto Rico, our longing for home, and our connection to one another.

We considered ourselves "revolutionary nationalists."[14] This idea expressed the intersecting and complex histories of Puerto Ricans exploited both in a US island colony and in the urban ghettos of the United States. Puerto Ricans suffered colonialism, class exploitation, and racism, and the Young Lords pointed to the US capitalist-imperialist system as the source of the problem. This view was distinct from that of other nationalists, who did not necessarily focus on a class analysis or on organizing the most economically disenfranchised, and from that of cultural nationalists, whose concerns were to promote and preserve Puerto Rican culture rather than transform the socio-economic-political system. For the Young Lords, revolutionary nationalism also meant internationalism—collaboration with people similarly exploited in the United States and throughout the world.

The first point of the Young Lords' Thirteen-Point Program and Platform declared, "We want self-determination for Puerto Ricans: liberation on the Island and inside the United States." These were dual and simultaneous demands. The Young Lords not only organized for the rights of Puerto Ricans in the United States but also mobilized thousands to support the decolonization of Puerto Rico.

Briefly summarized, the island's connection to the United States began when Spain ceded the colony of Puerto Rico at the end of the Spanish America War in 1898. Although the island had won agreement for local autonomy, the American government ignored it.[15] To complicate matters, Congress passed the Jones Act in 1917 imposing US citizenship on Puerto Ricans, and then drafted islanders into the military to fight in Europe in the First World War and then in every subsequent US war. Over a period of fifty years, fifteen successive US governors ruled the island, while the Puerto Rican people demanded the right to self-determination.

During the 1930s, a resistance movement grew. Under the leadership of the Nationalist Party, and its president, don Pedro Albizu Campos, a Harvard-educated lawyer, the Party organized workers' strikes and demonstrations, and other activities to free Puerto Rico from US control and domination. The US responded with unrelenting and brutal repression. In 1935, four Nationalists were killed and forty people wounded in an encounter outside the University of Puerto Rico in Rio Piedras. Two young Nationalists retaliated by killing Colonel Francis Riggs, the US police chief based on the island. In turn, the two men were picked up and executed in the Old San Juan police headquarters. After Riggs' was killed, a federal grand jury indicted Albizu Campos and others for sedition and "conspiracy to overthrow the government of the United States by force and violence." When the trial ended in a hung jury, the court retried them with a preselected jury and got a conviction.[16] Don Pedro Albizu Campos was imprisoned for ten years on this verdict. On March 21, 1937, a Palm Sunday, Puerto Ricans assembled in the city of Ponce to call for the release of nationalists held in US prisons. The police were there in force and indiscriminately fired their weapons into the crowd, killing seventeen persons and seriously wounding two hundred others. This date is remembered in our history as *la Masacre de Ponce*.

Laws intending to destroy the national liberation movement were enacted. The 1948 Ley de la Mordaza or "gag law" criminalized any discussion of independence; any writing, organizing, or meeting about the subject; and even singing patriotic songs or displaying the Puerto Rican flag. Thousands were arrested and jailed under this law. In 1950, President Harry Truman signed Public Act 600, in which the United States government "authorized" the nation of Puerto Rico to draft a constitution for autonomy over local affairs but permitted no change in its colonial status. The Nationalist Party opposed the law and, seeing no other recourse, began to organize for armed revolution. On October 30, 1950, Nationalist Party leader Blanca Canales led a takeover of the municipality of Jayuya and declared a free Puerto Rico; similar uprisings occurred in Peñuelas, Utuado, Ponce, and Arecibo. In retaliation, the United States bombed the towns, imposed martial law, and ordered the National Guard to crush the revolts.[17]

To bring international attention to the unending repression and colonial control of the island, the Nationalist Party acted. On November 1, 1950, two Nationalists entered Blair House in Washington, DC, in an attempt to assassinate President Truman. One man, Griselio Torresola, was killed; the other, Oscar Collazo, was wounded, captured, and imprisoned for twenty-nine years.[18] Across Puerto Rico, three thousand pro-independence supporters and patriots were arrested including don Albizu Campos who was sentenced to eighty years.[19] In 1954, Nationalist Party members, Lolita Lebrón, Rafael Cancel Miranda, Andrés Figueroa Cordero, and Irving Flores Rodríguez went to the Capitol Building in Washington. From the balcony in the US House of Representatives, they unfurled the Puerto Rican flag and opened fire with semi-automatic pistols; five representatives were wounded. The Nationalists were immediately arrested and imprisoned with sentences ranging from seventy to eighty-five years.[20]

Puerto Rican activists in the United States were intimately familiar with this history of struggle and repression on the island, and it profoundly influenced the direction of the Young Lords.

THE "DIVIDED NATION"

The Young Lords Party became a distinct national organization in May 1970 after separating from the Chicago Young Lords. Initially, the New York Central Committee remained the same. However, within months, the leaders announced that Felipe Luciano had been demoted from the position of chairman citing the reasons as his failure to follow the organization's rules and individualism. Luciano resigned. After his departure, Juan González, minister of education, was selected to serve as the minister of defense, the highest rank in the organization. (The details of the change in leadership were described in the previous chapters.) The other Central Committee members continued in their prior roles: Pablo "Yoruba" Guzmán as minister of information, David Pérez as field marshal, Juan "Fi" Ortiz as chief of staff, and Denise Oliver as minister of finance. A second woman, Gloria González (who subsequently used the surnames Fontanez and Wright) was promoted to the Central Committee in September 1970. González was born in Puerto Rico and identified as a strong supporter of the Nationalist Party. She had joined the YLO earlier in the year and celebrated a revolutionary wedding with Juan González that summer.[21]

The six-member Central Committee went into a retreat in December to evaluate the work of the Young Lords Party and set political objectives for the coming year. They summarized their deliberations in a retreat report distributed to all members. In a surprise announcement, it declared that the Young Lords Party would open branches in Puerto Rico in 1971,[22] a decision that signaled a shift away from its main focus on organizing Puerto Ricans in low-income communities across the United States.

Central Committee members had taken several trips to Puerto Rico to explore the feasibility of opening a branch on the island. Juan González, Gloria González, and David Pérez advocated strongly for the idea. In the retreat report, Pérez emphasized that all the Central Committee leaders were in full agreement with the new direction.[23] However, behind closed doors, it was another story as sharp differences emerged. Guzmán and Oliver firmly recommended against the move emphasizing that the role of the Young Lords was to organize Puerto Ricans in the United States and that a well-established pro-independence movement already existed in Puerto Rico. However, Gloria González countered that the main organizations, the Movement Pro Independence (MPI) and the Puerto Rican Independence Party (PIP), represented the middle and upper classes,[24] and that the Puerto Rican working class did not have revolutionary leadership. She argued that the role of the Young Lords Party would be to organize the most exploited segments of the population, "the working class, the poor, the lumpen, the jibaro, and the Afro-Puertorriqueño."[25]

Opinions about the responsibility of US Puerto Ricans to the island's liberation struggle had been the subject of debate for some time. As the argument got heated among Central Committee members, Oliver recalled that David Pérez questioned her right to vote on the decision saying that she was not Puerto Rican. While the others disagreed, Pérez's view foreshadowed a "narrow nationalist" outlook that would ascend in the Young Lords Party. In other words, an "authentic or real Puerto Rican" would support the move to Puerto Rico. Pérez's statements also implicitly opened up the question about the role of African American and other non-Puerto Rican members in the Young Lords Party to the island's national liberation struggle, but the issue was not addressed at this time. The dispute exposed other schisms among top leaders; those born in Puerto Rico were eager to open branches, perhaps because their personal connections to the country were stronger. Interestingly, the clearly identifiable Afro-descendants opposed the move recalling their experiences with racism in Puerto Rico, even within the pro-independence movement.

When the debate was exhausted, the Central Committee members brought the matter to a vote, and the proponents of the move to Puerto Rico won. Writing in Spanish for the winning position, Gloria González outlined the rationale for opening branches on the island. She declared that Puerto Ricans constituted a "divided nation:"

> [I]ndeed, we are divided physically—there's a million and a half Puerto Ricans in the US—⅓ of our people, ⅔ in the island. But in spite of being divided physically, we

are still one people like the Vietnamese (who struggle against the same oppressor).[26]

While the fact of geographic dispersal could have led to any number of interpretations, González theorized that Puerto Ricans in the United States represented one-third of a nation in exile severed from the two-thirds in Puerto Rico. She concluded that the YLP had to "reunify the Puerto Rican nation" and that, for this purpose, the Young Lords Party had to open branches on the island. The "divided nation" theory became the basis for defining the role of Puerto Rican activists in the United States to Puerto Rico's national liberation struggle. The decision, a hodgepodge of arrogance, opportunism, nostalgia, and inexperience, had a domino effect on everything that followed.

DEBATE SQUASHED

The announcement about Puerto Rico threw the Young Lords Party into turmoil. Members had many questions. Was it necessary to open branches in Puerto Rico to support the island's independence? Who would be assigned to go? Where would resources come from? What was the plan for the Young Lords in the United States? What did the move mean for non-Puerto Ricans, especially African American members? Would the Young Lords on the island support feminist campaigns and the battle for racial equality?

Of course, all Young Lords believed in Puerto Rico's right to self-determination and supported the struggle against US imperialism; this was the first point of the Thirteen-Point Program and Platform. But did these convictions mean that the Young Lords Party had to be physically present on the island? Richie Pérez, then Information Ministry captain, expressed the view shared by many of us:

> I understood the issue of Puerto Rican independence, and I was willing to die for it. But I didn't really want to go to Puerto Rico. I wanted to stay here. Couldn't I die for it here?[27]

Every Young Lord had a stake in the outcome, since each member was required to follow Central Committee decisions or face sanction, demotion, or even expulsion under the YLP's governing principle of democratic centralism. The rank-and-file understood that the move to Puerto Rico represented a major political change, although we did not yet grasp its implications for the future of the organization.

Carlos Aponte, a highly respected leader of the Young Lords and Education Ministry captain, also questioned the new direction. "*Why* is the Young Lords Party opening branches in Puerto Rico?" he asked. Aponte had considerable organizing experience and extensive knowledge of Puerto Rican history. His articles on Puerto Rican events and national figures were regularly featured in *Palante,* the YLP newspaper. With an excellent command of the Spanish language, he frequently represented the Young Lords to Spanish-speaking community organizations. Aponte was an officer in the Lower East Side branch and had previously opened the Bronx branch in April 1970 together with Richie Pérez of the Information Ministry. Before joining the Young Lords, Aponte had been a founding member of the Puerto Rican Student Union (PRSU), started up among students in the New York metropolitan area, and a community organizer in the Lower East Side. Returning from the Vietnam War as a medic, he developed political consciousness working with other veterans through the Vietnam Veterans Against the War (VVAW) and the Peace and Freedom Party (PFP) in California. The PFP, campaigning on an antiwar platform, ran third-party candidates in the 1968 primaries and elections. Through this work, Aponte learned the basics of community and political organizing side by side with members of La Raza, the Black Panther Party, and the student left radicals who were also part of the PFP coalition.

In a shocking turn of events, the Central Committee summoned Aponte and more than fifty other cadres to a secret meeting where Aponte was subjected to intense questioning and then accused of being a police agent. No actual evidence was presented or witnesses called, but we were led to believe that the Central Committee had conducted a thorough investigation to justify such an audacious accusation against such a highly regarded member. The Central Committee immediately expelled Aponte and published a special issue of *Palante* reporting his expulsion, along with expulsions of other alleged police agents. The newspaper featured Aponte's picture, listed his prior activist activities and affiliations, and paradoxically reported that he "was identified by friends in the Police Department as being a Bureau of Special Services" (BOSS) stringer.[28]

Aponte requested a public hearing—a people's trial—to answer the accusations. It was denied. Instead the Central Committee blamed him for spreading mistrust and trying to find out who had provided information against him. "We will not divulge our sources," the leaders answered.[29] Aponte was the fall guy, and the allegations against him introduced the practice of marking as "agents" those men and women who disagreed with the Central Committee members. It was a convenient means to cast suspicion on, isolate, and ostracize anyone so charged. Although it increased paranoia and distrust among the general membership, the Central Committee claimed that the Aponte episode had served to raise awareness about police infiltration throughout the political movement. Ironically, groundless accusations had the disastrous effect of providing cover to the real agents and informants, who stayed safely in the organization as they pointed a finger at others.

The incident with Aponte had a chilling effect. He was the first Young Lords Party leader of a high rank to be dishonorably ousted for raising questions about the Puerto Rico project. The public humiliation and shaming of someone so greatly respected and knowledgeable sent a strong statement that it could happen to anyone. Less experienced members were confused and became afraid to ask questions or express opinions, not wanting to be ridiculed, interrogated, or declared "an enemy of the people," or worst of all "a police agent." In retrospect, it is apparent that Aponte's doubts and questions about the efficacy and appropriateness of the YLP move to Puerto Rico made him an obstacle and, therefore, a target for the Central Committee members looking to take the Young Lords Party to the island. It was a disgraceful and shameful episode that successfully deflected the debate among members about the Puerto Rico venture and silenced opposition—at least for the time being.

Shortly after Aponte's expulsion, the Central Committee released another disturbing announcement. Denise Oliver, leading YLP member, and the first woman and only African American on the Central Committee, had resigned. A short statement published in *Palante* reported that Oliver had left to join the Eldridge Cleaver faction of the Black Panther Party.[30] At the time, the Black Panthers had divided into two factions; one led by Huey P. Newton and the other by Cleaver.

97

However, the Central Committee did not mention Oliver's dissent to the decision to open YLP branches in Puerto Rico.

OFENSIVA ROMPE CADENAS / BREAK THE CHAINS OFFENSIVE

The Young Lords Party's campaign to establish the organization in Puerto Rico, named Ofensiva Rompe Cadenas or the "Break the Chains Offensive," generated passionate and acrimonious debates about the role of Puerto Ricans in the United States to the national liberation struggle of the island—but it also created excitement in the movement. The premise that Puerto Ricans constituted one nation, whether living in Puerto Rico or the United States, gained popularity and had strong nationalist appeal because it defined "Puerto Ricanness" beyond geographic location and reflected the complexities of the Puerto Rican experience. The idea of "divided nation" insisted that, in spite of the transformative impact of the Great Migration, Puerto Ricans were still one people. It charged the United States with creating the economic conditions that forced Puerto Ricans to migrate and families to separate. As such, "divided nation" expressed familiarity with dispersal, the loss of home, and the longing for home; it captured the collective and unifying situation of being "here and there," "back here," and "there again." The colonial reality, back and forth migration, and the US influence on the island "kept the dividing line between Puerto Rico and mainland extremely fluid and boosted a common sense of identity."[31] "Divided nation" rejected predictions that the Puerto Rican uniqueness would cease to exist in the United States or that Puerto Ricans would assimilate into an "American" designation like generations of European immigrants. "Divided nation" merged ideas of identity and national liberation to advance the proposition that the *primary* duty of every Puerto Rican was to decolonize the island.

Ultimately, support for Ofensiva Rompe Cadenas and the move of the Young Lords Party to open branches in Puerto Rico can only be fully understood within the context of the island's colonial history, its struggles for self-determination, and the Puerto Rican migration experience discussed in this chapter. The Central Committee's decision in 1971 to move to Puerto Rico allowed Puerto Rican activists living in the United States to imagine playing a direct role in the island's national liberation. "Consolidate the Base to Prepare the Front!" was the Young Lords' rallying cry with Puerto Rico as "the front" and the United States as "the base."

RESTRUCTURING THE YOUNG LORDS

Moving the Young Lords Party to Puerto Rico was an immense undertaking, a transnational project requiring major coordination of people and resources across 1,600 miles. How would Ofensiva Rompe Cadenas be financed, and how would the Puerto Rico branches be sustained? The Central Committee devised a plan to focus US efforts on building a mass movement while also directing resources to the Puerto Rico project. Young Lord members were organized into "sections" for the purpose of developing "people's organizations" in different sectors. For example, Young Lords appointed to a "workers' section" were sent into factories and other workplaces to build a Workers Federation. Similarly, the Young Lords' "student section" organized in high schools and colleges. Likewise, other sections were created to mobilize women, prisoners, and other sectors of the population.

The Central Committee also formed a "community section," and renamed the YLP storefront offices the "Committees to Defend the Community" (CDC) with the idea that they would be "turned over to the community." However, the Central Committee failed to identify *whom* in "the community" would continue this work so critical to responding to and rallying neighborhood residents. Up to this point, Young Lords had staffed the storefronts and organized programs and campaigns from there. However, under the reorganization, most Young Lords were moved out to other "sections," and the local branch offices were left almost completely without staff. Moreover, the restructuring was executed in haste, almost overnight, without a transition of any kind. "Serve the people" programs and other initiatives came to an abrupt halt. "Only a few Lords were left in the offices to help community people organize,[32] explained Gloria González. People in areas where Young Lords offices had previously been located asked, "Where are the Young Lords? Despite the expressions of loss, the Central Committee leaders insisted that the pullback from the Puerto Rican communities in the United States was a necessary sacrifice to establish the Young Lords Party in Puerto Rico.[33]

The Central Committee set March 21, 1971 as the date for the Young Lords Party's arrival in Puerto Rico to commemorate the Ponce Massacre of 1937. Demonstrations took place in the United States and on the island. In New York, 7,000 people chanting, "¡Jíbaro Sí, Yanqui No! ¡Qué Viva Puerto Rico Libre!" marched to La Plaza Borinqueña[34] on East 138th Street in the Bronx to express solidarity. Hundreds also marched in Philadelphia, (Pennsylvania), Bridgeport, (Connecticut), Cleveland, (Ohio) and Syracuse, (New York).[35]

In Ponce, eighty nationalists joined Juan González, Gloria González, Richie Pérez, and other Young Lords. Pérez wrote:

When we put on our berets, people got excited. We lined up in three columns, looking strong, and began to march. There were hundreds of people lined up as we passed. The entire city was quiet. No chanting, only the sound of us half-stepping in cadence. We sounded like a small army."[36]

In an interview years later, Pérez recalled:

We were used to marching in military formation. When people in Puerto Rico saw this, it had a tremendous impact. As we began to march, I remember looking back and seeing [that] at least two hundred people fell in with us and were attempting to line themselves to march in formation and keep in cadence with us, and I thought the revolution was going to start then.[37]

Although the Central Committee members initially announced that the first branch would open in Ponce, they decided against it. Instead the Young Lords opened two branches; one named Julio Roldán in Aguadilla, a city in the northwest with one factory and one hospital built during the Spanish colonial period. A second, named for don Pedro Albizu Campos, was set up in the northeast in El Caño, Santurce, an area with high poverty, illiteracy, and unemployment. Gloria González led the advance group of two women and three men transplanted to the island. As the Young Lords Party focused on Puerto Rico and decreased its presence in the United States, other organizations filled the void. The New York chapter of the Movimiento Pro Independencia (MPI), renamed the Puerto Rican Socialist Party/PSP in November 1971, experienced amazing growth[38] as did El Comité, a group based in Manhattan's Upper West Side.

COUNTERINTELLIGENCE AND RED SQUAD ACTIVITIES

In Puerto Rico, the Young Lords Party came under intensified scrutiny by the Federal Bureau of Investigation (FBI). On one trip to the island, Juan González recalled meeting an acquaintance traveling on the same airplane who told González that the US Justice Department had assigned him to follow the Young Lords. "There will be agents with you every step of the way when you are on the island," he said.[39] Given Puerto Rico's strategic importance to the United States, the government had targeted pro-independence activists since the 1930s. In the sixties, FBI director J. Edgar Hoover instructed operatives to pry into the lives of movement leaders to gather information "concerning their weaknesses, morals, criminal records, spouses, children, family life, educational qualifications, and personal activities other than independence activities."[40] Similarly, the police in Puerto Rico collected data and accumulated tens of thousands of *carpetas* (files) about activists, which only became known many decades later.

When a group of US activists broke into an FBI office and removed files in 1971, their actions led to the exposure of the counterintelligence program known as COINTELPRO. The massive collection of files revealed extensive government-sanctioned surveillance, illegal tactics, and criminal activities implemented against a broad cross section of organizations and individuals, including the pro-independence movement in Puerto Rico and the Black Panther Party, labeled by the FBI as "the greatest threat to the internal security" of the United States. The Black Panther Party was a principal government target because of its domestic and international influence, and its leading role in the US social justice movements. Under Hoover's command, agents were directed to "expose, disrupt, misdirect, discredit, or otherwise neutralize" progressive organizations and leaders. The inner workings of the FBI and COINTELPRO are thoroughly examined and detailed in *The COINTELPRO Papers, Documents from the FBI's Secret Wars Against Dissent in the United States.*[41] The authors Ward Churchill and Jim Vander Wall explain:

> [The documents] expose the secret, systematic, and sometimes savage use of force and fraud, by all levels of government, to sabotage progressive political activity supposedly protected by the US constitution. They reveal ongoing, country-wide CIA-style covert action—infiltration, psychological warfare, legal harassment, and violence—against a very broad range of domestic dissidents."[42]

The Young Lords were also targets. Closely allied with the Black Panther Party, the Chicago Young Lords Organization was already heavily infiltrated when the New York chapter was formed. FBI agents were present at the rally that launched the YLO in New York in 1969 in Tompkins Square Park. Special agents, informants, infiltrators, and "confidential sources" monitored all meetings, rallies, public events, and leaders' travels. They gathered information using cameras, telephone bugs, and wiretaps, opened mail, and searched apartments without warrants. They questioned members' employers, landlords, neighbors, teachers, and family seeking information but also to spread fear and intimidation.

FBI operatives joined clandestinely and recruited informants. One infiltrator explained the process to become a Young Lord to his superiors in a May 12, 1970 report:[43]

> When an interested individual contacts the YLO expressing a desire to join the organization, his background is obtained and a schedule of availability for the next two weeks is worked out. This person follows the schedule . . . doing assigned tasks. This activity permits the YLO to determine if that individual is serious about becoming a Lord. After the two-week period, the perspective member fills out an application to become a "Lord-In-Training" which is followed by six weeks of political instruction under observation."

As members, these undercover agents participated in organizational activities and then reported to the FBI. They submitted a range of materials, including accounts of meetings, newspaper clippings, copies of speeches, flyers, verbatim transcripts of radio programs, articles, and other documents written by Young Lords. The FBI office in New York even had a special unit to translate Spanish documents into English.[44] Each FBI file was given a unique number. The individual files contained a person's entire political history and personal data, including social security number; a detailed physical description—height, weight, hair, and eye color—and any distinguishing marks; specifics of arrests and all activist activities; and details about family members. The FBI kept the same number for individuals who had a file prior to joining the Young Lords and consolidated all entries. Agents shared reports with multiple agencies and locations including the United States Department of Justice, Naval Investigative Services (NIS), the US Air Force (USAF), the US Secret Service, and the CIA and its offices in Albany, Boston, Buffalo, Chicago, Newark, New Haven, New York, Philadelphia, San Francisco, and San Juan, and the Office of Special Investigations, Ramey Air Force Base.[45]

In New York City, the FBI worked closely with local agents in the police department's Bureau of Special Services ("BoSS" or "the Red Squad"), which spied on organizations such as the Black Panthers and the Young Lords. BOSS carried out both overt and covert operations. "[B}etween 1968 and 1970, the New York red squad went from sixty-eight uniformed officers to ninety (plus fifty-five others assigned to undercover work)," documented researcher and author Kristian Williams.[46] Out on the city streets, the police routinely stopped Young Lords as we passed out flyers, sold *Palante*, or attended demonstrations. Members were regularly picked up, harassed, beaten, arrested, and put in jail on any number of charges ranging from felonious assault, obstructing government administration, and resisting arrest to inciting to riot or carrying a deadly weapon. BOSS detectives attended meetings and rallies, identified potential points of conflict, and repeatedly ransacked leaders' homes. *Palante* reported the police fire bombings of the Young Lords' offices at different times in the Bronx, Newark, Philadelphia, Bridgeport, and El Caño.

BOSS operatives also functioned as provocateurs planning frame-ups, promoting illegal activity, and stirring up violence.[47] In a well-known case, BOSS agents targeted the Black Panther Party with fabricated charges against twenty-one members that included conspiring to bomb department stores, a police precinct, a railroad yard, and the Bronx Botanical Gardens and assassination plots to murder New York City policemen. At the end of a long trial, all members of the Black Panther 21 case were acquitted. Despite the not guilty verdict, the trial had successfully disrupted and weakened the Black Panther Party as the organization was diverted from community organizing to raising funds for bail and legal defense. BOSS agents used similar tactics throughout the social justice movement. Against this backdrop, activists filed a lawsuit in 1971 charging the police with multiple constitutional violations. The suit settled in 1985 was known as the Handshu consent decree. It prohibited the police department from investigating political and religious groups unless there was specific information that the group was linked to a crime that had been committed or was about to be committed. After September 11, 2001, the New York Police Department (NYPD) sought and gained a modification of the Handshu decree that reduced the standard for investigating political groups. In 2013, Muslim communities brought a lawsuit charging unjustified and discriminatory surveillance, which was settled when the NYPD agreed to prohibit investigations where race, religion, or ethnicity were a "substantial or motivating factor."

During the 1960s and 70s, the government and police colluded and combined resources to destroy the people's movements. So many decades later, the full extent of COINTELPRO and police activities against the Young Lords are still unknown, especially their role in the shifting political directions, the move out of US communities, and the internal violence of the final years detailed later in this chapter.[48]

PEOPLE'S ORGANIZATIONS EXPAND MASS MOVEMENT

As the branches opened in Puerto Rico, the YLP focus in the United States turned to building the "people's organizations." Juan González described them as "organizations that involve the Puerto Rican people, wherever they are, at any level of struggle."[49] They intended to grow a mass movement by recruiting progressive-minded people who might not join the YLP because of its Marxist-Leninist ideology, paramilitary structure, or heavy time commitment. It was a promising strategy to expand the Party's influence as its membership was declining. Two groups, the Health Revolutionary Unity Movement (HRUM) and the Puerto Rican Student Union (PRSU), officially affiliated as people's organizations in 1971 and connected the Young Lords Party to thousands of hospital workers and students.

Puerto Rican and African American hospital workers, about 80 percent women, had formed the HRUM in New York's municipal hospitals to fight against proposed layoffs and cutbacks in services. The HRUM members and Young Lords had collaborated on several worker-patient-community campaigns in hospitals in the Bronx, East Harlem, and the Lower East Side, conducted door-to-door health testing, and developed a ten-point program focused on community control of health institutions. The HRUM's newspaper, *For the People's Health,* explained the organization's mission to expose the horrible health conditions, unite workers and patients, and stop the genocide of Third World people.[50]

The PRSU, formed by working class Puerto Rican and Latino/Latina students in 1969, organized across colleges and universities in the New York metropolitan area, and successfully expanded Latino/Latina student admissions, Puerto Rican studies programs, and the hiring of faculty of color. The PRSU appealed to fellow students in the language of the time:

> [W]e hope that you, brother and sister, who read this pamphlet do not just dig on it, and then go on bugalooing at the Saint George [dance club] or sniffing, popping and puffing your life away. Nor do we want you to become a social worker type liberal who suddenly decides to help "the people." We want you to dig yourself. . . . Begin to serve our community, fight for it to control every institution in it, and defend it by any and every means necessary.[51]

The PRSU and YLP successfully partnered in the first Puerto Rican student conference in 1970, launched "Free Puerto Rico Now" committees in high schools and colleges, and brought thousands of students to the march to the United Nations that same year.

In addition to the HRUM and the PRSU affiliations, the YLP proposed to create several new people's organizations. Top on the list was a Workers' Federation. While the YLP had strong links to hospital workers, this was not the case with other sectors of the working class.

As previously noted, the Central Committee assigned cadres to the YLP "workers' section" with the goal of building the Workers' Federation and a working class base for the organization. Section members got jobs in local garment and other manufacturing factories, telephone companies, daycare centers, and other workplaces. They organized with fellow workers to improve labor conditions and recruited members into the Federation. They conducted political education classes for workers and screened films about the history of the labor struggle in the United States. The Central Committee instructed the HRUM to continue organizing and mobilizing health workers. The idea was that the Workers' Federation would arise from these combined efforts.

ILLUSION AND REALITY: THE JULY 1971 RETREAT

During 1971, the Young Lords were busily involved in a wide range of organizing activities. In New York, the YLP cosponsored a Third World Health Workers conference with the HRUM and organized with the Inmates Liberation Front around prison issues. Young Lords worked in coalitions demanding the release of political prisoners: Carlos Feliciano, Martin Sostre, Eduardo "Pancho" Cruz, and the five Puerto Rican nationalists in US prisons since the 1950s. Members also protested the war in Indochina and held May Day rallies as workers' celebrations. In Philadelphia, Young Lords convened progressive religious leaders in a two-day Church Conference, while in Bridgeport, Connecticut, members led rent strikes. In Puerto Rico, Young Lords campaigned to improve services at a hospital in Aguadilla and supported students in their battles to expel the US Reserve Officers' Training Corps (ROTC) from the University of Puerto Rico. Two days later in New York, 2,000 people rallied to support the students. In East Harlem, the YLP opened a national headquarters on East 117th Street.

The Young Lords Party also prepared for the Puerto Rican Day Parade in New York City. The year before, a Young Lords' contingent had marched proudly down Fifth Avenue to cheering crowds and applause. In 1971, the Central Committee proposed that poor people, instead of the New York police, should march at the head of the parade to protest the city's budget cuts and layoffs, and US colonialism in Puerto Rico. Obviously, the parade committee opposed the idea, but so did the Movimiento Pro Independencia (MPI) in disagreement with the tactic. Nonetheless, members of the Young Lords, the PRSU, and El Comité arrived at the parade ready to march at the front. A confrontation with police ensued; and twenty persons were arrested, and many others wounded. The activists denounced the police and their use of brute force against parade goers. Within the YLP, members summed up the episode as the first public defeat and a mistake that lost the organization working-class support. Central Committee members admitted that the decision "was badly made, without sufficient ideological struggle."[52] Yet this style of decision-making, failing to take into account the opinions of members and allies, was becoming more and more characteristic of their leadership.

A month later, the Central Committee held an organization-wide retreat of all YLP branches in New York, Philadelphia, Bridgeport, and in Aguadilla and El Caño, Puerto Rico. Given the intense organizing schedule, the Young Lords welcomed the break and opportunity to evaluate the work of the prior six months. At the end of the retreat, the Central Committee delivered its main conclusion in a retreat document distributed to members. It said:

> From our point of view, this [Ofensiva Rompe Cadenas] was the most important offensive in our history, beginning the reunification of the Nation. The greatest impact was felt on the front [Puerto Rico] where thousands and thousands of Puerto Ricans came to know the Party for the first time, and in the base [the United States], where many workers who had been born in Puerto Rico began to support the Party.[53]

An impressive statement, except it was not based in reality. Despite the self-congratulations, the Young Lords' ideas and tactics were not taking hold on the island; members working there were demoralized, and the YLP was rapidly losing members and influence in the United States. In Puerto Rico, the Nationalist Party was the sole supporter. Other *independentistas* called the Young Lords arrogant and immature, criticized the group's lack of familiarity with the conditions of Puerto Rico, and rejected the YLP's "divided nation" theory as well as its ideas about the Afro-Boricua and women's liberation. Nonetheless, the Central Committee leaders sideswept the obvious question:

"Should the Young Lords Party continue in Puerto Rico?" Their single-minded obsession to position the YLP as a leader of the island's pro-independence movement overshadowed everything.

Although a multitude of problems had surfaced with the move to the island, the Central Committee made only one criticism; it had been launched with insufficient funds. Monies for the Puerto Rico project came primarily from *Palante* sales, the only source of steady income. At the high point, Young Lords had sold fifteen thousand issues every two weeks;[54] but with the organizational restructuring and branch closings; by mid-1971, fewer papers were being sold. The goal for the Puerto Rico branches to generate 25 percent of sales was unrealistic.[55] *Palante* was never a fundraising or effective organizing tool on the island and retitling it "newspaper of the divided nation" instead of "Latin revolutionary news service" did not improve sales. The Central Committee blamed the financial disaster on members' lack of "working class consciousness" and sent additional Young Lords to get factory jobs. This was both a political and a financial directive. On the one hand, organizing workers required dedicated organizers and consistent efforts. On the other, Young Lords with salaried jobs contributed a substantial portion of their earnings to pay for the expenses of the organization and the individual Central Committee members.

In Puerto Rico, islanders were appropriately suspicious of a group headquartered in the United States whose members arrived with such fanfare, allegedly to make revolution. Islanders knew that national liberation would not be achieved with imported revolutionaries. Richie Pérez, deputy minister of information, recalled,

> [T]he people told us, you got to make a choice. You
> can't be shuttle revolutionaries. You can't be back and
> forth from New York to the island.[56]

Young Lords wearing dashikis, blue jeans, and combat boots, some barely able to speak Spanish, were outsiders, and this reality haunted the YLP organizers during their year-and-a-half stay on the island.

AFRICAN AMERICANS AND THE YLP MOVE TO PUERTO RICO

The 1971 July retreat reframed the organizing priorities for the Young Lords Party. As explained in the last chapter, the national liberation of Puerto Rico and class struggles were declared the top priorities; issues associated with "sex and race" were secondary. As a result, feminist ideals and campaigns progressed no further. Likewise the secondary status accorded to matters of race also had a detrimental impact on the Young Lords Party and African American members.

Approximately 20 percent of the Young Lords were African Americans, some with both African American and Puerto Rican ancestry. African Americans had joined the YLO/YLP attracted by its radical politics, bold campaigns for the rights of Puerto Ricans and African Americans in the United States, and its Afro-Latino and African American leadership and membership. Pablo "Yoruba" Guzmán, minister of information, summarized the significance of the relationship:

> It is important for us to study the history of Blacks in the Americas, because it is a part of Puerto Rican history, in terms of Black slaves in Puerto Rico and how they came into the culture, and in terms of better understanding the development of Blacks [African Americans] in the united states, who are the major force in the Amerikkan revolution. We realize that one of our most important allies in the national liberation struggle will be Black people [African Americans].[57]

However, the YLP move to Puerto Rico had raised questions for African American members. With the shift in focus to the island and the secondary status accorded issues of race, African American members no longer saw their interests represented. The Central Committee members responded to their concerns in the July report. They wrote:

> The reality that the Puerto Rican nation speaks Spanish and that [US] Blacks speak English means that [US] Blacks that want to do better organizing should, during a period of time, learn Spanish not to forget your culture and language but to better your work.[58]

The long-awaited answer hit like a bucket of ice water thrown in the face, a patronizing lecture about maintaining an internationalist outlook and learning Spanish. Dismayed and heartbroken, many African American members left or drifted away from the organization.

The Central Committee's retreat report, full of political analysis, unrealistic proposals, and lofty rhetoric, failed to delineate between conditions in Puerto Rico and the United States, and the strategies and tactics appropriate to each. What it revealed was a widening gulf between the theorizing of the Central Committee and the reality of on-the-ground organizers, a chasm between leaders and the rank-and-file. The leaders offered no solutions, action plans, or guidance to members' day-to-day organizing concerns. The focus on Puerto Rico weakened the YLP in the United States. Did the Central Committee leaders really believe what they said about achieving a great success in Puerto Rico? Or did they just want *us* to believe it? Or was the Puerto Rico project just a setup for failure? As members, we kept hoping for a change in direction. We had a sort of blind faith, like hoping someone you love who has a terminal illness, will get well. As members, we hoped for the best still believing in the need for an organization like the Young Lords Party to fight for social justice in the United States.

FORESHADOWING THE PRISON INDUSTRIAL COMPLEX

Conditions in low-income communities continued to deteriorate. With factories moving out of the United States, joblessness soared. Cutbacks in government services and programs pushed working people below subsistence existence. Heroin flooded poor neighborhoods. President Richard Nixon's 1971 "war on drugs" increased street harassment by police and arrests. Politicians' cries for "law and order" accelerated the incarceration of people of color, positioning the United States as the world's leading jailer, and setting the foundation for the "Prison Industrial Complex," with Wall Street investors making huge profits by warehousing and contracting out prison labor.

Prisoners across the country fought to end horrendous living conditions, like those at the Attica Correctional Facility near Buffalo, New York. In September 1971, approximately 1,200 men, mostly African American and Puerto Rican, seized the prison. Their demands were basic: decent food, a minimum wage, medical treatment, expanded work-release programs, better educational facilities, and Spanish books in the library. The prisoners set up a committee to negotiate with prison officials. Two Young Lords, Juan "Fi" Ortiz, 17-year-old Central Committee member, and José "GI" Paris, a former prisoner at Attica, joined the negotiations committee, which consisted of well-known activists, journalists, lawyers, and politicians. However, Governor Nelson Rockefeller would not negotiate. Despite worldwide humanitarian appeals for a peaceful outcome, he sent in five hundred state troopers with "shoot to kill" orders. Forty-three men were killed, and eighty others injured.

Immediately, thousands of people of conscience took to the streets in protest. Young Lords, Black Panthers, and members of I Wor Kuen, the Third World Women's Alliance, the PRSU, the HRUM, the Black Workers' Congress, the Women's Union, and dozens of others, demonstrated daily, twenty-three marches over the course of twenty-five days.[59] We demanded that Rockefeller and prison chief Russell Oswald be indicted for first-degree murder. We demanded that an international committee made up of nonimperialist nations investigate the massacre and the American penal system in general. We called for the formation of community groups as commissions of inquiry and demanded reparations to the families of the massacred inmates. Decades passed before New York State acknowledged the killings. In 2000, the state settled a lawsuit brought by victims or their families and conceded to pay $8 million, but no official has been held accountable for the deaths.

THE 'DIVIDED NATION' DEBATE RESURGES

Around the time of the Attica prison uprising, minister of information, Pablo "Yoruba" Guzmán, represented the Young Lords Party in a delegation to the People's Republic of China. (Washington did not recognize Beijing at the time, still recognizing Taiwan as "China.") Guzmán toured the country and exchanged ideas with officials. When he presented the "divided nation" theory to them, the Chinese responded that the people of Puerto Rico would determine the island's fate, not the Young Lords Party from its headquarters in East Harlem.

When Guzmán returned to New York after six weeks in China, he met with Central Committee members Juan "Fi" Ortiz and David Pérez. (Juan González was on a book tour in California and Hawaii promoting the recently published, *Palante: Young Lords Party*,[60] and

Gloria González was living in Puerto Rico.) Guzmán listened to reports of how quickly the YLP was losing members—twenty-nine had left the organization just in New York during the short time he had been away. Community organizing was inconsistent; programs were being started up and then dropped.[61] *Palante* was not being published regularly and was rarely found in the streets. Members complained about lack of democracy in the organization and too many meetings.[62]

"We need a 'Rectification Movement'!" Guzmán exclaimed. Inspired by the China trip and determined to get the Young Lords Party back on track, he outlined his analysis of the key problems in a written report: 1) lack of integration with the daily life of working people; 2) poor analysis of the strategies and tactics of the American and Puerto Rican revolutions and their relation to one another; 3) lack of democracy; and 4) breakdown of collectivity.[63] Most importantly, Guzmán concluded that the "divided nation" theory was wrong. "The nation of Puerto Rico is on the island, and Puerto Ricans migrating to the United States form a 'national oppressed minority' part of a multi-racial, multi-ethnic working class. While Puerto Ricans living in the United States have a unique and special relationship to Puerto Rico, the people on the island will determine its political status,"[64] he said.

Guzmán's ideas challenged our views about the Puerto Rican diaspora and the mission of the Young Lords Party. Were Puerto Ricans in the United States part of a "divided nation" or an "oppressed national minority"? Should the Young Lords close the branches in Puerto Rico? Juan "Fi" Ortiz and National Staff members, Richie Pérez, Juan Ramos, and myself, united with Guzmán. We were eager to reconceptualize and revitalize the organization, and we shared the ideas of the Rectification Movement with enthusiastic rank-and-file members who expected a full discussion in the organization.

When Juan González and Gloria González returned to New York City, they were furious. The Rectification Movement directly challenged their beliefs and authority. But instead of bringing the Young Lords together to discuss issues so fundamental and vital to the organization, they pulled Guzmán, Ortiz, and David Pérez into a closed-door meeting. Guzmán and Ortiz maintained that the YLP was headed for disaster and that the move to Puerto Rico was based on an erroneous premise of "divided nation." They stood together, but the two men made no progress in persuading the others. Finally, they gave up, and the fight was lost. Even though Guzmán believed that an "overwhelming majority of Lords would have left" with him and Ortiz, and Ortiz was willing to take that risk, Guzmán explained that he wanted to avoid a split in the organization. He added: "I was haunted by the corpses of factionalism that littered the Left."[65] Guzmán and Ortiz relinquished their leadership to a newly formed Executive Committee, a decision-making subgroup within the Central Committee consisting of Juan González, Gloria González, and David Pérez.

After three weeks, the Central Committee issued a communiqué titled "Deviation in Party Line," in which Gloria González characterized the Rectification Movement as "a departure from national liberation." She further announced, "Discipline is coming to those participants."[66] As "discipline," the Central Committee and National Staff members who participated in the Rectification Movement were demoted from leadership and sent out to different branches, making it difficult to mount another challenge—at least for the time being.

Guzmán was transferred to the Philadelphia branch. Because he had been the leader of the Rectification Movement, the Executive Committee made an example of Guzmán, even though he had a court case pending for refusing induction into the US military and was likely going to prison. He could have benefited from staying in New York to consult with lawyers, build support, and spend time with his family. Central Committee member Juan "Fi" Ortiz and education ministry cadre Gloria Colón were sent to El Caño in Santurce, Puerto Rico. Juan Ramos, cofounder of the Philadelphia chapter, was transferred to Aguadilla, Puerto Rico. I was assigned to Philadelphia. When I heard the outcome, I was angry and demoralized. "How could this be?" Even with strong cadre support, we lost, and those of us who tried to revitalize the Young Lords Party were to be uprooted from our work and communities, our homes, families and friends, and sent to other cities to start over. I did not want to leave New York. None of us wanted to leave home. Still, we packed our bags and said our goodbyes. We respected the chain of command and went as directed, believing that it was our duty to do so. It was early in 1972, and we still believed that the Young Lords Party was an organization with the possibility of fighting for revolutionary change. I went to Philadelphia and organized with the branch there for two years.

AMID RESIGNATIONS IN PUERTO RICO, A PARTY CONGRESS

During the early months of 1972, the Young Lords prepared for a Congress scheduled for June 30 through July 3 intended as an assembly of Young Lords and delegates from the various people's organizations: the Puerto Rican Workers Federation, the Committee to Defend the Community, the Puerto Rican Student Union, the Third World Student League, and the Women's Union. The stated purpose was to unite the "mass movement" and decide the future direction of the Young Lords Party.

Before the highly publicized event took place, Central Committee member Juan "Fi" Ortiz, National Staff member Juan Ramos, and five other Young Lords in Puerto Rico appealed to the Executive Committee to close the branches seeking to avoid a split in the organization. They explained that their time in Puerto Rico had convinced them that the role of the Young Lords Party was in the United States. However, the Executive Committee rejected their recommendation, and the Puerto Rico members resigned. Ramos explained:

> I took the side that said that we needed not to be in Puerto Rico. *La experencia de nosotros*—our experience—was strictly a mainland experience, with Puerto Rican hearts and culture and history, *pero* outside of that, the way people moved and did things in Puerto Rico was different.[67]

Not surprising, the Central Committee members accused them of "factionalism" in a full-page attack in *Palante* with photographs eerily reminiscent of claims made against alleged police agents the year before.[68] They announced that the YLP would continue working in Puerto Rico; however, the Aguadilla branch closed immediately and El Caño branch shortly after.

Despite the resignations, the Central Committee proceeded with the Party Congress. Attendees accepted a name change from the Young Lords Party to the Puerto Rican Revolutionary Workers Organization (PRRWO). The expressed mission was to organize Puerto Rican and Latino/Latina workers in the United States and build a new US multi-national revolutionary party in collaboration with other left organizations. Secondarily, the PRRWO would give "direct and resolute aid to the national liberation struggle of Puerto Rico."[69]

The Congress appointed a Central Committee. Gloria González, now using the name Fontanez, had flown out of Puerto Rico back to New York City to take the reins as chairwoman and head of a "Standing Committee" that included herself, Carmen Cruz (her cousin who had officially joined the YLP three months earlier),[70] and Juan González. The other members named were: Pablo "Yoruba" Guzmán, Lulu Limardo, Willie Matos, David Pérez, Richie Pérez, and Elba Saavedra.

The Puerto Rico resignations compelled the Central Committee to clarify PRRWO's viewpoint on the role of Puerto Ricans in the United States to the decolonization struggle of the island. The Standing Committee members admitted that the "divided nation" theory, which Fontanez had so staunchly promoted, was false.[71] They admitted that the strategy of one organization for island and US Puerto Ricans was also wrong, and that Ofensiva Rompe Cadenas had been a mistake. About the move to Puerto Rico, they simply wrote:

> We proceeded, however, with this partial analysis [divided nation] to make our second gravest error, as we began to plan to take leadership of the revolution and movement in Puerto Rico.[72]

However, no Central Committee member faced any consequences. After two years of debate about the Puerto Rico project, the admission of an "error" was too little, too late; irreversible and irreparable damage had been done. Hundreds of members of the Young Lords Party had already left the organization.

NAILING THE COFFIN SHUT

In 1974, I was reassigned to New York and was eager to return home. However, I was uncertain about continuing with the Puerto Rican Revolutionary Workers Organization. Though I had little contact in Philadelphia with the New York group from 1972 to 1974, we heard through second-hand accounts of family and friends about the endless ideological debates and the PRRWO's pullback from community organizing. We heard about the many members who resigned or drifted away, and I never saw or heard from them again. Most of the

Central Committee members in leadership when I was transferred were now gone. Juan "Fi" Ortiz resigned in 1972. Fontanez had removed Juan González from the Standing Committee in 1973. Pablo "Yoruba" Guzmán resigned in 1974 when he returned to New York after being locked up for a year in a Florida prison for refusing induction into the military. "It was obvious that the organization was spinning its wheels,[73] he concluded.

As I began to attend the PRRWO meetings in New York, I felt like an outsider, completely alienated from the group. The organization bore no resemblance to the one I remembered. I was a stranger among people wearing false smiles, arguing meaningless theories, and speaking words with no soul. I witnessed self-designated leaders and unthinking followers, who had no relationship to the community, the workplace, or each other, rip the heart and spirit out of revolution. It was like sitting in a windowless room with little air and only one exit.

In January 1975, I submitted my resignation at a meeting held at Fontanez' Lower East Side apartment. Fontanez instantly hurled personal attacks at me; the others chimed in, even a few former friends from the YLP days. Fontanez demanded books that she claimed as the PRRWO's property. "All books belonging to the organization are downstairs in the truck of my car. Come with me to get them," I offered as a way to exit. Fontanez ordered someone to go with me. He had been a close friend, but now he just said, "You're making a big mistake." When we got to the car, he took the books. On the drive home, I felt a weight lifted, but a threatening feeling lingered, and I decided to remove all personal files and books out of my apartment.

A few weeks later on a Sunday morning, I had just returned from a trip to Philadelphia with Pablo "Yoruba" Guzmán when there was a knock at the door. "Who is it?" I asked through the door since there was no peephole. I recognized a women's voice, a PRRWO member from Philadelphia, whom I considered a friend. "Iris, it's me; let me in." She sounded desperate. As soon as I opened the door, she ran toward the stairs yelling, "I'm sorry; they made me do it" and shot me an embarrassed look of knowing betrayal. Two PRRWO members arrogantly shoved their way in. I pushed past them into the hallway frantically knocking on neighbors' doors, shouting for help. No one was home. Everyone was at church. When I turned, I realized that Yoruba was still inside and banged on the apartment door to get back in.

One of the men opened, and I saw the other one pointing a gun. I went straight to him, yelling at him, but I stopped when his cold stare let me know he was ready to inflict violence. I had worked closely with both men in East Harlem; they had been like brothers. Now they were unrecognizable to me; there was no reasoning with them. They went through the small apartment, opening closet doors, rifling through boxes and drawers, saying that Fontanez had sent them to retrieve all books and documents. When they turned up nothing, they left. Stunned and fearful for our lives Yoruba and I reached out to trusted family and friends, including several former Young Lords. For weeks, they accompanied me to work and picked me up at the end of the day, staying through the night until the next day when the routine repeated. Years later, one of the intruders appeared at my new address. Speaking through the door, I asked, "What do you want?" He said, "I want to apologize." I accepted his apology.

Fontanez imposed a reign of terror over the PRRWO. In 1976, she and her clique of followers picked up Diana Caballero, a PRRWO member and educator, and Richie Pérez, a Central Committee leader, and took them to an apartment where they beat them for several days, all the while accusing them of being police agents. Pérez recalled:

> Looking back on it and seeing when we had debates about the "divided nation" and who participated in the beatings and interrogation, the most enthusiastic participants, among our leadership was Gloria Fontanez Wright who changed her name a number of times; her cousin, Carmen Cruz, also participated very enthusiastically in the beating and in directing defense cadre. Other people participated. Some were dupes. Just as I was able to turn on friends and say they're enemies of the people and discredit them in the community.[74]

He added:

> I allowed actions to be taken against people that later were taken against me. I allowed the birth of the monster that eventually destroyed the organization—not so much personal cowardliness as a *political cowardliness*. I

mean I would still go out and be willing to risk my life and challenge the system, but it was political cowardliness, to be politically incorrect, to be ostracized, to be thrown out of the family. Never allow yourself to be in an organization that becomes so narrow that it doesn't speak to the larger society that you don't listen to the people you claim you are serving.[75]

Pérez further elaborated that members tended to keep silent about disagreements with leaders because they were used to agreeing; they gave the leaders the benefit of the doubt; or they feared being ostracized or isolated within the rank-and-file.

News about the PRRWO beatings spread. Angry and sickened, former Young Lords gathered to express support for Pérez and Caballero. The fact that PRRWO was carrying out violence and beatings against members and dissenters was not generally known. We resolved to expose them in the community and social justice movement. We wrote a statement denouncing the shameful and reprehensible actions of the PRRWO and Fontanez, and we circulated it widely.[76]

Undeniably, Gloria Fontanez betrayed the YLP/PRRWO, its principles, and members. Several former PRRWO members described her role in a pamphlet published in 1976. They wrote:

We want to state that we see that Gloria Fontanez, the mastermind of the destruction of PRRWO is clearly an agent-provocateur, as her work of sabotage has been at too high a level to have been planned by any one person, no matter how opportunist.[77]

However, Fontanez' treacherous role was only one factor in the organization's deterioration and demise, and most former members reached this conclusion recognizing that many other conditions and dynamics played a role in the destruction of the YLP/PRRWO and the broader social movements of the late sixties.

Richie Pérez was the last leader remaining from the early days, a member of the Young Lords Organization since 1969. The violence against him and Diana Caballero in 1976 marked the end of the YLO/YLP/PRRWO. It nailed the coffin shut.

WHAT HAPPENED TO THE YOUNG LORDS?

As years passed, former Young Lords evaluated what happened. In the midst of our community organizing, we had not fully grasped the factors converging to destroy the social justice movements. As young people of color, mostly in our early twenties and from working class homes, we tackled big issues of self-determination, class, national liberation, racism, and sexism while struggling to sustain revolutionary organizations with few financial resources. Visionaries, people of conscience, and revolutionaries joined the Young Lords. We risked our lives to fight for poor and working people in the middle of a shifting world order, government sanctioned-violence, and betrayal. Global power and economic conditions were rapidly changing as Western capitalists adopted neoliberal policies, transferring economies from the public to the private sector. By 1971, US capitalists had shifted to an export-based economy that relocated manufacturing outside of the country. Black and brown communities were devastated as jobs disappeared, and workers faced unemployment with no prospects.

Puerto Ricans had the lowest income, level of education, and housing quality, and the highest percentage of people living in poverty among all New Yorkers during the 1970s.[78] As Edna Acosta-Belén and Carlos E. Santiago write, "There is no doubt that Puerto Ricans, more than any other group in the United States, suffered disproportionately from the deindustrialization of this country."[79] Thousands of Puerto Ricans migrated back to the island desperate to find work, but Puerto Rico was also in crisis as US corporations moved out to other countries seeking cheaper labor costs and bigger profits.[80] Through this bilateral flow, stateside Puerto Ricans connected to the island but were treated as outsiders "*de afuera*," not "authentic" Puerto Ricans, and mocked as "Nuyorican." In turn, Puerto Ricans in New York appropriated the word and sparked a cultural movement. "Nuyorican" poetry, literature, and arts exposed the economic and social realities in New York City's negative spaces[81] and abandoned neighborhoods. The exchange between mainland and island Puerto Ricans reflected deteriorating socio-economic living conditions, and the political vacuum left by waning protest movements. Without grassroots organizing and concrete strategies to respond to worsening poverty and industrial decline, organizations like the Young Lords lost their appeal.[82]

The YLP/PRRWO did not degenerate overnight nor was it possible for it to decline by the actions of one or two "evil persons" alone as some former members wrote. Informants assaulted the organization like an unshakeable virus. They fueled divisions and conflicts, and preyed on the psychology of members. Infiltrators mixed in with opportunists, individualists, and misguided youth who carried out the final beating, disgracing, and burial of the revolutionary Young Lords. The vicious role of COINTELPRO was described earlier, and it is worth repeating that the government targeted the Young Lords from Chicago to New York, from the East Coast to the West Coast, and to Puerto Rico. The scope and details of the government and police activities in the YLO/YLP/PRRWO have still to be fully revealed.

The Young Lords Party made a series of mistakes in strategy and tactics that steadily moved it away from its base of support.[83] Sincere leaders made severe mistakes resulting from inexperience, misguided analysis, ill-advised opinions, and political cowardliness. Members also, willingly or unwittingly, enabled the directional shifts that took the organization down. Some opened the way to destructive individuals, and others enabled their influence through silence, conspiracy, and ego. Members allowed accusations against others without question, and the Young Lords/PRRWO deteriorated under the weight of the resulting tensions.

The move to Puerto Rico was the biggest political mistake, not only flawed in conception, but also paternalistic and arrogant toward islanders. Puerto Ricans had fought against US imperialism since 1898 and Spanish colonialism before that. The Young Lords Party from its East Harlem headquarters would not be the savior. The proponents of the Puerto Rico project failed to appreciate the difference between providing support to Puerto Rico's national liberation movement and trying to take it over. Inexplicably, the obsession to dominate Puerto Rico's pro-independence struggle prevailed even when leading and trusted members counseled against the move, and members resigned in protest or drifted away in frustration. In 1970, more than a dozen active Young Lords' branches thrived across the United States; but by 1973 only four were left.[84] The move to Puerto Rico was a disaster as the shifting of people and resources steadily dismantled the organization and precipitated an exodus of members from which it never recovered. The Puerto Rico fiasco depleted the Young Lords financially, politically, emotionally, and spiritually. The YLP lost its revolutionary heart—gone was its rebel spirit and imagination. Narrow nationalism and a politics of expediency took hold, and the organization's character and integrity declined. The "revolution within the revolution" was discarded. Gender and racial equality struggles were deprioritized, although they had strengthened the organization, expanded membership, introduced innovative thinking and practices, and launched vital community-based campaigns.

The turn to organizing US workers opened another movement building possibility but sending members into factories and other work sites without support, resources, training, or strategy was a losing proposition that ultimately also failed. Totally divorced from the reality of working people's everyday lives and struggles, the Puerto Rican Revolutionary Workers Organization became consumed with ideologies and abstractions. Arguments about 'correct' and 'incorrect' political lines replaced interaction and organizing with workers and community members.

The governance model of "democratic centralism" was out of balance, heavy on centralism and woefully light on democracy. A few persons at the top of a hierarchy made all decisions, and they stifled creativity and initiative. Without mechanisms to engage differing points of view, the YLP/PRRWO degenerated into dogmatism. Those who advocated for democratic processes or who raised questions, criticisms, or doubts were branded "anti-leadership," "anti-working class," "petit bourgeoisie," "enemy of the people" or "police agent." By the end, a couple of self-anointed leaders with a clique of unthinking followers resorted to physical violence to squash anyone who expressed a different point of view.

Given the importance of leadership to the success or failure of any organization, it is worth contrasting the Young Lords' hierarchal, top-down style with Ella Baker's group-centered tradition and movement-building approach as described by the historian and activist Barbara Ransby.[85] Baker, an organizer and adviser to the Student Nonviolent Coordinating Committee (SNCC) and other organizations, believed in the collective power of everyday people to assess their situation, shape solutions, take action, and fight for social change. Leadership's role, in her view, was "to strengthen the group, forge consensus, and negotiate a way forward"[86] through open, democratic, and collaborative structures. Although the Young Lords were familiar with Baker's work, the organization did not adopt her ideas.

The Young Lords took many twists and turns. Without the benefit of ties to the community and collective deliberations, PRRWO turned rabidly violent and anti-revolutionary, and it inevitably imploded. By 1976, the YLO/YLP/PRRWO had faded into history. Our collective dream was hijacked, trashed, and buried—a cautionary tale.

SUMMARY

The Young Lords represented a new chapter of Puerto Rican militancy in the United States—a powerful activism that championed a people and roused a generation. Although we did not have the Internet, cell phones, or the social media tools of today, we utilized every available resource and strategy to build a people's movement. We mobilized our communities through door-to-door canvassing, street protests, civil disobedience, mass demonstrations, takeovers of institutions, the building of coalitions and networks, and legal, political, media, and cultural work. Determined to change the deplorable living conditions of our people, we organized at the grassroots to confront powerful elites.

As the people's movements of the late sixties and seventies were destroyed, former members of the Young Lords/PRRWO went their separate ways, disillusioned. Like a plague, sadness and pessimism spread. The official myth that social change was impossible permeated and demoralized us—at least for the moment. In the years after the organization's demise, former members appeared wounded, disoriented, heartbroken, and dazed. Some totally defeated had lost faith and never wanted to speak of revolution again. Others disappeared into middle America as if activism had been a youthful and embarrassing indiscretion. Those who participated in violence against other members pretended like it never happened.

Still, others emerged committed to the principles we had embraced as Young Lords. In 1977, former members together with other activists brought international attention to the plight of Puerto Rican Nationalists in US prisons since the 1950s by occupying the Statute of Liberty and placing the Puerto Rican flag on her crown.[87] Two years later, President Jimmy Carter pardoned the Nationalists who returned to Puerto Rico to a triumphant welcome. Former Young Lords also organized for the freedom of another generation of political prisoners, who were released in 1999.[88] Many former members joined to expel the US Navy from Vieques, an island off Puerto Rico's east coast used for bombing exercises. Countless others helped to form the National Congress of Puerto Rican Rights in the United States, and several built educational institutions and women's organizations. Former Young Lords organized grassroots movements against police brutality, demanding justice and supporting victims' families. Others became labor organizers providing leadership to national campaigns for a living wage and immigration reform, or become health care workers. A few became journalists or reporters. Many former women members became educators and professors in public schools and universities, or lawyers, judges, and doctors. Former Young Lords also continued to organize public events to commemorate important dates in Puerto Rican history and celebrate Puerto Rican culture.

I took the journey with the Young Lords from the group's beginning in New York through its painful decline and saw the organization crumble. We cannot forget that those in power—the ruling class, the exploiters, those who oppose justice—strike not just for one day, but relentlessly and remorselessly to incapacitate generations to come, using all their resources—every tactic imaginable or not, with no shame or trace of humanity of any kind—to annihilate and obliterate all who resist their control and domination. Silence will not free us. For us to remember and exchange experiences is to bring healing to reinvigorate the movements for social justice to take action and fight again another day.

The Young Lords were first- and second-generation Puerto Ricans in the United States, also African Americans, Cubans, Dominicans, and Mexicans primarily from working class homes—people marginalized and scorned by mainstream society. Yet we dared to imagine a civilization "where the needs of the people come first, and where we give solidarity and aid to the people of the world, not oppression and racism." I end where I began, believing in rebel imagination, freedom dreams, and the power of the people to achieve human liberation. Our dedicated actions in pursuit of these ideals as Young Lords are the legacy that continues to inspire new generations.

PART 2.
PALANTE SIEMPRE REFLECTIONS

(Edited transcripts of interviews conducted for
¡Palante, Siempre Palante! The Young Lords in 1995
Essay written by Martha Arguello (Duarte) in 2015)

The Excitement Was in the Streets!
Denise Oliver-Vélez

Woman, Dominican, and Young Lord
Martha Arguello (Duarte)

From Young Lord to Union Organizer
Minerva Solla

Philadelphia Young Lords and the Role of Women
Gloria M. Rodríguez

The Final Days and the Struggle Continues
Diana Caballero

Cultural memory is the elixir on which we must raise our children to keep them healthy and whole.

If you forget where you came from, why should anyone else give a damn?

Remember and Resist.

Magdalena Gómez
from *Shameless Woman*

The Excitement Was in the Streets!

Denise Oliver-Vélez

I WAS A MEMBER of the Central Committee of the Young Lords, first as minister of finance, then as minister of economic development. Before the Lords came into existence, I was living in Washington, DC, and I was going to Howard University, a black university. I had gone there because I thought it was going to be a political experience for me, but I found out it was basically a very bourgeois institution where people were interested in joining fraternities and sororities and marrying the right person. Since I wasn't looking for a doctor or a lawyer to marry, I was unhappy.

While I was in Washington, a group of Puerto Ricans came down for some kind of conference. A friend of mine called me and said, "You're from New York, and you probably know how to talk to Puerto Ricans." I was invited over as sort of an honorary Puerto Rican because I had lived in East Harlem and had cousins and friends who lived there, and I was familiar with Puerto Rican culture. They were members of an organization called the Real Great Society (RGS) who were just opening a branch in East Harlem.

I left Howard University, came back to New York, and joined the Real Great Society. I was sent to El Barrio to work as a teacher in their prep school for high school dropouts. I moved onto 110th Street between Madison and Park, a block notorious at that time known as "Death Row." My salary was paid through VISTA, which was the "urban Peace Corps" at the time. I felt like I was doing something important in the community. I was happy doing what I was doing. I was glad to be out of school; I enjoyed teaching, and I was assigned to teach Puerto Rican history, which I had to study in order to do.

At that time, there were recruiters from a new university being founded on Long Island called SUNY Old Westbury. They came to East Harlem looking for poor, poverty-struck Puerto Ricans to recruit because they wanted to have the perfect ethnic mix. They found a few blacks; they brought in some foreign students from Ethiopia and Thailand, and what they were missing were Puerto Ricans. When they met me they had absolutely no idea what class background I was from. They saw me in East Harlem living in a tenement; they assumed that I was this underprivileged person who had never been to college, and they recruited me, and Roberto [Ortiz], whom I was living with, and two other students in the prep school to go out to college at Old Westbury. They were paying for everything. It was an experimental school. They had seminars, and you could do fieldwork. You would get credit for work you were doing in the urban environment. All of us leaped on this opportunity to go to this school. At that time at RGS, there had been founded an organization called the Sociedad de Albizu Campos. Mickey Meléndez was one of the organizers, and a number of Westbury students used to attend those meetings. We'd commute from the campus to RGS.

At Westbury, there were ninety-five students in the original class. The sixteen non-white students, and I say non-white, because there weren't enough blacks, or enough Puerto Ricans; enough Asians; so we banded together and formed a non-white caucus in defense of our situation. We wanted course work that would relate to our urban communities, to our cultural background. We took over the campus; we shut it down. We made some demands. One was that we get lecturers who related to our background. One of those people who we invited to the campus was Juan González, a Puerto Rican student who was at Columbia University around the time of the big takeover. We also invited Felipe Luciano, who had come out of prison, was at Queens College, and was also a member of a black cultural, nationalist poetry group called the Last Poets. On campus was a young man named Paulie Guzmán from Bronx Science High School. He was in his freshman year; and, as a result of a trip to Mexico, he discovered his Puerto Rican and Cuban identity and became Pablo Guzmán. Roberto Ortiz was one of the Puerto Rican students, and there was myself; I'm black American. There was a young black American student named Bob Bunkley who took the name "Muntu." Mickey Meléndez was still at the campus. This was sort of the beginning of a portion of the Young Lords in New York right on campus. We started using the school facilities, the school car, the mimeograph machine, to do political work, and we maintained ties to the RGS office in East Harlem.

Around about that time, the Panthers were in existence in New York, and we were all reading the Black Panther paper. We were sort of fascinated with what they were doing. Pablo, who had tacked on the name "Yoruba" being of Afro-Latino heritage, and "Muntu" went to New York to try and join the Panthers, but something went wrong, and they came back a bit disgusted. But in that issue of the Panther paper was a very interesting article. It talked about Fred Hampton, the chairman of the Illinois Black Panther Party. Fred had developed a concept called the Rainbow Coalition. Jesse Jackson uses the term; he co-opted it from the Panthers. In Chicago, Fred Hampton had been in jail at one point with a young man named "Cha Cha" Jiménez, who was a member of a street gang, the Young Lords. Due to his exposure to Fred, when Cha Cha got out of jail, he went to his gang and decided to convert them into a political organization. Fred pulled together not only the Young Lords but also a white group of Ozark hillbillies who became the Patriot Party [Young Patriots Organization]. He reached out to a number of Chicano groups. He was really trying to form a Rainbow Coalition—black, white, Latino, Asian, and Native American.

So there was this article about this group of Puerto Ricans in Chicago—the Young Lords. A decision was made by some of the guys to hop in a car and drive to Chicago and go and meet Cha Cha. And when they got back from Chicago, they were very excited. They had met Cha Cha; they were very impressed with him, and they had made an agreement to start an East Coast branch of the Young Lords Organization. Of course, we didn't have any money, no office, but we liberally borrowed the facilities of the State University at Old Westbury. We liberated Xerox paper and office chairs and started to have meetings. The guys would go into the city; and, by that time, they had hooked up with members of some other youth organizations, and that formed the core of what became the Young Lords. Pretty soon it became impossible for me to continue my education because becoming a member of the Young Lords was a full-time job. Before I knew it, I had left school. All of us abandoned school. The excitement was in the streets!

There were a lot of cultural and psychological reasons why I became a Young Lord. Several years before, I had attempted to become a member of a pan-Africanist organization, and I was rejected for my color. I was told that if I really wanted to make a revolution among black people I would have to assassinate my grandmother when the time came because my grandmother is white. I was called a half-breed. A lot of the politics at that time were politics of skin analysis. It was ugly. I was unhappy and disillusioned.

I was rescued once. I was working in a place called the True Coffee Shop in Harlem, and a crazy nationalist came there to shoot me. The person who intervened was a very nice gentleman who used to sit in "the Truth" and play chess. He had reddish hair, and he stepped in front of the brother with the gun and told him, "Brother, it's not about skin analysis today." Later, I found out that the man was Malcolm X, and I'll never forget his intervention. Not a lot of people listened to that part of Malcolm's message, and I retreated from the black struggle at that time. I wasn't around for the development of the Panthers; I was out on the Old Westbury campus. After the Panthers turned down Pablo and Muntu, it seemed the route for me, to follow my revolutionary dream, was to join the Young Lords.

I had always felt really comfortable in El Barrio. I had always fit in, in terms of color; I was neither too light nor too dark. Many of the people I grew up with as kids and had gone to Orchard Beach with, to the Palladium, to the Corso, and to the Tropicoro were Puerto Rican. Many of them had known me since I was a kid and made the assumption that I was Puerto Rican. But I wasn't. But that core group of people who formed the Young Lords were not all Puerto Rican, and I think that's something very important, and something that's very different about the Young Lords. It was not locked into a very tight cultural definition of who you had to be, to be a Young Lord.

The politics in the late 1960s were a mess. Through the late 1950s and the early 60s, of course, there was the civil rights movement. But as younger people began to feel frustrated with concepts of pacifism, of turn-the-other-cheek, the ideals of Martin Luther King, the NAACP, CORE, and SNCC, groups splintered off, and you had the development of a more militant wing of the Student Nonviolent Coordinating Committee, which was no longer nonviolent. You had the Deacons for the Defense of Justice in Bogalusa, Louisiana,[1] and the development of the Black Panther Party.

The politics in East Harlem were non-existent within the framework of the Democratic and Republican Parties for Puerto Ricans. Even though Puerto Ricans were the majority in that area, there was always an Italian assembly person. There was no effort to organize Puerto Ricans in the United States even within the confines of straight politics. The organizing within the Puerto Rican community was basically only people who had grown up in Puerto Rico and had experienced either the Nationalist [Party] struggle or some other movements on the island. But their focus was back in Puerto Rico; it had very little to do with what was going on with Puerto Ricans in the United States, their conditions as workers, their conditions in housing, food, clothing, shelter. There was a vacuum. Some of the void was filled during the time of President Johnson when a lot of anti-poverty money poured into the community. You had what was called a new breed, "a poverty pimp." These were people who got money to run programs that were set up to fail. They became very self-important, spent that money mostly on themselves; it didn't trickle down to people it was supposed to be for. So, the Young Lords—this developing, fledgling organization—walked into a community that had been crying out for somebody to address these needs. People had taken a look at the poverty programs and, in most cases, rejected them because people in the community are not stupid, and they saw where that money was going. They saw that these people ended up with big shiny cars and nice houses on Long Island, but nothing was coming back into the neighborhood. And the conditions in the community were dire. There were a lot of drugs. The housing was abominable. The health care was non-existent. There was no bilingual education in the schools so a lot of Puerto Rican children were just thrown by the wayside. The Young Lords were in the right place at a time when the world was in foment. There were rebellions all around the world.

The Young Lords had to develop politics by osmosis and take a little bit of this and a little of that. We liked certain things from Marxism and that was implemented. But there were certain concepts that were cultural/nationalist, particularly influenced by Felipe, who was coming from a more cultural/nationalist/pan-Africanist/black background, also by Pablo. Because Juan was coming out of the Columbia University student struggle and out of the SDS, he had a more clearly defined intellectual perspective on the history of politics, probably more Marxist, or socialist at that time. I don't know where I was coming from; I had participated in SNCC, CORE, and other civil rights organizations and had attempted to become a pan-Africanist, which I rejected. I had communists in my family, so I was already an eclectic, a rather confused one. Other people brought other things, and we attempted to make a synthesis of these varying perspectives as well as incorporate the history of struggle that came from Puerto Rico. There was a lot of time spent doing political education and teaching Puerto Rican history, which the majority of people were not familiar with. All of this came together to form this growing and developing politic of the Young Lords. We had somebody from the Communist Party coming and teaching us about Marxism. Early on there were certain relationships with black cultural nationalists. With the Black Panther office, we worked together on a number of projects. Something that was very unique to the Young Lords' programs was dealing with lead poisoning detection. That became one of our massive outreach mobilization techniques to get the community involved by addressing issues of concern to their health. Health was one of the primary things we dealt with in terms of organizing.

At that time the anti-war movement was expanding. The country was becoming more overtly racist. In reaction to the racism and the political confusion, on the ground there was a developing militancy. For myself, I was a lot more comfortable with the Young Lords' point of view. The Black Panthers became more and more suicidal. The extreme positions they were taking were the result of having developed in California, where there were no laws against having guns. So the carrying of guns was expected of Panther chapters across the United States, and they had to arm themselves. In states where it was not legal to carry guns, it put them in a situation where they were constantly involved in shootouts, and people started to die.

The Young Lords stepped back from that position and understood that there's a big difference between an above ground organization and one that's an underground militant arm or an army. I think that had to do with the fact that there was an active Puerto Rican underground, CAL and MIRA, in Puerto Rico.[2] It left the Lords free to develop mass organizations, do community organizing, and take a militant stance. We got into a lot of situations where we battled with police, but we were not armed outright, or in the open, with the exception of the second takeover of the People's Church. We weren't ready to commit revolutionary suicide at that point in time, and I was very comfortable with that, too.

Though I ran away from some of the reactions to my own particular ethnic status within the black community and hid out in the Young Lords, I'm not going to say everything was perfect. There is racism in the Puerto Rican community. And there was a very strong reaction to the Young Lords' politics; it was very heavily stressed that people were from an Afro-Taíno culture. The already-in-existence Puerto Rican political organizations reacted negatively to that position. One, because of the separation between Puerto Ricans on the island and in the United States, but two, because there was a lot of denial about there being any African roots in Puerto Ricans at all. That was reality. We tried to deal with those things in the Young Lords.

Puerto Ricans have a unique placement in that triplicate identity of European history, African history, and indigenous American history, to become a bridge group between disparate cultural, and ethnic and racial identities; that was one of the important things that the Young Lords did. The Lords, with ties to both the black community and the white movement, became that *puente*, that bridge between groups, the cultural/nationalist, the Marxists, the whites, the blacks, and the Asians.

In the early days, the structure of the organization was paramilitary. We borrowed that from the Panthers. There was a Central Committee; each member of the Central Committee was called a minister. Within each ministry, you had different ranks, like lieutenants and sergeants, and each ministry had different tasks. My particular opinion is that the women did most of the work. I know I'm being a little biased. But since a lot of the work involved actually going out and doing community organizing and running the different programs, the women took on a lot of those tasks. The health organizing, in particular, was one of the things that women were involved in. Many of us, the original women in the Young Lords, made it very clear that we were not going to be just secretaries, that we were warriors too, and that we had a right to be in every area. Most of the tasks that involved feeding children, breakfast programs in the morning, that involved clothing drives, collecting and distributing things in the community, and testing the children for lead poisoning was work carried on by women. Ultimately, we found out that about a third of the children in East Harlem had high levels of lead in their system. As a result of this program, this was under the John Lindsay administration (Lindsay was mayor then), legislation was passed in New York City banning the use of lead based paints in tenements, in apartment buildings, and also a law was put into effect that landlords would have to go back and take that lead paint out of the apartments, which has not been followed up on. The Young Lords were in the vanguard of that and that was one of the major changes in New York as a result of Young Lords activities.

We were going to put out a Young Lords newspaper, *Palante*, in Spanish and English. The problem was doing the Spanish part. Everyone could write in English, but we would spend hours trying to translate. It was really better when we got people in the organization whose Spanish was better because people in the community started to complain. But that had a lot to do with who we were. The Young Lords were not Puerto Ricans from Puerto Rico; they were people who grew up here, who had English basically as a first language in terms of what they dealt with on a daily basis, and then you had Afro-Americans, and some other people sprinkled in, too. So it was rather adventurist to even attempt to do something in Spanish. Since I went to music and art high school and majored in art in college, and knew something about layout and design, one of the first jobs I had was working on the paper doing layout, and some of the editing, as well as doing this school book translation of the Spanish.

One of the most powerful positions not on the Central Committee was the Officer of the Day (OD), that's like the staff sergeant. You sit behind the desk, you have to know where everyone's going, who's in, who's out, who has to go and sell newspapers. That was our source of money, cadres who went out and sold newspapers on the street. It was real important to make people go and do their quota of newspaper selling on a daily basis and keep track of that. The Officer of the Day was the person who answered the phone calls and also had the power to hand out discipline. Discipline was if you messed up on something, you had to do pushups, or run around the block ten times, or you were sent to study hall where you were given some boring document by Lenin to read, and had to write a paper on it. You stayed up all night, and then you had to get up at five or six o'clock in the morning to do the free breakfast program. People did not like going to study hall. Because the Central Committee was all male, the highest rank that any woman could aspire to was Officer of the Day. I had been around for a while and contributed things, and as a token gesture, because the original OD had been a male, I was given the position.

We suffered from all the problems that exist in contemporary society between the sexes, the male chauvinism, the sexism, that's amplified when you become a paramilitary organization. Then you have the particular cultural bent of machismo that exists within the Puerto Rican community, and the combination of factors made life rather miserable for the women in the organization for a period of time. We were incredibly committed to the struggle. I know that I worked hard from early in the morning until late at night; sometimes I had no sleep. But the men were the ones who went out there as the "warriors," and the women did all of the work. At least that's the way I felt about it.

I was very proud of becoming Officer of the Day, and Central Committee members were very surprised when they would bop into the office late, and I would make them do push-ups. I wasn't supposed to be disciplining them, but I pointed out their own rules and regulations. Women were secretly happy to see a woman dishing out some discipline. The structure of the Young Lords was called democratic centralism. It was more central than democratic. There was a lot of flow from the top down, from the men down to the rest of us, and very little input from the bottom up. The women felt that we didn't have a voice on the Central Committee. We sat down, and we wrote a list of demands. I don't remember how many, but we presented them to the Central Committee. They were not requests: they were demands. One of the demands was that there be a woman on the Central Committee, and that the program and platform of the Lords be changed because there was one line in the program that said that machismo must be revolutionary, and we didn't see how machismo, as a concept, could ever be revolutionary. It's reactionary. And that was done. I was put on the Central Committee. I became the token woman. We got our demand met, but then, my orders were that my allegiance had to be to the Central Committee, that if I took any discussion from the Central Committee out to the women, I would be breaking security.

We understood that, as women, we were equal to our brothers, and we never wanted to separate. We had to achieve a balance. The black movement was going through a certain kind of intersexual warfare, with the cultural/nationalists taking a position that men were superior, and women had to walk four steps behind. You had the Muslim movement developing, and then you had the revolutionary movements, which had an uneasy relationship between men and women. But it was important for the growth of the organization that this kind of conflict developed. It got ugly at times; it got rough at times, but it never destroyed the organization. What it did was make it stronger when women could feel they were equals; when women could participate on all levels. The conflict itself caused the breakup of a number of relationships. There were people who, as a result of the revolution within the organization, left because they could not politically go along with these changes. Though it was painful, it was necessary. We were a lot stronger afterward.

A few months after I got on the Central Committee, another woman came on. Later, a Central Staff was formed, and there were women involved in that, as well as women put into the Defense Ministry. So many things were changing in our world. We looked, and we searched in revolutionary literature. Maybe we found a few pieces, but there really wasn't much because the world had never really dealt with this. We did take as heroines of our struggle Lolita Lebrón and Blanca Canales because they had been in the Nationalist Party struggle in Puerto Rico. We looked to women like Angela Davis. There were two women in the Panther 21 case at the time, Afeni Shakur and Joan Bird, who had been arrested with the brothers. We were proud that women were going on posters. That was real important because this was new. The face of the civil rights movement had been male. Then with the strong pan-African groups, you never knew the names of any of the women; they just wrapped their heads in galeas and stood around holding baskets of fruit.

I was very molded and shaped by that early education. I came to understand and believe that I have a right as a person to express the fullness of myself, to be proud of being female. We didn't try to be men. We struggled to know our strengths and weaknesses, which stood me in good stead throughout my life, something that can never be taken away. But some men accused us of being disruptive. "The most important thing is the struggle; forget about your petty problems as women." But if there is no unity within an organization as long as there is a disparity between men and women in the struggle, there will not be that ability to strive for change in the world.

Many marriages broke up because we were trying to be different, and we didn't know how to maintain marital ties, or even know how to define what marriage was. We looked at it as chains, *cadenas*. You're not free! You're this new, liberated woman, but your husband keeps telling you what to do. What happens if the wife gets promoted, and she's a higher rank than the husband, and she can give him orders? There were very few Puerto Rican men who wanted to put up with that. A majority of the people, who came in relationships, didn't leave in the same relationship. There are scars that people have to this day. But again, it's part of a process of change, and I don't want to talk about it as isolated. Most young people were going through this in America at that time. That's an issue we still haven't resolved. Divorce is now par for the course in most families. Women are still trying to cope with how to run an organization, work a job, go to school, raise a family, and almost become superwomen. Maybe generations to come won't have to deal with these issues because we dealt with them then, and we're dealing with them now.

I left the Young Lords in 1971 to go into the Black Panther Party. My leaving didn't make me bitter; in fact, I watched the Young Lords' activities from outside as things changed. But I had to leave for a number of reasons. In my opinion, my leaving was at a time of major change in the organization, which I feel was almost the beginning of the end, of the dissolution of the organization. I've walked through the streets in East Harlem, and people have said, "Dónde está los Young Lords?" Where did they go? People miss the Young Lords. They had been an integral part of that community in the South Bronx, the Lower East Side, Philadelphia, New Haven, Hartford, and New Jersey. What happened? Let me backtrack just a bit. The organization was trying to increase its ties to Puerto Rico to develop a relationship to revolutionary organizations on the island, particularly MPI [Movimiento Pro-Independencia], which later became the Puerto Rican Socialist Party. An advanced group was sent to Puerto Rico. It was Gloria [González, Fontanez], Pablo, and myself. Gloria was very comfortable there because she had been born on the island; she spoke Spanish perfectly. Pablo, who looked like one of the Black Panthers, had a big afro, dark glasses, dark leather jacket, and, because he's black, was not accepted with open arms. They were very confused about me. I made an attempt to give a speech in Spanish, and I got attacked for being a

137

Nuyorican and mangling the language. I kept trying to explain that I was black, and they kept saying, "That's what's wrong with you Nuyoricans; you keep saying that you're black." I kept saying "No, but I *am* black." Finally, when it got through, they apologized. But the racism in the island, nobody wanted to deal with because I was told, "No hay racismo en Puerto Rico." But that was not true. Color, caste, class were major contradictions, even within left-wing political groups. I had very ominous feelings in the pit of my stomach, and to this day I regret that I wasn't strong enough in expressing the feelings I had, or maybe I felt that I didn't have a right to really push my perspective because I wasn't Puerto Rican. I was the only non–Puerto Rican on the Central Committee.

The decision was made to shut down the entire organization in the United States. Close the offices, which means to break away from the economic support that came out of the community, the sale of the newspaper, all the things that we had going in the community, and to focus the struggle on the liberation of Puerto Rico. The decision was made to take an essentially US-based organization of people of Puerto Rican heritage and ship them lock stock and barrel to Puerto Rico, where there were already three highly established left-of-center organizations. Also, remember the Young Lords was an ethnic and racial mix pushing this Taíno/Afro culture. It was my gut feeling that it wasn't going to work. If we wanted to open a Young Lords office to make ties, that would be one thing, but to wipe everything out that had taken several years building, and take everybody to Puerto Rico, to me, was committing suicide. And within the confines of the Central Committee, I fought the decision. There were other people in the Central Committee who felt differently, some who had much closer roots or ties with Puerto Rico, others that were sort of wavering and didn't know what to do. At one point, I had an argument with somebody who said, "Well, you're not Puerto Rican. You can't vote on this." I said, "To hell with that, I'm on the Central Committee, and I'm going to vote." The vote took place, and I was outvoted. There were two other people who voted with me, that it was not correct. I thought it was going to be a political disaster. I had ties to the Panthers and ultimately just committed my time to the Panther Party. Then I got a phone call and was asked to leave the country and go to the Panthers' Information Section to do work with Eldridge Cleaver and the Information Section in Algiers.

I kept my eyes on what happened to the Young Lords. I watched them go to the island. I watched it not work. I watched them come back and do a reassessment of what had gone wrong. That didn't work either because the move severed the roots; the base of El Barrio and the other communities had been lost. The grassroots orientation that the Young Lords Party had, no longer was there, and without those close ties to the community, it couldn't work, and it didn't. I'm not saying that this is isolated from the effect of police intervention, infiltration, COINTELPRO, the FBI, and the political change in America that came at the mid-seventies, and the destruction of a massive revolutionary movement. I think the primary factor in the failure of the Young Lords was the decision to leave its roots here. These were the children of the *Marine Tiger*.[3] Most of the Lords had parents perhaps who had been born in Puerto Rico, but some had parents who were born here. That last migration in 1947 spawned a generation who had one foot in the United States, and maybe they had dreams of Puerto Rico, but the reality of their existence was here. The moment that was abandoned, they were like a boat without an anchor. They were adrift. The boat doesn't go backward. You can't go home that way.

The destruction to the Lords and other movements was a traumatic experience. I've learned similar to what Vietnam vets go though. They call it post-traumatic stress disorder; I call it post-traumatic revolutionary failure stress disorder—I have my own name for it. After the collapse of this revolution, many of us had to go on journeys of self-exploration. I had to bottom out. I got into drugs, alcohol, workaholism. The Young Lords were my family. It was my dream. I didn't know what to put there. I didn't know how to deal with it. And I did it in isolation. Many of us did it in isolation. It's only now, years later that I can look at it more comfortably and understand what happened. I did become very disillusioned and didn't want to have anything to do with organizing anything for a period of time. But that healed. It's taken twenty years. The wounds are not there anymore—as open wounds. And the scabs are no longer there. There is some scar tissue, but it's not uncomfortable so I can look at things from a different perspective. And I keep returning to doing the kinds of things that I feel are necessary for social change. We need another Young Lords.

Woman, Dominican, and Young Lord

MARTHA ARGUELLO

I DO NOT RECALL the specific moment when I decided to become a Young Lord; rather it seemed a natural transition, a way to live many of the beliefs that I had grown up with. It was about justice, creating a new world and being a part of a movement that actively worked to change a system that I deemed racist and unequal. Still a teen, proudly Dominican, a woman trying to pave my own path in the world, I joined the Young Lords Organization during my first year at New York University. It was a defining moment, one that would thrust me into a history that continues to inspire me. I became a Young Lord amid a period of growing activism with episodes of incredible solidarity. While the organization lasted only a few years, for most of us who donned the purple beret, its impact would last a lifetime.

By the time I joined the YLO in El Barrio, political meetings and marches were a part of my life. As a young teen, I participated in civil rights and antiracist demonstrations, attended a "freedom school" for young activists, and marched against the draft and the war in Vietnam. Malcolm X, Albizu Campos, the Mirabal sisters,[1] the Fort Hood Three[2] were familiar names to me, their political actions, *actos de consciencia,* inspirational. Some of these historical figures entered my life through the teachings of my activist brother, Tito, who publicly advocated independence for Puerto Rico, recruited members to the Movement Pro Independence for Puerto Rico, and was among the founders of an early political organization of New York-based Dominicans calling themselves *Juventud Patriótica Dominicana* (JPD). An organ of the 24 de Abril Movement in the Dominican Republic, the JPD aligned itself with the civil uprising remembered as the April Revolution that began on that date in 1965. Within days of the uprising, US troops landed in the Dominican Republic and began a military occupation that lasted more than a year. US president Lyndon Johnson intervened allegedly to protect US citizens, while officials publicly expressed fears that the country would become another Cuba.

Although I was not formally a member of the JPD, largely composed of recent immigrants from the Dominican Republic in their twenties or thirties, I did sketches for its newsletters and flyers, helped in the production of the news organ, and participated in JPD protests and political events. While I strongly identified with their ideals; the ages, life experiences, and prior involvement in island politics of most members set me apart. As a Dominican brought to the United States as a little girl, my experiences were informed by my neighborhood, news gathered from local sources, and the civil rights and black power movements. The JPD, activist family members in New York, as well as stories about politically active relatives in the Dominican Republic expanded my consciousness of movements beyond US borders.

In addition to my involvement with the JPD, antiwar, and student-worker coalitions, I was also active in LUCHA, NYU's Latino student organization, and worked with the Black Allied Student Association. The combined efforts of these two groups resulted in the creation of a free summer camp program at NYU for children of the Lower East Side. My experiences with these organizations prepared me for the level of service and engagement expected of Young Lords.

Like other Young Lords, I embraced the position that local, national, and international movements for social justice and equality represented a common cause. While I understood the strength of solidarity and felt impassioned about the sustained struggle for independence in Puerto Rico, it was the Young Lords' identification of, and approach toward, community issues that eventually drew me to their ranks. The YLO's bold and innovative actions, the young cadres and leadership, as well as the visible presence of strong women in the organization moved me to join. As a Young Lord, I experienced the incredible and the mundane. We organized, worked, studied, celebrated, and mourned. We drew energy from small victories, the opening of new branches, and the addition of new members. We felt angered by the conditions of our neighborhoods, and mourned the deaths in our communities and ultimately of one of our own: Julio Roldán. We went beyond meetings and study groups and became active in direct action and targeted protests. In addition to the publicized protests and offensives, as a member, I swept sidewalks, sold *Palante* newspapers, recruited members, attended political education and women's caucus meetings, stood guard in branch offices, and, on occasion, spoke at rallies and press interviews. I worked in East Harlem when it was our only East Coast branch, later moving to the Lower East Side branch when it opened in September 1970.

I was one of the first women assigned to the Defense Ministry; I felt empowered by our actions and inspired by our collective spirit. While some may describe us as dreamers, which to a degree we were, we aspired to create a new society. How else do you change a community, a society, without dreaming about another and daring to act and work toward bringing that about? The inclusion of both personal and public issues in our repertoire of challenges resounded with my ideals for a new society. In our internal and external struggle for women's liberation, our quest for justice, quality education, health services, community control of institutions, we engaged in personal and public conversations. In bringing attention to sterilization practices in local hospitals and in Puerto Rico, by exposing the high incidence of lead poisoning among children in urban housing while also talking about living conditions in island neighborhoods like La Perla or El Fanguito, we were able to link our urban, local existence to island folk, our lives to those of our parents and grandparents. As Young Lords, we brought these issues into community spaces in New York, introducing them to a generation physically removed from but connected to Puerto Rico.

Among the Young Lords who were not of Puerto Rican descent, our embrace of the YLO/YLP reflected our belief in a common cause, our shared neighborhood experiences, and the growing political awareness and activism of young people of color. An estimated 20 percent of members in Young Lords were African American, with additional representation from various Caribbean and Latin American countries. It is not by accident that these numbers existed. Rather, they reflected the blended communities we came from, the work done by the YLO and later the YLP, and the emphasis on building solidarity movements among the Lords, student organizers, and other community activists. While there are earlier examples of combined efforts of African American and Puerto Rican communities in New York, particularly in education and fair housing, the work of the Young Lords within this arena provided a strong new voice.

I relocated with my family to California shortly after the book *Palante: Voices and Photographs of the Young Lords* by the Young Lords Party and Michael Abramson was published. Juan González and a young woman in the Defense Ministry visited me en route to Hawaii. I learned of YLP plans to potentially open branches in Hawaii and California. Although these plans did not develop, the organizational shift and branch openings in Puerto Rico occurred shortly thereafter. I did not experience the final chapters of the Young Lords Party; the swift dismantling of an organization so many had sacrificed for. When I think about the external and internal factors that precipitated its demise, it is with a pain, similar to my memory of the deaths of Malcolm X, Fred Hampton, don Pedro Albizu Campos, and the Mirabal sisters. While these individuals left an incredible legacy, I still wonder, "what if . . ." Similarly, I ask myself: what if the YLP had lived longer, survived as an organization? During those moments, the teacher and organizer in me reminds me that there are new dreamers, organizers, and fighters, who, guided by principles of social justice, have developed their own platforms and methods for mobilizing, who have staged their own offensives, and who will write new pages in movement history.

Cha Cha Jiménez is fond of saying: "there are no ex-Lords, only 'Old Lords.'" While he jokingly speaks to the reality of our aging, his words also point to the need to continue working towards the ideals we so fervently embraced, even as we operate on different planes or in different ways. As a woman in the Young Lords, I am compelled to share this history. I am mindful that as activist women, we claimed our rightful places within the organization: as leaders and cadres, members of different ministries, performing tasks beyond those that had been historically assigned to us. We embraced and sought to emulate the lives of the strong women and men who came before us and dreamed of those who would follow.

From Young Lord to Union Organizer

MINERVA SOLLA

WHEN I JOINED THE Young Lords, I joined the Young Lords out of anger. It was a struggle as I was growing up in New York City, and I saw a lot in the communities, and I saw the healthcare system, and I saw the educational system in this community not helping any of the people that I relate to every day. I joined the Young Lords out of anger. I was eighteen years old when I heard Felipe Luciano, the then chairman of the Young Lords, speak at Brooklyn College about what was going on in our communities. Out of that meeting, there was a group of us, and we just decided to go join the Young Lords.

My work in the Young Lords was to reach out to the community trying to educate around what is actually going on in the system. The same way I did not know what's going on around my community, other people didn't either, so we used to educate people about what was going on with the system, and how we are oppressed as women, and as students, and as Latinos and African Americans in our communities. We used to sell *Palante* every day and that was a tool to start the conversation. We used to have clothing programs. We also had breakfast programs. We had political education classes to educate people on the history of Puerto Rico.

I was stationed in East Harlem, and I saw how the people lived. There was no reason for us to be living in this way in a country as rich as it is. There was no need for people to be treated as they were treated. And people trying to struggle every day, and the only thing that they had was going on the welfare line and looking forward to just going to pick up a welfare check. They had no self-esteem. There was no ambition for them to do anything. The children ran into drugs, into alcohol, and that bothered me. Also the lack of health care bothered me. The way people were being treated in the emergency rooms bothered me. And it hasn't really changed now, and that's why I'm in the healthcare industry fighting for better health care with the union.

144

I was one of the first women in the Ministry of Defense of the Young Lords. The Ministry of Defense was a very heavy role to play. As a woman in the Defense Ministry, we had problems sometimes with the men thinking that the women couldn't do the same job that they could. So it was almost trying to compete with the men so that we could prove to them that, yes, we could do the job as well as them, and maybe even better. So I felt really strengthened by being in the Defense Ministry in the Young Lords Party. I was trained in different security measures that had to be taken. We had to secure buildings. We had to secure the Central Committee members. Basically it comes down to, you actually have to put your life down on the line. We saw the importance of that because we did see the need for an organization. As a woman in the Defense Ministry, I can say that I was really risking my life by being in the Defense Ministry, but I saw the need for us to be there.

We used to go in back of the sanitation trucks and steal their brooms so that we could clean up the streets because the sanitation did not clean our streets as well as they clean other parts of the city. One time we stole a truck for it was a healthcare mobile, and we brought it into the community because they were not servicing the community at that time, they were servicing other areas in the city.

Most of the people were enthusiastic because I think that they saw there was a need for social change, and they saw that there was somebody doing something about it. The Young Lords Party was talking about we want respect and dignity for the people in these communities. We want better education. We want better housing. We want better healthcare, and the people in the community related to us because they saw that we were the only group actually working in the communities besides the Black Panther Party. People gave us that respect that we stood for change so that we could better our lives, so that we could better our futures as the younger generation. At the same time we were trying to educate the people in the community that they also had to stand up next to us, so that they can better their lives in the community.

Today, I'm a union organizer with 1199 SEIU, United Health care Workers. We represent one hundred thousand healthcare workers in this country. The Young Lords Party inspired me in fighting for social justice in the healthcare system. I see myself as a woman in the struggle, and I always backtrack to what I learned in the Young Lords. In 1973, I was able to bring in the union at Roosevelt Hospital in New York as a result of being part of the Young Lords. The organization inspired me to stand up for my rights. Union organizing is not an easy job, especially for a woman. I have the ability now to do the job as a result of what I learned in the Young Lords.

In my job now as a union organizer, we get calls from different people that want to join the union. We set up meetings, and we ask people, why do they want to join the union? We get an organizing committee going inside the healthcare facility, and we direct them—give them guidance. We help them understand that *they* are the union. Just like when we were in the Young Lords, we believed that the people in the community have the power to change things. In the union also, we say *they* are the union. In the union, the workers for the first time have an opportunity to voice their opinion on what they want and what they want to negotiate in their contract, not what management imposes on them.

It's very important for the young people today to understand and know what the Young Lords Party was about. There is a history as to why a Young Lords Party was formed. Many years ago, people did consider us as a gang. We were not a gang; we were an organization fighting for social change. I believe we still need an organization for social change.

Philadelphia Young Lords
and the Role of Women

GLORIA M. RODRÍGUEZ

I JOINED THE YOUNG LORDS in the early seventies. Originally from Brooklyn, the Lower East Side office was my home branch, and I was later transferred to the Philadelphia branch, where I was in the leadership. My parents were involved in the civil rights movement, union organizing, and community issues. They took us to every demonstration and rally they attended. So social activism is in my DNA. I read and stayed informed on what was happening in the country and around the world. I was an activist as early as junior high and high school, organizing student organizations and advocating for black and Puerto Rican studies. I lived in the Red Hook projects in South Brooklyn, a black and Puerto Rican community. It was predominantly black, so I got involved in the black movement interested in Malcolm X and the Black Panther Party. At that time, the only representation that I saw in the Puerto Rican community was PSP [the Puerto Rican Socialist Party]. This organization was primarily concerned with the liberation of Puerto Rico. As a young activist, I was concerned why there wasn't a strong stateside Puerto Rican organizational presence.

Everything changed when my dad began doing some political work with a new organization called the Young Lords. I graduated high school and was enrolled in the City College of New York. I was hanging out, not sure of my direction. My dad was concerned that his daughter was going to lose herself, so he took me to an activity that the Young Lords was initiating up in the barrio. It was the People's Church. When I walked in, I felt like I was home. It was so gripping; it felt like that was really where I was meant to be, it was where I belonged—that the struggle, the concerns that I saw that all these people had about equal rights and really making a difference in the world, standing up for what they believed in and being really committed to that, moved me so, it moved everything I felt that I was about at that time.

Shortly after, I became involved first as a "friend of the Lords," taking political education classes and participating in community initiatives. I became familiar with the Thirteen-Point Program and Platform that united the organization around these principles and guided our political work. I decided to drop out of college to become a full-time member and, as mentioned, began working out of the Lower East Side branch. About a year later, I was asked to relocate to Philadelphia. Our platform stated that women had to be represented on all leadership levels, and there was a need for a woman to be included in the branch leadership there. Also, the man I was engaged to marry was a member of the Philly branch, so I said yes to the transfer.

The personal adjustment to living in another city that I knew nothing about was challenging. The majority of Puerto Ricans in Philadelphia were first generation and Spanish dominant with strong ties to the island. So all community organizing, newsletters, and political education classes were done in both Spanish and English. On a personal note, I wasn't used to strong divides between the African American and Puerto Rican communities, and I experienced major culture shock.

As a branch of a national organization, we followed the platform of the YLP. However, we addressed specific local matters important to the Puerto Rican community. At that time, [Frank] Rizzo, who was known to be a right-wing conservative, was the police commissioner and later became the mayor. The amount of police brutality that was not only affecting the Puerto Rican community but the African American community as well was astounding. We did a lot of work basically trying to bridge the different communities together because the amount of separation and segregation, again the question of divide and conquer, was so clearly evident. As Young Lords, we coalesced with different organizations (Puerto Rican, African American, white, Asian) so we could bring our communities together and deal with common issues. The police were unbelievable. We were constantly under surveillance, stopped for no reason, and harassed. Our phones were tapped. They were doing this to the Black Panther Party and to the Young Lords Party.

We were involved in the student movement, organizing on a high school and college level. Most members in Philly were young, and some were still in school. The Federation of Puerto Rican Students had recently formed, and many of their leading members began to take political education classes with us and began initiatives to include Puerto Rican studies and cultural events on campus.

One issue that was really important was addressing the needs of migrant workers. Large numbers of Latinos were unemployed and, during the summer months, would go to the farms in Jersey to pick fruit, and get paid just two, three dollars an hour. They had no job protection, security, or benefits—nothing! We worked on this campaign in Philadelphia and in South Jersey where the farms were located. We covered the workers' struggles through *Palante*, the national newspaper of the YLP, and our local newsletter called *La Lucha* published every two weeks. The newsletter was bilingual, and it was well received. It was one of few, if any, bilingual community newsletters that existed [in Philadelphia] other than the Puerto Rican newspaper, *El Diario. La Lucha* was a necessary educational and organizing tool.

I began working at Temple Hospital. In the mid-seventies, there were no unions in the hospitals, so our task was to organize a union. I became a part of a team of workers working with the local office of 1199. It didn't take long for the workers to unionize and vote in a contract that addressed issues of job security, protection, benefits, promotions, salaries, grievances, etc. Once we became unionized, other hospitals followed suit.

I was the only woman in the branch when I first arrived, which was challenging and difficult. The response from the community to a young Puerto Rican woman being out in the streets organizing, engaged in militant politics, was not great. My activism challenged the predominant cultural and traditional mindset of women as homemakers. I absolutely did not fit that mode. So in my experience, the men in our community were dismissive and resentful. I also experienced much of that behavior within the YLP. It was tough to work within a branch of all men who resented my presence. For many of them, I was "Mike's girlfriend" and wasn't taken seriously. My ideas and leadership were not received well. There were many instances where I was involved in meetings, and my proposals were rejected, but if a brother said the same exact thing, it was welcomed. One brother in particular was very angry at my being one of three leading the branch. He felt that I had usurped his position, and he tried to make my life miserable. His attitude was hostile and challenging toward me, and the overwhelming majority of the brothers (who started this branch together) were complicit in their silence and lack of support. Conceptually, they agreed with the organization's position on women, but practically, it wasn't aligned. So, I often felt frustrated, isolated, and alone. There weren't any other female full-time members, so unlike New York, no women's caucus or built in support system. I had to deal the best way I knew possible because my commitment to the Puerto Rican community and to the struggle for human rights was my priority, and I wasn't going to leave.

In January 1972, the Central Committee transferred Iris Morales and Pablo "Yoruba" Guzmán to the Philadelphia branch, and things began to slowly change. Some of the Philly founding members left the organization.

In 1973, two brothers in leadership were sent to jail for political cases. It was now Iris and I providing leadership for the branch. We began to see a change in the community as a result of the work we were doing. Women involved in organizing in the hospitals and factories were joining the organization. Also a substantial group of women out of the student struggle actively engaged in our community initiatives. We witnessed an increase in women attending our political education groups. The presence, leadership, and community and workplace activism were undeniable. This was a reflection of a few things: the work and commitment that we as Puerto Rican women leaders were exemplifying and a collective evolution of consciousness. During this process, we began to see the fruits of our labor.

On a personal level, I was involved in all our efforts. I worked at a hospital that was nonunion. I did the footwork to organize a union. I was voted the union delegate of my division and represented our concerns to the union. I was also active with the Puerto Rican student organization at Temple, setting up Puerto Rican studies programs. And I focused my energy on organizing women in the community. I would hold political education classes in my backyard and organized a women's group composed of community, working class, and students. I developed strong personal and community relationships.

The Young Lords set the foundation in consciousness for other organizations. Many of us supported and participated in cultural organizations and forged relationships with community service groups. When the organization [the Puerto Rican Revolutionary Workers Organization] ceased to exist, former members began creating or joining existing organizations, continuing political work. I think that really was our contribution to the Puerto Rican community in Philadelphia. I am inspired and happy at having been a part of laying that foundation for future generations. In addition to the Thirteen-Point Program and Platform that guided me, I felt my life was one of purpose and contribution to our people. We were young people willing to put ourselves on the line for the Puerto Rican people. I felt my purpose was the higher cause—about service. It's about looking at where we are and where we have to go as a community. I always felt a deep love in my heart for justice, fairness, and freedom. That was why, at eighteen years old, I joined the Young Lords and remained for five years, sacrificing the "personal for the political." My mentors and members united around our commitment and love for our people. It was the most impactful and life altering experience in my young adult life.

In order to make a difference in the world, it's not enough to identify, complain, or talk about it. We have got to get active. Wherever you are—find your place of activism. Changes that need to be made are not going to be made just by talking about it, nor will they happen overnight. It's a process. But certainly, it's going to require commitment, purpose, and determination to make the most impact. We all have to be guided by a deep call of what's true to our hearts.

The Final Days and the Struggle Continues

DIANA CABALLERO

I WAS A YOUNG LORD at heart for a very long time but didn't start working with the organization until about 1972. Prior to that I did work with El Comité, another Puerto Rican organization. I started working with the YLP when it was changing to the PRRWO [Puerto Rican Revolutionary Workers Organization]. I worked in education with parents, but I also worked [for the release of] Puerto Rican political prisoners. My main work was in Community School District 1 on the Lower East Side. It was the first time there was a Puerto Rican superintendent in that district, Luis Fuentes. There was a Support Los Niños slate; it was very active in terms of getting Puerto Rican parents involved in local school board elections.

But the push [in the PRRWO] was mostly for doing work as close to the working class as possible so that meant working in factories. It meant organization members being pulled out of either student work or work in public schools with parents to go into the factories. Organizing in the unions, organizing in the shops was the thrust in the organization. When I look at it now, I have one analysis. When I think of it then, I felt it was the correct thing to do. If we're about to make proletarian revolution, it makes sense to be where the workers are, and that's in the factories, so it made a lot of sense to me. But I also found myself in conflict because being involved in education and working with parents, I knew that our people feel oppression everywhere, not just in the factories. It's our kids; it's the parents; it's our families; and so I had that conflict. I was being told [by the PRRWO], "you're such a petit bourgeois element; you don't want to leave education work, and the reason is because it's hard labor." I felt that's not the reason; there's work that has to be done here as well. This was one of the reasons why, in 1976, I was purged from the organization.

By this time, there was no storefront or anything like that. The visibility of the organization was through individuals. We were organized into sections. I was part of the community section that involved people who were working in the public schools, in daycare centers. We met at people's homes. Meetings would go on till two or three o'clock in the morning. First, we'd have a study section on politics, economy, on Marxism-Leninism; then the last thing on the agenda was a discussion about the work in that particular area, and many times we never got to that. Most of what was happening was the study and preparing for the development of a new political party and for proletarian revolution. Everything had to be geared in that direction. If you had a dissenting voice, it was internal; you couldn't verbalize, or you were in trouble. It was a very interesting period of repression on a number of levels.

It was 1976. At that point, PRRWO was uniting with other groups from around the country. Different groups that had started as the organization did, being community oriented, eventually evolved into groups that talked about revolution and organizing in a very abstract way. People have blamed the police for infiltrating and moving the organizing in that direction. I don't think it is all due to that. I think there were still some people who were coming to this from a good place and felt it was the right thing to do, and then I think some people were into some grandiose plans to make a mark.

Whenever I verbalized that you have to organize the grass roots, you have to work with parents; you have to think about what's happening in classrooms as well, I'd be criticized. I kept doing my work a certain way, and I kept getting criticized. I was singled out, and so was my compañero at that time because his ties to the student movement were very strong. We were targeted, and I would say that at that time we probably were the two in the New York area that had the closest ties with community and were criticized for having those ties. The leadership targeted us because we were not kowtowing to them.

I was at a meeting of the community section and saw leadership people coming in. They said they had to talk to me because they felt that I was conspiring against the organization. I felt they were honestly making a mistake about what I was doing. I was taken from that meeting and kept for three days, questioned, terrorized. Terrorized verbally, terrorized physically, terrorized by people in leadership who at one time I respected very much and being questioned and interrogated and being told to stay awake all night; or if I fell asleep, I would be hit so I would be awake to answer questions. It took about a day and a half for me to realize that I was being accused of fractionalizing and doing the work of the police. At this time, I was alone trying to figure out how long this would go on before I could leave, and go home. I was looking out the window to see if there were ways that I could escape. I was trying to be as honest as I possibly could about things I was asked. I was very afraid. I didn't know what was going to go on, and I didn't know where my compañero thought I was. I didn't know what was happening with him.

Meanwhile, he had also been kidnapped and taken someplace, beaten and also questioned. Finally, they had me for three days; they had him for two days, and they brought us together on the third day, beaten up, with a group of about ten to twelve people. Some people whom I didn't know were involved in this. They brought us together in the home of one of the members and beat us in front of each other.

The leadership convinced the others that we infiltrated and were working with the police to destroy the organization. In fact, when things were happening to us during that three-day period and even after that, people didn't know. People didn't find out for months later, so it was very well kept secret, very well kept. It's difficult to remember all their questions, but I remember a couple of things having to do with my relationship with Iris [Morales]. Basically it was brought up a couple of times, how interesting it was that we had a relationship in terms of our similar thinking and that we were still in connection. Some of the people who participated were people whom I had considered close friends, whom I supported economically. We had to give half of our paychecks to the organization. We did it with good intentions because we felt that it was our responsibility. These were people we knew, people whom I worked with in the community section, and people whom had been in leadership of the organization since the beginning whom I had tremendous respect for, and others whom I didn't know.

I started realizing there's some irrationality going on, and things were happening that I didn't completely understand. There was a point where my feeling was, if you want to hear me say that I don't want to work with the working class, even though that's not in my heart, that's what I was going to say. I felt whatever I said, didn't matter. But it didn't start like that. It started with what I thought was going to be the honest exchange, which turned into something very irrational, very sick, and very traumatic.

At the point when they brought my compañero and myself together, we realized the quicker we said what we had to say, the quicker we could get out. They left us alone after they beat us up. I said, "they're going to kill us," and he said they possibly could. We knew they were coming back. We knew we had little time. This was all instinct. It was get up now, or we don't get out. They left us with a younger person, and we were able to physically get out of there fast. Where the strength came from, I don't know, after not having slept or eaten for three days, but we were determined to get out of there. So we had to find our way out. I had to break a bottle over the man's head who was watching us; tear the phone out of the wall; grab our stuff, and get out of there. It was March in the middle of the night.

Our first instinct was to go to family. For the next weeks, we lived in terror, in fear. It's amazing because we felt that these people were omnipotent, that they could find us, that they could tap our phones. Although they didn't have that power, we were so vulnerable and scared, and weak, because it was their intention to do that, and we feared for our lives. So in this period, we didn't speak with anyone. We needed to put our strength together and reflect on what had just taken place, and try to figure out what to do with our lives because we were now totally disconnected from a world that we had been very intensely a part of for a number of years.

The disruption was very traumatic, and it was not easy to put ourselves together, but we had the support of family that helped us. At some point, we were saying, we don't want to know about community organizing work. But I kept thinking, if I really believed in this before the kidnapping, then I should still believe regardless of what happened. If I believed in social change, and that we have to work and be organized to make real change, then I'm going to believe it, even now. But I was also worried about how we would protect ourselves, where would we live, how would we move around in the world, in the city, never mind the world. But it took us weeks. We talked about it every day.

Then we started making connections with people who we felt we could trust. We thought about the people who had gone through this. We didn't know how this would be brought out in terms of the movement and how people would know what happened, but we started making connections with some of the people who had left the organization, either voluntarily or been traumatized to leave. So those connections started happening, and we had to put our lives back together. We received a telegram through one of the family members. Mixed feelings, you know; on the one hand it was, wow, there are people reaching out to us. We saw the list of people who were reaching out to us; we said, "my God that's some mighty mixed group of people." Mixed in the sense of who united and were coming together for this; it was real important, that reaching out.

Well, after putting the pieces together, it meant getting our personal lives together in terms of a safe environment, to live, in terms of work. I continued my work in education outside of New York City. I went to work on Long Island with parents, with teachers, doing work in bilingual education. My work on Long Island was very good work. Though I was still afraid for my life, looking around me at all times, wondering if anyone was going to grab me and kidnap me again.

We also knew that where there is injustice, you have to organize against that injustice. How we would do that, we didn't know. We eventually came back and started doing more political work. Our coming back was working with the committee to free the Nationalist political prisoners and some people who had already been organizing for a number of years. Going back to that kind of work meant putting out a newsletter, speaking about the case of the Nationalists. Little by little, making ties with different people, and getting our strength back and our ability to be able to do the things that we believed.

When I first came into the movement in 1970–1971, I came in because of the Nationalist prisoners. My learning about being Puertorriqueña, my learning about these revolutionaries from Puerto Rico who committed these acts, to me were acts of a fight against injustice and had to do with the self-determination of Puerto Rico. It was important work for me to again say, I want to get involved, and I did.

I remember the first time that it was shared with me that there was going to be this action—taking over the Statue of Liberty. I said, "Wait a minute, we just got kidnapped, tortured; we're just putting our lives back together. How are we going to take over the Statue of Liberty?" I was not going to do what I did before, which was to follow blindly. They've got to convince me. I have to understand it. I have to embrace it, not be forced into it. It was really about having a dialogue about why this was important for us to do, and I got involved.

I drove the car. It was timed just right. I had to get to the ferry to take that ferry to the statue at a certain time, and everything had to be timed just right. It was putting together the best skills of the people involved, the skills to organize, the skills to educate because it was an educational campaign as well. You organize; you educate; you involve people; there's dialogue; there's process; and it's not just cut-and-dried. It was bringing together a good group of people that knew exactly what to do, and it was an act that went down in history and that I'm very proud to have been part of it. Taking the Statue of Liberty brought international attention to the imprisonment of the Nationalist political prisoners, important because we had to get them out of jail. The time was right. It brought together people and organizations from our own community that many times did not work together, because it was an issue that we could find unity around. Seeing the Statue of Liberty with the Puerto Rican flag on her head on every major newspaper in this country and internationally was significant in terms of El Puertorriqueño and our struggle.

The role that I played contributed to that action because as our community started coming down to South Ferry, people had started hearing it on the radio or reading about it in the paper. Myself and another compañero were the ones responsible for organizing what had to be done on this side, while the other compañeros were at the statue. Our work involved the press; it involved the education and bringing together of the people who came down. At one point, I was almost flown out on a helicopter to bring food to our prisoners at the Statue of Liberty. It was something that brought people together, and we were able to really execute this act. The Nationalist prisoners were not just an issue belonging to the Left or an issue belonging to the Puerto Rican movement, it was an issue belonging to the Puerto Rican people.

Bueno, the release, the final release was an incredible day. We were over at the church on Fifty-Ninth and Tenth Avenue, and there they were, these people that we had read about. There they were in person: Lolita, Rafael, Irving, Oscar, and Andrés. The release of the Nationalists was an amazing celebration in our community. This was something that touched the heart of all Puerto Ricans, all Puerto Ricans who were there to greet them. Lolita was given the Puerto Rican flag that hung on the Statue of Liberty, so that was also quite an experience to see her get this flag, and then take it to Puerto Rico and put it at don Pedro Albizu Campos's grave. It was incredible. I guess looking at the Puerto Rican prisoners that we have today, it is important to take lessons from the work that was done to free the Nationalists, and always know that it can be done.

During the late 1970s, beginning of the 80s, was when a lot of us got involved around issues of media racism, and the depiction of Puerto Ricans especially since the movie with the great white liberal, Paul Newman, was coming out, *Fort Apache, the Bronx*. An incredibly effective campaign because, even though the movie did come out, the issues about racism historically, not just with the Puerto Rican community, with the Chicano community, with the Asian community; those issues were finally brought to the forefront in a very organized way. It was a campaign on all fronts from the press, to organizing, to disrupting the filming of the movie. For a lot of us in New York, the issues around the political prisoners and the media racism got us involved again. We saw the need to build an organization of Puertorriqueños. It couldn't just be getting involved in an issue. It had to be something more than that. It also meant all of us accepting the fact that we were ready to do this, and we were. Not just in New York, but also in Philadelphia. Some of our folks from Chicago, from New Jersey, began to talk about the need to bring together our people to organize something that would struggle for the democratic rights of our people. It took two years of discussions and dialogue, people meeting in different Puerto Rican communities and parts of the country to form the National Congress of Puerto Rican Rights, an important organization that had its founding convention in New York City in 1981. The mission of the Congress was to fight for the basic democratic rights of the Puerto Rican people in this country. We had chapters in Philadelphia, New York, and New Jersey. We were looking at the base, because one of the mistakes we made in the past was just mechanically applying things to different situations, and it just doesn't work that way.

The National Congress had different areas of work and actual involvement in the electoral arena. The organization didn't run candidates but did support people's efforts to run. That was something very different. My involvement in education naturally took me to work around school board elections, which was work that I'd done for a number of years, but it gave me a different approach, a different outlook about school board elections and learning to negotiate the system. The National Congress was different from the traditional Puerto Rican leadership. We wanted to find our way to do this, learning from their good things, avoiding the bad things from that traditional leadership. It's not the usual power broker–type mentality. How you negotiate the system for it to work, to change it, to impact on it, because it's got to work for us. It's a very different approach.

Bilingual education was a constant issue, the cornerstone of our civil rights issues. It brought together Puertorriqueños with other Latinos, with undocumented workers, with new immigrants, not just Latinos but also with the Asian and the Haitian communities. It was coalition building. An issue that was very significant and still is because we've got the 1994 version of English Only[1] right before us now. In the National Congress, my work was to organize the national task force for bilingual education, which brought me together with people from Pennsylvania, New Jersey—Puerto Ricans from different parts of the East Coast. That work meant testifying in Washington, DC, which was also something I never thought I would be doing, actually testifying at federal hearings about bilingual education. The work was national in scope; it meant also organizing parents, which was local in scope; it meant bringing those things together.

When I was elected to leadership in the National Congress for Puerto Rican Rights, it indicated something that took a long time for me to recognize in myself, which was the ability to be the leader of something. I never look at leaders as individuals. One good things about doing the work in the organization during the seventies is this collective thinking. Collective spirit is something very positive and very important. There is not one leader; there is a collective of leadership. I did get elected to leadership twice. I became the president in 1983, and I served two terms until 1987. The first elected woman president in the organization. Not an easy period. Difficult, a major responsibility I took on with all heart and soul behind it.

I've been a community activist for the last twenty-five years, and most of my work has been education. I believed then, as I believe now, that there has to be a fundamental change in the way that children are educated in this country, in particular the Puertorriqueño and Latino children. One real positive experience that the [National] Congress [of Puerto Rican Rights] gave me was to organize different sectors and build coalitions. Many education activists here in New York felt that we had to build a coalition effort among Puertorriqueños and Latinos because what we kept doing was responding to the crisis as opposed to having a plan on how to deal with the crisis of education. So in 1984 many of us got together. There was ASPIRA, the Centro de Estudios Puertorriqueños, the Puerto Rican Educators Association, the Association of Progressive Dominicans, a parents' group from District 3, the National Congress of Puerto Rican Rights—and we talked about what we were going to do and how. We organized the Puerto Rican Latino Education Roundtable, a coalition of community organizations of educators, of parents, to respond proactively to the crisis. In that response, it meant knowing how to do things on a policy level and continuing with the grassroots ties. This coalition was very important because it wasn't just the usual good government–type group that talks about advocacy and policy but has no ties with their community. We knew we had to do the work in all different levels, but all those levels had to be done and brought together.

We've been together for over ten years. We have organizational and individual memberships, people who have a mission in education, people who feel there has to be educational transformation. We've been involved still with our bilingual education issue. Also taking it out of that framework and looking at the education of Latino kids because bilingual education is not just where our kids are. In New York City, only one in every four Latino kids is in a bilingual program, but embracing the issue of bilingualism and biliteracy, the right to speak and learn in your language. We've been involved with fighting the English Only movement and participating in school board elections every few years, coalition building with groups involved in education in New York City, dealing with decentralization and legislation to change the way the New York school system is governed.

Right now [1996], my involvement, especially for the last two years, has been with a new initiative on school reform in New York City to build small schools within this large institution of one million kids. We've got about 350,000 Latino kids in this system, and they're in the worst schools, the most overcrowded and segregated situations. We still have the highest dropout rate of any other group. Even though we're organizing, if we weren't there, it would be worse. My work right now has been very directed toward helping to build a school, the Leadership Secondary School, which looks at our kids as leaders and tries to develop that potential. Our work is in terms of impacting the direction of school reform, especially in New York City. With Latinos creating a vision, articulating and implementing it. Our school, along with El Puente Academy for Peace and Justice, are the only two schools in this whole initiative to build new schools that are guided by a Latino vision.

I was nationalist just like everyone else. When the YLP went to Puerto Rico, it was developing pride and nationalism, so I found it a good thing. With the National Congress of Puerto Rican Rights, our focus is on the democratic rights of Puertorriqueños, but our platform also supports the self-determination of Puerto Rico, but it does not mean going there. The community there has the right to its self-determination, that means the people in Puerto Rico determine.

That sixties period was so important, and I'm so glad I was a part of it. A lot of people also became role models for me, men and women from the YLP, especially those who are here today still doing their work—tremendous role models and tremendous inspiration. But these days, my role models are the young people. Usually the role model is the older person, *la que sabe*, the experienced one. This next generation of our young people, you know, we've lost one generation, but there's another generation that I'm not about to lose and that we can't lose. The kind of organizing, thinking, participation, and work that they're doing is incredible. It just keeps me going, and it helps me realize that all this was worth it because of what I see happening today.

Sexism in the media is one of the most capitalist ways of controlling the emancipation of women. An emancipated woman is a dangerous woman, one who threatens an entire system with all its distortions that manage to keep the possibility of real freedom in check.

Ana Tijoux
"La Cultura de la Basura"
www.walkerart.org/magazine/2014

WOMEN IN THE YOUNG LORDS

Young Lords Party March (1970)

Photographs courtesy of Michael Abramson

Top: Young Lords at United Nations demonstration (October 1970)
Bottom: Doleza Miah at rally in support of prisoners' rights (1970)

Mirta González speaking from a TB-testing truck (1970)

Jenny Figueroa selling *Palante* (1970)

Denise Oliver speaking at Randall's Island (1970)

Young Lords line up to march (1970)

Iris Morales marching at Julio Roldán's funeral procession in East Harlem with pallbearers from I Wor Kuen, the Inmates Liberation Front, the Puerto Rican Student Union, and the Black Panther Party (1970)

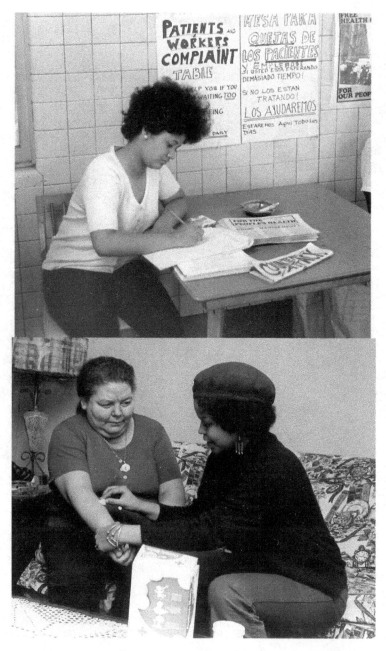

Top: Lincoln Hospital, Patient-Worker Complaint Table (1970)
Bottom: Letty Lozano conducting TB testing (December 1970)

Iris Morales, Denise Oliver, Nydia Mercado, and Lulu Carreras after a meeting of the Women's Caucus in East Harlem (1970)

Connie Morales marching to the United Nations (1970)

PART 3.
FROM THE FRONTLINES

(1969–1973)

(Original documents and newspaper articles)

POWER TO THE PEOPLE!

It is our duty to fight for our freedom. It is our duty to win. We must love each other and support each other. We have nothing to lose but our chains.

Assata Shakur
Assata: An Autobiography

First Years In The United States:
History of the Puerto Rican National Minority

PUERTO RICAN REVOLUTIONARY WORKERS ORGANIZATION

We came over on ships like the *Marine Tiger* and first settled in the Navy Yard section of Brooklyn, on the Lower East Side, and in Harlem. As more and more of us came over, our communities began to stretch from the Brooklyn Navy Yard into Williamsburg, from Harlem into East Harlem and across the Harlem River into the South Bronx. We began to move into neighborhoods abandoned by other ethnic groups as they continued to run away from the increasing numbers of Blacks and Puerto Ricans in the city in their never-ending search for "a better neighborhood." Today, the buildings Puerto Rican live in are the oldest in the city. . . .

Many of our people came to the US as migrant farm workers. They would work in the US from July until the end of October or November and go back to Puerto Rico for the beginning of the sugar cane season in January. The migrant farm camps were like concentration camps, and our people were forced to live under inhuman conditions, squeezed into tiny, unheated, and unventilated shacks, without sanitary facilities. . . . The key problem we faced in New York was finding jobs. Our employment problems were intensified because many of us had very little education. For example, in 1960, more than half the Puerto Ricans in NYC 25 years of age and older, had less than an eighth grade education. Some 87% of us had not graduated from high school.

But the main factor in determining what kind of jobs we could get was, what did the US need? In the 1940s when Puerto Ricans started migrating in large numbers, the labor needs in the US were for manual labor, semi-skilled and unskilled workers. There were many routine and repetitive jobs in light industry that had to be filled, and many services that had to be performed. When we found jobs, the majority of them were in small factories, in the hotel and restaurant trades, and in the Garment District. . . .

These jobs were very different from the way we had made our living in Puerto Rico. Not only had we come to a new country, a new territory; but we had a different way of working, lived under different conditions—life in an overcrowded New York apartment in the winter is very different from the life in one's own small house where, whatever the shortcomings, we had all of the outdoors to live in all day, every day.

Added to this, besides the low wages, long hours, and bad conditions on our jobs, we also were faced with constant discrimination and hostility because we are a people of color and speak Spanish.

In the 1950s, American advances in technology led to many of our jobs being taken over by machines. . . . To us, it meant displacement from our jobs and more unemployment.

We were not alone with these problems, however. Many Black people had come from the South just like we came from Puerto Rico, looking for a better life too. Like us, they thought they would be able to find a better life for their families in the more industrial cities. Together we shared many of the same run-down neighborhoods and worked side by side in many industries. We also shared the burden of being the "last hired and the first fired." Every day, there were many little things to remind us that we were "niggers" and "spics" whether it was being fired for fighting with a racist foreman that started it by calling us a bad name, or coming home to hear that our kids' teacher had called them stupid, because they couldn't talk good English. . . .

It was during this time that the mass media began to portray all Puerto Ricans as ignorant troublemakers. Every time someone who looked Latin was involved in something, the *Daily News* would say a "Puerto Rican murderer" or a "group of Puerto Rican hoodlums." Films, too, degraded us. Movies like *Blackboard Jungle* were as much an insult to the Puerto Rican people in the 1950s as *Badge 373* in 1973.
. . .

The early years in the US were not easy, but we are a strong people. We worked hard, we sacrificed, we adjusted to life in the US; we wanted our children to have what we couldn't have.

Palante, vol. 5, no. 8, October 1973

YLO Feeds

CONNIE MORALES

In this capitalist society, we are denied certain basic necessities such as food, clothing, and decent shelter. We go to school without eating a hot breakfast and can't concentrate on our schoolwork as a result. How can we concentrate on learning when our stomachs are growling? We are then told by teachers that we are stupid and can't learn, giving us a defeatist attitude for the rest of our lives.

The YOUNG LORDS ORGANIZATION realizes this, so we have instituted breakfast programs in our communities. One such program is at Emmaus House at 241 East 116th Street. This breakfast program feeds 30 young Brothers and Sisters before they go to school. At this Program, they receive nourishing meals, such as fruit, juice, bacon, and hot chocolate. We do this in order to educate our People as to how a socialist society cares for the basic necessities of a People. The 13th Point of our Thirteen-Point Program states, "We want a socialist society," meaning complete liberation, free food, clothing, shelter, education, health care, transportation, utilities, and employment for all.

If the YLO can feed hungry children, then people should . . . question why, under this present system, where they have the money to put a man on the moon, people should go hungry. We realize that the reason for this is that the man is out there for himself, and that he couldn't care [less] if young Puerto Rican and Black Brothers and Sisters go hungry, as long as the man is making his money.

This pig talks of our violence while we are brutalized by his violence, by the violence of hungry children, illiterate adults, and diseased old people. This is why the 12th Point of our Program states, "Armed self-defense and armed struggle are the only means to liberation."

The YOUNG LORDS ORGANIZATION is educating our people to the fact that when a government oppresses the People, we have the right, and it is our duty, to abolish it and create a new one.

Palante, vol. 2, no. 2, May 8, 1970

Message from a Revolutionary Compañera

BLANCA CANALES

I address myself to the members of the Young Lords Party and to all Puerto Rican, Latin American, and North American patriotic organizations of New York, in short to all men and women in the new struggle for people's liberation who have made the independence of Puerto Rico their cause, and who will unite in front of the United Nations building on October 30th to demand the immediate withdrawal of the *yanqui* invading forces from our land and the recognition of Puerto Rico as a sovereign and independent nation. I send you my most cordial message of fraternity and gratitude on behalf of the free-dom loving people of Puerto Rico who on that same day will gather solemnly in a National Assembly in the town of Jayuya to proclaim and reaffirm the validity of the cry for liberty that we uttered in those mountains exactly 20 years ago.

That October 30th a general uprising took place in the whole is-land. There were shootout battles in the barrio Macana of Peñuelas, in Utuado, Ponce, Arecibo, and in front of La Fortaleza, the official resi-dence of the colonial governor in San Juan. In Jayuya, the revolution-aries took over the town, battling the police in their own headquarters, setting fire to the city hall and US federal offices—the post office and the army recruiting office (which at that time was recruiting Puerto Ricans to serve as cannon fodder in Korea). The municipality of Jayuya was under the power of the revolutionaries for three days un-der the command of Elio Torresola. Elio is the brother of our martyr, Griselio Torresola, who fell November 1st in front of Blair House in Washington when as a participant in this revolution he went with Os-car Collazo to shoot the president of the US.

In Jayuya, US flags were lowered from all public buildings for three days and the Puerto Rican flag was raised in a building in the center of the town from where we issued our freedom proclamation with the cry of VIVA PUERTO RICO LIBRE! The colony's lackey government under the command of the traitor Muñoz Marin mobi-lized the pigs, the badly named National Guard, and launched it against Jayuya, occupying the town after having bombed it from its planes. Our people overcome, the lackeys at the service of *yanqui* imperialism handed over the town's control to the insular, federal, and municipal functionaries in a public ceremony. This ceremony, photographed by newspapermen, is the tacit reminder that our people proclaimed their independence for three days and repudiated the US intervention. This struggle of 1950 was nurtured with the blood of our people. Once more the sacrifice of our martyrs consecrated our sovereignty; for in that glorious step, we reaffirmed our desire to be free, continuing the chronology of our independent republic begun in Lares.

The intervention of the United States in Puerto Rico has been disguised with different names—the last one, the so-called "free associated state." This intervention has been fought in whatever form this island has been able to. This small island has known how to rise up, especially in the last 40 years under the inspiration of the hero and teacher don Pedro Albizu Campos. Puerto Rico has kept up a war for its liberation from the first encounter in 1932 in which Rafael Manuel Suárez Díaz offered his life on the stairs of the capitol building to the recent death of another student, Antonia Martínez, who less than a year ago fell, beaten down by the imperialist's bullets in the University in Río Piedras, and the burning of 2,000 draft cards in Lares on September 23. The struggle has had many martyrs and hundreds of Puerto Ricans have suffered imprisonment, which demonstrates our unbeatable determination to reestablish the independence of Puerto Rico, which was proclaimed in Lares and Jayuya.

Today Puerto Rico is suffering the most monstrous intervention as our territory is surrounded with land bases and submarine bases with powerful atomic weapons that, because of the smallness of the island, can cause the destruction of all Puerto Ricans and the total disappearance of the island from the world map. And as if this horrible menace were not enough, genocide is being perpetrated in the most shameless way with a massive house-to-house campaign to force the women to use a US form of birth control. The plan is to prevent the birth of more Puerto Ricans. At the same time, they stop the advancement of our youth when they recruit them to take them to their deaths in the fields of Vietnam. On the other hand, they have no qualms in firing over the heads of the Puerto Ricans who live on the island of Culebra, and the US marines have the audacity to ask that the people of Culebra abandon their island because the almighty marine of the biggest empire in the world has decided to use this island as a target for their military practices.

Friends of the demonstration in front of the United Nations, I invite you to prepare a document including these and other violations to the human and political rights of Puerto Rico and to present them to the delegates of the United Nations and to the chiefs of all countries of the world. I ask you to continue picketing periodically at the United Nations to demand the liberty of our prisoners of war in the jails of the United States, our patriots—Oscar Collazo, Lolita Lebrón, Rafael Cancel, Andrés Figueroa, Irving Flores, and Carlos Feliciano.

To all of you gathered on that day, we say to you, forward, always forward, every day with more faith in the ultimate victory. If on that day or in the following days, the United Nations plays deaf to your demand, you Puerto Ricans who are there, come back to our Puerto Rican countryside, and let us redouble the fight without mercy and without rest from all the angles and by whatever means necessary until we obtain the liberty of Puerto Rico. From Bayamón, Puerto Rico, says hello one who was imprisoned for 17 years only for the crime of loving her country.

Palante, vol. 2, no. 14, October 1970

Whenever any people are victims of abuse, it's only natural that they fight against it. The Third World Woman, as the most oppressed person in the world today, is no exception.

The Women's Union (1971)
People's Organization of Young Lords Party

THE REVOLUTION
WITHIN THE REVOLUTION

As women everywhere, we are still suffering injustice, contempt, bad treatment, discrimination, humiliation, and the violation of our rights.

This unjust situation that we women live . . . has to change.

Comandanta Hortensia
Zapatista Army of National Liberation
In Motion Magazine, March 13, 2006

Young Lords Party Position Paper on Women

CENTRAL COMMITTEE

Puerto Rican, Black, and other Third World (colonized) women are becoming more aware of their oppression in the past and today. They are suffering three different types of oppression under capitalism. First, they are oppressed as Puerto Ricans or Blacks. Second, they are oppressed as women. Third, they are oppressed by their own men. The Third World woman becomes the most oppressed person in the world today.

Economically, Third World women have always been used as a cheap source of labor and as sexual objects. Puerto Rican and Black women are used to fill working class positions in factories, mass assembly lines, hospitals, and all other institutions. Puerto Rican and Black women are paid lower wages than whites, and kept in the lowest positions within society. At the same time, giving Puerto Rican and Black women jobs means that the Puerto Rican and Black man is kept from gaining economic independence, and the family unit is broken down. Capitalism defines manhood according to money and status; the Puerto Rican and Black man's manhood is taken away by making the Puerto Rican and Black woman the breadwinner. This situation keeps the Third World man divided from his woman. The Puerto Rican and Black man either leaves the household, or he stays and becomes economically dependent on the woman, undergoing psychological damage. He takes out all of his frustrations on his woman, beating her, repressing, and limiting her freedom. Because this society produces these conditions, our major enemy is capitalism rather than our oppressed men.

Third World Women have an integral role to play in the liberation of all oppressed people as well as in the struggle for the liberation of women. Puerto Rican and Black women make up over half of the revolutionary army, and in the struggle for national liberation they must press for the equality of women. The woman's struggle is the revolution within the revolution. Puerto Rican women will be neither behind nor in front of their brothers but always alongside them in mutual respect and love.

HISTORICAL

In the past women were oppressed by several institutions, one of which was marriage. When a woman married a man she became his property and lost her last name. A man could have several wives in order to show other men what wealth he had and enhance his position in society. In Eastern societies men always had several wives and a number of women who were almost prostitutes, called concubines, purely sexual objects. Women had no right to own anything, not even their children; they were owned by her husband. This was true in places all over the world. In many societies, women had no right to be divorced, and in India it was the custom of most of the people that when the husband died, all his wives became the property of his brother.

In Latin America and Puerto Rico, the man had a wife and another woman called *la corteja*. This condition still exists today. The wife was there to be a homemaker, to have children and to maintain the family name and honor. She had to be sure to be a virgin and remain pure for the rest of her life, meaning she could never experience sexual pleasure. The wife had to have children in order to enhance the man's concept of virility and his position within the Puerto Rican society. *La corteja* became his sexual instrument. The man could have set her up in another household, paid her rent, bought her food, and paid her bills. He could have children with this woman, but they are looked upon as by-products of a sexual relationship. Both women had to be loyal to the man. Both sets of children grew up very confused and insecure and developed negative attitudes about the role.

Women have always been expected to be wives and mothers only. The community respects them for being good cooks, good housewives, and good mothers but never for being intelligent, strong, educated, or militant. In the past, women were not educated, only the sons got an education, and mothers were respected for the number of sons they had, not daughters. Daughters were worthless, and the only thing they could do was marry early to get away from home. At home, the role of the daughter was to be a nursemaid for the other children and kitchen help for her mother.

The daughter was guarded like a hawk by her father, brothers, and uncles to keep her a virgin. In Latin America, the people used *dueñas* or old lady watchdogs to guard the purity of the daughters. The husband must be sure that his new wife never has been touched by another man because that would ruin the "merchandise." When he marries her, her purpose is to have sons and keep his home but not to be a sexual partner.

Sex was a subject that was never discussed, and women were brainwashed into believing that the sex act was dirty and immoral, and its only function was for the making of children. In Africa, many tribes performed an operation on young girls to remove the clitoris so they would not get any pleasure out of sex and would become better workers.

THE DOUBLE STANDARD, MACHISMO, AND SEXUAL FASCISM

Capitalism sets up standards applied differently to Puerto Rican and Black men from the way they are applied to Puerto Rican and Black women. These standards are also applied differently to Third World people than they are applied to whites. These standards must be understood since they are created to divide oppressed people in order to maintain an economic system that is racist and oppressive.

Puerto Rican and Black men are looked upon as rough, athletic, and sexual, but not as intellectuals. Puerto Rican women are not expected to know anything except about the home, kitchen, and bedroom. All that they are expected to do is look pretty and add a little humor. The Puerto Rican man sees himself as superior to his woman, and his superiority, he feels, gives him license to do many things— curse, drink, use drugs, beat women, and run around with many women. As a matter of fact these things are considered natural for a man to do and he must do them to be considered a man. A woman who curses, drinks, and runs around with a lot of men is considered dirty scum, crazy, and a whore.

Today Puerto Rican men are involved in a political movement. Yet the majority of their women are home taking care of the children. The Puerto Rican sister that involves herself is considered aggressive, castrating, hard, and unwomanly. She is viewed by the brothers as sexually accessible because what else is she doing outside of the home. The Puerto Rican man tries to limit the woman's role because he feels the double standard is threatened; he feels insecure without it as a crutch.

Machismo has always been a very basic part of Latin American and Puerto Rican culture. Machismo is male chauvinism and more. Machismo means "mucho macho" or a man who puts himself selfishly at the head of everything without considering the woman. He can do whatever he wants because his woman is an object with certain already defined roles: wife, mother, and good woman.

Machismo means physical abuse, punishment, and torture. A Puerto Rican man will beat his woman to keep her in place and show her who's boss. Most Puerto Rican men do not beat women publicly because in the eyes of other men that is a weak thing to do. So they usually wait until they're home. All the anger and violence of centuries of oppression that should be directed against the oppressor is directed at the woman. The aggression is also directed at daughters. The daughters hear their fathers saying, "the only way a woman is going to do anything or listen is by hitting her." The father applies this to the daughter, beating her so that she can learn *respeto*. The daughters grow up with messed-up attitudes about their role as women and about manhood. They grow to expect that men will always beat them.

Sexual fascists are very sick people. Their illness is caused in part by this system, which mouths puritanical attitudes and laws and yet exploits the human body for profit.

Sexual Fascism is tied closely to the double standard and machismo. It means that a man or woman thinks of the opposite sex solely as sexual objects to be used for gratification and then discarded. Sexual fascists do not consider people's feelings; all they see everywhere is a pussy or a dick. They will use any rap, especially political, to get sex.

PROSTITUTION

Under capitalism, Third World women are forced to compromise themselves because of their economic situation. The facts that her man cannot get a job and that the family is dependent on her for support means she hustles money by any means necessary. Black and Puerto Rican sisters are put into a situation where jobs are scarce or nonexistent and are forced to compromise body, mind, and soul; they are then called whores or prostitutes. Puerto Rican and Black sisters are made to prostitute themselves in many other ways. The majority of these sisters on the street are also hard-core drug addicts, taking drugs as an escape from oppression. These sisters are subjected to sexual abuse from dirty old men who are mainly white racists who view them as the ultimate sexual objects. Also he has the attitude that he cannot really prove his manhood until he has slept with a Black or Puerto Rican woman. The sisters also suffer abuse from the pimps, really small-time capitalists, who see the woman as private property that must produce the largest possible profit.

Because this society controls and determines the economic situation of Puerto Rican and Black women, sisters are forced to take jobs at the lowest wages, and at the same time take insults and other indignities in order to keep the job. In factories, our men are worked like animals and cannot complain because they will lose their jobs—their labor is considered abundant and cheap. In hospitals, our women comprise the majority of the nurses' aides, kitchen workers, and clerks. These jobs are unskilled; the pay is low, and there is no chance for advancement. In offices, our positions are usually as clerks, typists, and no-promotion jobs. In all of these jobs, our sisters are subjected to racial slurs, jokes, and other indignities such as being leered at, manhandled, propositioned, and assaulted. Our sisters are expected to prostitute themselves and take abuse of any kind or lose these subsistence jobs.

Everywhere our sisters are turned into prostitutes. The most obvious example is the sisters hustling their bodies on the streets, but the other forms of prostitution are also types of further exploitation of the Third World woman. The only way to eliminate prostitution is to eliminate this society, which creates the need. Then we can establish a socialist society that meets the economic needs of all the people.

BIRTH CONTROL, ABORTION, STERILIZATION-GENOCIDE

We have no control over our bodies, because capitalism finds it necessary to control the woman's body to control population size. The choice of motherhood is being taken out of the mother's hands. She is sterilized to prevent her from having children, or she has to have a child because she cannot get an abortion.

Third World sisters are caught up in a complex situation. On one hand, we feel that genocide is being committed against our people.

We know that Puerto Ricans will not be around very long if Puerto Rican women are sterilized at the rate they are being sterilized now. . . . Part of this genocide is also the use of birth control pills, which were tested for 15 years on Puerto Rican sisters (guinea pigs) before being sold in the US market. Even now many doctors feel that these pills cause cancer and death from blood'clotting.

Abortions in hospitals that are butcher shops are little better than the illegal abortions our women used to get. The first abortion death in NYC under the new abortion law was Carmen Rodríguez, a Puerto Rican sister who died in Lincoln Hospital. Her abortion was legal, but the conditions in the hospital were deadly. On the other hand, we believe that abortions should be legal if they are community controlled, if they are safe, if our people are educated about the risks, and if doctors do not sterilize our sisters while performing abortions. We realize that under capitalism our sisters and brothers cannot support large families and the more children we have, the harder it is to support them. We say, change the system so that women can freely be allowed to have as many children as they want without suffering any consequences.

DAY CARE CENTERS

One of the main reasons why many sisters are tied to the home and cannot work or become revolutionaries is the shortage of day care centers for children. The centers that already exist are overcrowded, expensive, and are only super-baby-sitting centers. Day care centers should be free, should be open 24 hours a day, and should be centers where children are taught their revolutionary history and culture. Many sisters leave their children with a neighbor, or the oldest child is left to take care of the younger ones. Sometimes they are left alone, and all of us have read the tragic results in the newspapers of what happens to children left alone—they are burned to death in fires or they swallow poison, or fall out of windows to their death.

REVOLUTIONARY WOMEN

Throughout history, women have participated and been involved in liberation struggles. But the writers of history have never given full acknowledgment to the role of revolutionary women.

MARIANA BRACETTI was a Puerto Rican woman who together with her husband fought in the struggle for independence in Lares. She was called "El Brazo de Oro" because of her unlimited energy. For her role in the struggle, she was imprisoned. She sewed the first flag of El Grito de Lares.

Another nationalist woman was LOLA RODRÍGUEZ DE TIÓ, a poet who expressed the spirit of liberty and freedom in "La Borinqueña" in 1867. Besides being a nationalist, she was a fighter for women's rights. She refused to conform to the traditional customs concerning Puerto Rican women and at one point cut her hair very short.

BLANCA CANALES was a leader of the revolution in Jayuya in 1950.

LOLITA LEBRÓN, together with three other patriots, opened fire on the House of Representatives [in Washington, DC] in an armed attack in 1954 bringing the attention of the world to Puerto Rico's colonial status. She emptied a .45 automatic from the balcony of the Congress onto the colonial legislators. She then draped herself in the Puerto Rican flag and cried, "Viva Puerto Rico Libre." The result was five legislators [were] shot, and one critically wounded. She was imprisoned in a federal penitentiary and sentenced to 50 years and is still in prison for this heroic act.

Only recently, a 19-year-old coed, ANTONIA MARTÍNEZ, was killed in Puerto Rico in a demonstration against the presence of amerikkkan military recruiting centers. She was murdered when she yelled, "Viva Puerto Rico Libre!"

SOJOURNER TRUTH was born a slave in New York around 1800. She traveled in the north speaking out against slavery and for women's rights. She was one of the most famous Black orators in history.

KATHLEEN CLEAVER is a member of the Central Committee of the Black Panther Party. The Black Panthers are the vanguard of the Black liberation struggle in the United States. Another Panther sister, ERICKA HUGGINS, is imprisoned in Connecticut for supposedly being a member of a conspiracy. She was forced to have her child in prison, and was given no medical attention while she was pregnant. Her child was later taken away from her because of her political beliefs.

ANGELA DAVIS is a Black revolutionary sister who is being hunted by the f.b.i. and is on their 10 most wanted list because she has always defended her people's right to armed self-defense and because of her Marxist-Leninist philosophy.

In other parts of the world, women are fighting against imperialism and foreign invasion. Our sisters in Vietnam have struggled alongside their brothers for 26 years; first against the french colonizer, then against the japanese invaders, and now against the amerikkkan aggressors. Their military capability and efficiency has been demonstrated in so many instances that a women's brigade was formed in the National Liberation Front of the North Vietnamese Army.

LA THI THAM was born in a province constantly bombarded by US planes. After her fiancé was killed in action, she sought and got a job with a time bomb detecting team. She scanned the sky with field glasses and when the enemy dropped bombs along the countryside, she would locate those that had not yet exploded, and her teammates would open them and clear the road for traffic.

KAN LICH, another Vietnamese sister, fought under very harsh and dangerous conditions. She became a brilliant commander, decorated many times for her military ability. Her practice to "hit at close quarters, hit hard, withdraw quickly" proved to be valid.

The Central Committee of the Young Lords Party has issued this position paper to explain and to educate about the role of sisters in the past and how we see sisters in the struggle now and in the future. We criticize those brothers who are "machos" and who continue to treat our sisters as less than equals. We criticize sisters who remain passive, who do not join in the struggle against our oppression. We are fighting every day within our party against male chauvinism because we want to make a revolution of brothers and sisters, together, in love and respect for each other.

Palante, vol. 2, no. 12, September 25, 1970

Why a Women's Union?
June 1971

The Third World Woman is exploited in many ways.

First, we are used as a source of cheap labor. As workingwomen, we get the dirtiest jobs at the lowest wages. We get paid less than men and less than white women for the same amount of work. Because we work out of necessity, we have to put up with abuse and manhandling from the bosses to keep our jobs. We are worked like animals in factories, especially in the garment industry where we spend most of our lives making clothes for other people while we can barely clothe ourselves. Our labor is considered abundant and cheap. If we speak up against the mistreatment, the boss fires us and gets himself another "girl." In the hospitals, we make up the majority of the workers as nurses' aides, kitchen workers, and clerks. In offices, we work as clerks and typists. They squeeze out our sweat and blood and still we don't make enough for a decent life.

Second, we are the women that are forced to prostitute ourselves in order to survive within a system that excludes us because there are no jobs. We sell our bodies like merchandise in order to stay alive. We are forced into a situation where we depend on the streets for our survival. Most of us are the street hustlers selling our bodies and barely making a living at it. A lot of us are prostituting because we depend on drugs that the rich pushers bring into our communities, and the government doesn't do anything because it benefits them. Or we're on welfare taking government handouts that are not enough to support ourselves and our children.

Third, as women our bodies are used for experimentation. Puerto Rican women have been sterilized to stop us from having "too many babies." This kind of murder leaves ⅓ of Puerto Rican women sterile today. The birth control pill was tested on Puerto Rican women for 15 years before it was sold in the u.s. Puerto Rican women have the highest death rate from butcher performed abortions, like the case of Carmen Rodriguez who was killed at Lincoln Hospital in New York City when she went for an abortion.

This government also uses us as sexual objects. We have always been portrayed as very exotic and sexual, but with no brains. We are used as objects with which to sell different things, which we then are brainwashed into buying. Women buy the most products. We are taught from the time we are born to look at ourselves negatively. Puerto Ricans refer to a baby girl as a *chancleta*—a slipper. Consciously and non-consciously, we believe we are inferior. So then businessmen make products promising us that we will look better and be happier. Things like padded bras, girdles, false eyelashes, wigs, make-up, vaginal sprays, and crash diets are just a few examples. We are taught to look pretty, get married, have children, take care of them, do the housekeeping, and serve the husband as his slave. Depending on how well we do these things, determines how good a woman we are. A good woman does all the housework alone, even if she works [outside the home as well]. A good woman obeys her husband and never talks back to him. We're not supposed to have the brains to think and we're supposed to remain passive and conform to the role of being shy, timid. Women aren't supposed to be fighters.

Yet our history has always had women fighters. . . .

Why a Women's Union?

Because as women we can best organize other women for the liberation of Puerto Rico and for the self-determination of all oppressed people. Because as women, we best understand our own oppression and can organize ourselves for our liberation, always remembering that we will not be free until all our people are free.

We don't want to be cheap labor horses anymore. We don't want to be used as guinea pigs anymore. We want to be respected and treated as human beings by our men. We want all our people to be treated like human beings, and if not, we will fight till we are.

La Luchadora, vol. 1, no. 1, June 1971

Women's Union Twelve-Point Program

1) We believe in the liberation of all Puerto Ricans—liberation on the island and inside the U.S.

2) We believe in the self-determination of all third world people.

3) We want equality for women—down with machismo and sexism.

4) We want full employment and equal pay for all women with day care facilities provided by the work institution.

5) We want an end to the present welfare system; community-worker boards must be established in all welfare centers to [e]nsure the protection of women and their needs.

6) We want an end to the particular oppression of prostitutes and drug-addict sisters.

7) We want the withdrawal of the American military force from our communities and an end to their sexual abuse of women.

8) We want freedom for all political prisoners and prisoners of war and an end to the sexual brutalization and torture enforced on sisters by prison officials.

9) We want an end to the experimentation and genocide committed on sisters through sterilization, forced abortions, contraceptives, and unnecessary gynecological exams.

10) We want a true education of our story as women.

11) We believe in the right to defend ourselves against rapes, beatings, muggings, and general abuse.

12) We want a socialist society.

La Luchadora, vol. 1, no. 1, June 1971

Women's Union Rules of Discipline

1) All sisters shall know all information put forth by the Women's Union and adhere to the policy and ideology put forth by the Women's Union.

2) All members must attend P.E. (Political Education) classes regularly.

3) No sister in the Women's Union is to commit any crime against the people.

4) All contradictions (differences or disputes) that arise between sisters must be resolved at once.

5) Any sister found using or selling drugs will be expelled at once.

6) No sister may speak for the Women's Union unless authorized by the Women's Union.

7) All sisters will have criticism and self-criticism sessions at the weekly general meetings.

8) We are to keep a United Front before all forms of the enemy at all times.

9) Each Committee will submit a written report to the steering committee regularly.

10) All sisters must wage a constant struggle against machismo and female passivity.

La Luchadora, vol. 1, no. 1, June 1971

Sterilized Puerto Ricans

IRIS MORALES

Genocide is being committed against the Puerto Rican Nation through the mass sterilization of Puerto Rican women! In no other nation has sterilization been so prevalent as a means of genocide against an oppressed people. Why Puerto Ricans? First, the united states needs Puerto Rico as a military stronghold to maintain "political stability" and control in the rest of Latin America. Second, Puerto Rico is the fourth largest worldwide consumer of amerikkkan goods and yields massive profits to American capitalists. Also, Puerto Rico supplies fighting men and a cheap labor pool, both necessary to u.s. capitalism. One way to control a nation of vital importance is to limit its population size. The u.s. is doing exactly this through sterilization.

The practice of sterilization in Puerto Rico goes back to the 1930s when doctors pushed it as the only means of contraception. As a result, throughout the island, Puerto Rican women of childbearing age were sterilized. In 1947-1948, 7% of the women were sterilized; between 1953 and 1954, 4 out of every 25 Sisters were sterilized; and by 1965, the number increased to 1 out of every 3 women. This system was practiced on Sisters of all ages. But, since 1965, the trend has been to sterilize women in their early 20s when they have had fewer babies. This is especially true among lower class Sisters where future revolutionaries would come from. Committing sterilization on young Puerto Rican mothers with fewer children means that the u.s. is able to significantly reduce and limit the Puerto Rican population in a short period of time.

Genocide through sterilization is not only confined to Puerto Rico. It is also carried out within the Puerto Rican colony within the u.s. In El Barrio, sterilization is still practiced as a form of contraception among women, especially young Sisters. One out of four sterilized women in El Barrio has the operation done when she's between 20 and 30. But the system justifies the shit saying the Sisters go to Puerto Rico to get it done. Yet the evidence says that over half the Sisters get the operation done right here in New York City and are strongly encouraged by doctors to do so. Again, sterilization in the early reproductive years of a woman's life limits the Puerto Rican population substantially and permanently.

Sterilization is also a form of oppression against Puerto Rican women. We are oppressed by our own culture that limits us to the roles of homemaker, mother, and bearer of many children, which measures male virility. We have been made dependent on family and home for our very existence. We are used by u.s. corporations to test the safety of birth control pills before placing them on the market for sale. Our bodies are used by capitalists for experimentation to find new money making and genocidal gadgets. We are prevented from getting adequate birth control information and legal abortions. As a result, one of every four Sisters who try it die from self-induced abortions, giving Puerto Ricans the notoriety of having the highest death rate casualties from abortion than any other group. Sterilization is just another form of oppressing us.

Sterilization is irreversible and as such the u.s. can control the Puerto Rican population. Sterilization once done cannot be undone. We must stop sterilization because we must leave the option to ourselves to control the Puerto Rican population. Our men die in Vietnam, our babies are killed through lead poisoning and malnutrition, and our women are sterilized. The Puerto Rican Nation must continue. We must open our eyes to the oppressor's tricknology and refuse to be killed anymore. We must, in the tradition of Puerto Rican women like Lolita Lebrón, Blanca Canales, Carmen Pérez, and Antonia Martínez, join with our brothers and, together, as a nation of warriors, fight the genocide that is threatening to make us the last generation of Puerto Ricans.

Palante, vol. 2, no. 2, May 8, 1970; reprinted, August 28, 1970

Abortions

GLORIA COLÓN

A sister we know went to a clinic where they perform D 'n' C (abortion that's performed up to the 12th week of pregnancy by means of a suction machine that pulls the fetus from the womb).

"You're 18 weeks pregnant. We can't do it here. You'll have to go to a hospital for a saline induction," the doctor said. (A saline induction is an abortion performed after the 12th week of pregnancy where the woman is injected with a saline solution that induces labor as in normal birth.) She went to a hospital where a Puerto Rican attendant directed her to the abortion ward adding, "That's where they kill babies!" There another doctor estimated that she was 14 weeks pregnant and would have to return when she reached her fourth month salting out.

The sister returned and was sent to still another hospital where a long line of women waited with $400 in hand to pay in advance for their abortions. Since she had no money, she was sent to another hospital, a city hospital, where a doctor examined the sister and said that she was 6½ months pregnant and that it was "too late." The sister returned home to her other children and her unemployed husband to do more hustling to allow her future child to survive when she gives birth. In a certain sense, she went home relieved because, being a Puerto Rican woman, she knew that for her entering an abortion clinic in New York City hospital was either risking her life or the possibility of ever being pregnant again. And she was scared!

The case of this sister is no different from that of other Third World (Puerto Rican, Black, Chicana, Asian, Native American) women who face the situation of choosing between the risk of an abortion from a racist hospital administration, or of inventing new ways of hustling to clothe, feed, and shelter an addition to her family.

In Puerto Rico, the amerikkkan government has been pushing sterilization as the only means of contraception since the 1930s with the result that by 1965 ONE OUT OF EVERY THREE WOMEN WERE STERILIZED. The Puerto Rican woman was also used as a guinea pig for the contraceptive pills that were tested on the island for 15 years before being sold on the u.s market, while even now these

197

pills are believed to cause cancer and death from blood clotting. In a San Juan slum known as El Caño de Martin Peña, one out of every eleven children born dies before he or she is one day old. One out of every four women in Puerto Rico who attempts a self-induced abortion dies from it.

If a Puerto Rican woman decides to have an abortion, the Church that charges her around $3 for a baptismal certificate but that won't feed her children, tries to make her feel guilty. The man who gets drunk and beats her while she's pregnant and tells her that he doesn't want to be a *chancletero* makes her feel guilty. And the "welfare" department tells her that it's going to be rough if she doesn't have an abortion.

The government forces us to live like roaches, always in the garbage. When we can't produce in the sweatshops to make them more money because of high unemployment rates; when we can't buy their junk because they won't give us credit to legalize the rip-off; when we're no longer of any use to them and become a threat of possible revolutionaries, they exterminate us like roaches, always in the garbage. . . .

So we have the Third World woman holding on to her pregnant body, watching her already born children nibble on lead paint in place of food, watching the rats that gather to nibble on the toes of her children, worrying about having her insides ripped-up during an abortion.

Point Number 6 of the Young Lords Party Thirteen-Point Platform and Program states, "We want community control of our institutions and land." This means that we want institutions, like hospitals where sisters go to have abortions, to be under the control of our people to be sure that they really serve our needs. Until we struggle together to change our present situation, women will not be allowed to have the children they can support without suffering any consequences.

Palante, vol. 3, no. 5 March 19 – April 2, 1971

Free Our Sisters

MECCA ADAI

For the past few months, newspapers and magazines all over the country have been writing articles about the prisons. But if we look at these articles closely, we can see that in every article the author deals only with what's been happening inside the concentration camps for men. No attention has been paid to our sisters who are being held inside of the Women's House of Detention. This again is an example of how we are taught in this society to ignore our sisters and only pay attention to our brothers.

The Young Lords Party says, "We want equality for women. Down with machismo and male chauvinism." Because of this belief, we write articles in *Palante* to educate our people about our sisters and to explain that we must fight for the liberation of all our people—not just for half of our population.

On Sunday, December 20, a demonstration was held at 2:00 p.m. in front of the Women's House of Detention. The demonstration had three purposes:

1. To celebrate the 10th anniversary of the NLF (National Liberation Front of the people of South Vietnam),
2. To announce the beginning of a bail fund for the sisters inside the prison,
3. To demonstrate against the conditions in the prison.

Among the speakers were representatives of the Black Panther Party, Women's Bail Fund, Puerto Rican Student Union, and Young Lords Party.

The demonstration was held on the 20th, celebrating the anniversary of the NLF, because just as the Young Lords Party and the Black Panther Party serve and protect our people over here, the NLF serves and protects the people of Vietnam. Just as the Lords and Panthers are fighting for our people's liberation here, the NLF is fighting our common enemy—amerikkka—for the liberation of the people of Vietnam. As the 11th point of our Program says, we give solidarity to our sisters and brothers around the world who fight for justice and are against the rulers of this country.

The Women's Bail Fund was started a short time ago with the purpose of bailing out sisters who are not involved in the "movement" and who have bail less than $500. So far, they have been able to raise $6,000 and will continue to raise more. At [this] point, there are two ways that the Bail Fund can determine which sisters with bail less than $500 they can bail out. One is by writing to sisters inside the House of D. The second is by people on the 'outside" contacting members of the Bail Fund about friends and relatives. As of yet the Women's Bail Fund hasn't been able to bail out anyone because the courts are purposefully convicting sisters just as they are about to be released. It is also hard to find out any information because security inside is so tight. So once again we are going to have to get together and show that with the power of the people we can overcome anything. . . .

The third reason for the demonstration was to publicize the conditions inside the prison and the need for change:

1. Basic necessities, such as toothbrushes, soap, and deodorant are missing.
2. In order to get the basic necessities from the matrons, inmates sometimes are forced to sell their bodies.
3. The sisters are paid only from 3 cents to 10 cents an hour for work done inside (work in laundry, kitchen and library, etc.)
4. The allowance of only $1.50 is given only on request.
5. There is no instructive education taking place inside. The UFT (United Federation of Teachers) boycotted the prison and refused to let any of its members teach the sisters inside.
6. The most recent legal book in the prison library is dated 1950. All of the Legal Aid lawyers are too busy and overworked now to handle the cases of our sisters properly, and without proper legal defense sisters are forced to plead guilty. If they plead innocent and are later found guilty, it's up to the court to decide if their pre-trial detention (the time they spent waiting in jail for their case to come to court) counts toward their sentence. If, on the other hand, they're found innocent, they've already

served time. So we may be innocent, but if we're too poor to make bail, we have to spend time in jail anyway.

7. If women with money are picked up for shoplifting, they are dismissed as kleptomaniacs (people who don't need money but like to steal anyway for the fun of it) and are released. If by some chance they are arrested, they're usually let off with a much lesser penalty than if they were poor and needed the money or goods to survive.

8. The cells inside the Women's House of Detention are divided racially—Black on one side and white on the other. Sisters are encouraged to be antagonistic towards each other. The pigs are still using race to "divide and conquer."

9. Sisters from the streets are picked up for prostitution, yet the businessmen who buy and use their bodies are never prosecuted. We have to understand that prostitution, along with drug addiction, pushing, and stealing, exists among our people because of the poor conditions under which we are forced to live. If we are not allowed to get an education, if we are not allowed to learn skills, we have few alternatives left for survival.

We have to stick together to fight to improve the conditions in the jails for all our people—sisters and brothers alike. In doing so, we have to keep in mind two basic things—the present and the future of our people. At present, we have to realize that the whole prison system is a form of genocide of all Third World people. As for the future, we must understand that this situation will be changed totally only when WE, as a people, decide to change it. . . . Only by waging struggle will we free our sisters and brothers from amerikkka's concentration camps.

Palante, vol. 2, no. 17, December 1970

RACISM AND
COLONIZED MENTALITY

Puerto Rican Racism

IRIS MORALES

The Taíno Indians were the first people of Borinquen, the Indian name for the island that is still used today. The Spaniards came to Borinquen in 1493, changed the name to San Juan Bautista, and forced the Taínos into slavery, exploiting their labor in the gold mines and on plantations. The enslavers divided the land and people among themselves getting all the benefit and profit from the work of the Indians. The Taíno women were also exploited, not only their labor, but also their bodies. In the early days the Spanish did not bring any women, so they took, abused, or raped our Indian sisters. They justified this inhumanity and murder saying the Indians were savage, unchristian, and of another race.

Quickly, the colonizer killed, enslaved, or chased into the mountains our first ancestors. The Spaniards then had to look to Africa for new slave labor. In 1558, the first contract to bring in large numbers of Africans was signed. The oppressor accepted slavery as normal, the church never condemned it, and the government never enforced laws against it. Our African sisters were also raped and used as breeders. The number of African slaves was important to the sugar plantation owners who made a lot of money off the sugar cane fields where they put the African to slave. Again, the Spanish justified slavery and rape, saying that the African was inferior, uncivilized, and of an alien race.

From the 16th to the middle of the 19th century the Africans and Taínos rebelled against spanish colonialism, many times uniting to fight the common oppressor. By 1868, when the Puerto Rican nation emerged and fought the Spanish in El Grito de Lares, Blacks were still slaves. Black slavery was not abolished in Puerto Rico until 1873.

Puerto Ricans don't like to talk about racism or admit that it exists among Puerto Ricans. Boricuas talk of an island free from racism, or they say that the amerikkkans brought it. Although the amerikkkans did make it worse, racism in Puerto Rico began with the Spanish. According to them, one drop of white blood meant you were white and better than your Black compatriot. Acceptance was given according to the "degree of whiteness." The upper classes were white, descendants of the Spanish or Creoles. The colonizer had economic interests in Puerto Rico and Latin America; that's why they used racism as a justification for exploiting labor to get economic profit.

When the u.s. invaded Puerto Rico in 1898, racism was reinforced and intensified by them. The white upper class, empowered by the Spanish, now made deals and got money from u.s. industries to stay in power in return for supporting u.s. policies. The u.s. took advantage of the racial and class divisions within our country to better control by playing one group against the other. Puerto Ricans have developed a phrase that is constantly referred to and taught to all Puerto Ricans from generation to generation as a basic axiom of life; "Hay que mejorar la raza," which means, "One must better the race." Every Puerto Rican grows up with this concept and learns to view as ugly—dark skin, thick lips, a broad nose, and kinky hair. . . . Puerto Ricans believe that to better the race you must marry a light-skinned Puerto Rican. Every Puerto Rican family has light and dark Puerto Ricans. We say, "el que no tiene dinga, tiene mandinga," which basically means, "Everyone is Black." That's why we ask, "y tu abuela, donde esta?" And your grandmother, where is she?

During the 1940s Puerto Ricans were forced to emigrate to the US. Here the formula for racism says, "one drop of Black blood makes you Black." Puerto Ricans as a mixed people are considered Black and become victims of US racism. Amerikkkans cannot accept us because they believe that the racial mixture has caused a decline in our mental and physical capabilities. . . . Puerto Ricans and Blacks are in the same communities. Both are victims of racism, drugs, unemployment, the draft, bad health care, bad housing, and miseducation. Each is taught that the other is inferior and to be avoided or hated. For Puerto Ricans this means that the light-skinned Puerto Ricans start viewing themselves as white and their compatriots as Black, reflecting amerikkkan society. Many Black Puerto Ricans cling to being Puerto Rican to negate their blackness. Many light-skinned Puerto Ricans say, "I'm American. I'm Spanish, or I'm White" in order to avoid identification as Puerto Rican. Both Black and light-skinned Puerto Ricans adopt racist attitudes toward Afro-American brothers and sisters.

We in the YLP are revolutionary nationalists and oppose racism. [. . .]

Palante, vol. 2, no. 7, July 17, 1970

Colonized Mentality
and Non-Conscious Ideology

DENISE OLIVER-VÉLEZ

We are fighting against an enemy, the Yankee, and the Puerto Rican lombrices. The one major thing that holds us back in our fight to liberate Puerto Rico and all oppressed people is a lack of unity. If we are not united, like a fist, we are weaker in our battle. In unity there is strength; a nation divided is a weak nation. We have been divided geographically, with one third of the nation on the mainland and two thirds on the island. To be stronger we must unite. But even this unification will not be enough if we still fight against each other. . . . Capitalism is a system that forces us to climb over our brothers and sisters' back to get to the top. It is like a race, in which the prize is survival. . . . We fight against each other to live, and we are divided into groups that fight against each other. These groups are formed out of artificial division of race and sex, and social groupings. . . .

Many of these divisions that exist are a result of colonization. . . . As a result of the oppression suffered for generations and generations, first under Spain and then under the amerikkkans, we all develop a "colonized mentality." The colonizers divide us up, teach us to think we are inferior, and teach us to fight against each other, because as long as we fight against each other we won't deal with our real problems—slavery, hunger, and misery. We are so brainwashed by the newspapers we read, the books they write for us, the television, the radio, the schools, and the church that we don't know what our real thoughts are anymore. We are afraid to lead, because we are taught to be followers. We have been told that we are docile so long, that we have forgotten that we have always been fighters. . . . We can only unchain our minds from this colonized mentality if we learn our true history, understand our culture, and work toward unity.

This colonization is responsible for the racism that exists in our nation. We do not see it all the time, and most Puerto Ricans believe that we don't have any racism. Most people will tell you "we are all Puerto Ricans, we are all different colors, none of us are black or white, we are just Puerto Ricans." But that doesn't mean that racism

205

doesn't exist. It is so deep that we just don't see it anymore. The darker members of every Puerto Rican family have felt it all their lives. We have been so brainwashed that it has become unconscious. The Young Lords Party calls this non-conscious ideology. We believe that Black is bad and ugly and dirty, that kinky hair is *pelo malo*, we call Black Puerto Ricans names like *prieto, molleto,* and *cocolo.* We are not proud that our ancestors were slaves so many of us say we are "spanish" or "castilians." Our birth certificate says white even if the reality when we look in the mirror is very dark.

The Spanish treated the slaves as if they were animals, and none of us want to believe that our ancestors were animals, so we "non-consciously" reject the Blackness we are all a part of. All Puerto Ricans have a Black heritage in our culture; in the way Spanish is spoken, in the blood that flows through our veins. Having slaves for ancestors is not something to be ashamed of; one should be proud to know that one's ancestors were strong enough to live through the horrors of slavery, strong because of the rich and beautiful history of Africa. We are taught that Africans were savages, and this makes us non-consciously ashamed of our past.

We must study true African history of the civilizations of Mali and Songhay, for this is part of our history. The Young Lords Party is a Party of Afro-Americans and Puerto Ricans. Both have the same roots, similar culture, and the same types of "colonized mentality." Because of the Black Power movement inside of the united states, American Blacks are now able to hold their heads up high and be proud of their past. It is necessary that we study Puerto Rican history, much of which is African history, so that we can move on ridding ourselves of the barriers that exist between Afro-boricua and jibaro.

We should not be afraid to criticize ourselves about racism. We are all racists, not because we want to be, but because we are taught to be that way, to keep us divided, because it benefits the capitalist system. And this applies to racism toward Asians, other Brown people, and toward white people. White people are not all the oppressor—capitalists are. We will never have socialism until we are free of these chains on our mind. [. . .]

"Ideology of the Young Lords Party," February 1972

World of Fantasy

JENNY FIGUEROA

Television is used to brainwash and confuse our nation here and on the island. The programs provide false images and ideas that do not relate to the reality of oppression of Puerto Ricans, especially sisters. These lies come in many forms. One way is through the novelas (soap operas) shown on TV. These novelas are geared toward our sisters in the Puerto Rican Nation. They are supposed to be entertainment and are used to make us passive to our daily oppression. The stories revolve around upper middle-class people, racism, sexism (male chauvinism—female passivity), and religion, all of which are products of the capitalist society and all designed to enslave us and our minds. The racism scene usually involves a young couple, one who is Black. Problems develop when the couple wants to get married—they know that the Black person will not be accepted. What happens to a sister who looks at a program like this? It will create racist attitudes that being Black is not good and that somehow the best thing to be is white.

Television, especially novelas, also conditions us to roles that we have to play as "men" and as "women." This is what is called sexism. The model families sold to us in those novelas define how we're supposed to act and what we're supposed to do. For example, you have the typical mother who cooks, cleans, washes, shops, takes care of the kids, etc.; the typical father works, is out all day; and the typical children want to be just like their mommies and daddies. The man is the "head of the house" and the breadwinner. He comes home from work and expects to have his dinner ready and see the house spotless. The wife, of course, is loving, fragile, and if her husband has another woman on the side, she is patient and understanding because after all, he is a "man." When our sisters watch these novellas, they make us passive to oppression as Third World People and to our oppression as women. We accept our brothers' male chauvinism because we are taught that that is what a man is.

Taking another example, let's say that on TV there's a story where one of the children becomes ill. The doctors can't find the cause. There's no medicine that can help. Then an elderly woman comes to visit and stays with the child for a while. Within days the child, miraculously, recovers. The doctors, bewildered, want to know what the old woman did to cure the child. The woman pulls out a statue of the Virgin Mary or Jesus Christ and says that through her faith in God, the child was cured, and that we should all slave very hard because someday a savior will come who will lead us to a new kingdom. Religion is another way that we are kept pacified.

The people shown in these novelas are upper middle class people. They own their houses and cars. The husband is a doctor or lawyer, or he owns his own business. Their children go to private schools. The reason these people are shown to us is so we can think that our problems and theirs are the same. We become involved in these stories, and we begin to sympathize with these people, and we try to act like them, forgetting ourselves, and, most importantly, our people and the reality of our oppression. But these novelas are not real. They don't show the truth of our oppression. They don't show how in a capitalist society, poor people work hard and yet barely survive, while a few play in all the riches of our island and the world. TV is used as a tool to sell lies and to try to make us believe those lies. It shows nothing of how sisters die of abortions forced upon us because in the land of plenty, we can't "afford" another human life. It shows nothing of how doctors tell us to take the pill, making us believe that it is safe, when in fact they were using us as guinea pigs and all the time making us sterile. It doesn't show how hard we work and yet how little paid. It doesn't show the housing conditions we are forced to live in. It doesn't show how we work all day in a factory only to return home at night to a husband who is drunk, out all the time, or beats us constantly. Television is unreal, but our oppression isn't.

In a socialist society, television will be put to better use. It will be used to serve our people by having educational programs, for example. Programs where our people can be taught to read and write. Programs that show us what is really happening in the world around us, not like the television now that shows us only what the rich capitalists want us to know.

In this society, being Third World and a sister means we are oppressed not only by the society but also by our brothers. This is what we call the Triple Oppression—we are oppressed because we are Third World, because we are sisters, and because we are poor. This system, through television, tells us that is the way that it's supposed to be. Sisters, they say, are supposed to be weak and inferior while brothers are strong and superior. This society has in the past succeeded in making us think that we're all inferior. Brothers have directed their frustrations into themselves and have taken it out on sisters. Sisters have directed our frustrations into ourselves, developing self-hatred. We must stop competing with each other, trying to be like somebody on TV, and we must look for ourselves as what we are, how we live, and where we stand.

For now, sisters and all oppressed people are moving. We know that in this society there is no freedom. The 5th Point of the Young Lords Party Program and Platform says, "We want equality for women. Down with machismo and male chauvinism." The Young Lords Party also is fighting for the "liberation of all Third World People" as stated in our 3rd point of the Program. We are going to fight for our liberation and the liberation of all oppressed people, and we know that there is power only in unity.

Palante, vol. 3, no. 2, January 29, 1971

Make-Up and Beauty

LULU ROVIRA

Many Puerto Rican, Black, Asian, and other Third World women try very hard to look "beautiful" and often compete with each other for who is more "attractive" and who can "get a man." Let's look deeper into this and see why this happens.

We live in an economic system called capitalism. Capitalism is based on selling things for profit, so capitalists (big businessmen) create certain standards of "beauty" through advertising, television, magazines, newspapers, and movies. Then we are told that to become "beautiful," to meet the standards they have set up, we have to buy certain products—like lipstick, make-up, wigs, etc.

The society makes us believe that sisters have to be "beautiful" for men, because women aren't supposed to have anything else. They put commercials on television to make us believe this. Television always shows a white woman with blonde hair, blue eyes, and a certain kind of figure. They say this is the "perfect woman" that men are always after. So, many Third World women try to change themselves to look like this. This is impossible because we are not white, but Third World. When we try to look like the Clairol blondes, we look ridiculous. We dye our hair, straighten it, and go on diets (that many times get us sick). We do all this because we are trying to look like that "perfect woman" in the advertisements.

Take make-up for example. Commercials say that make-up will make your face more "beautiful," and men will be attracted to you. First of all, this is implying that our natural beauty is not enough, that we must add artificial things to our faces. Many of us develop complexes and begin to think we are ugly and that make-up can hide our "ugliness" and make us look good. Second, the commercials don't say that make-up has a lot of chemicals that mess up our faces. After years of wearing make-up, we start getting blemishes and wrinkles. We start getting all kinds of skin diseases and discoloration. Our hair begins to fall out from so much dye, sprays, teasing, curling, and straightening. It starts to feel like dried-up straw. When this happens, we start to feel "old," and we get scared. We are afraid to look old because everything focuses on youth, and when a woman gets old, she isn't wanted anymore—she is no longer "attractive," because she is only an object.

Basically, what is happening is that we are being trained to believe that the way we look is not good and that we need a bunch of external (outside of ourselves) things to make us look "attractive." We are made to feel ashamed of the way we are—our bodies, our hair. For example, we are often made to feel that our natural hair is "bad" or "nappy." This feeling is created in us, and then the businessmen rush to sell us something to eliminate the bad feelings we have about our hair—wigs with straight hair. And it's like that with everything else.

Some people feel that the businessmen are changing because they are putting out afro-wigs. First, why should women have to wear any kind of wig? Every woman should be proud of her natural hair. Second, businessmen put out afro-wigs because it's a way to make money. They will try to sell anything because their whole life is based on making profits for themselves.

All of us go through a lot of changes. We are made to feel ugly, inadequate, and inferior when we don't live up to the false standards of "beauty" the businessmen create. We're always dissatisfied with what we are. We're either too short or too tall, or too skinny or too fat, or our hair is too curly or too straight. And on and on. So we're very unhappy with what we are. We have to think a lot about this because it is part of our everyday lives. The more I think about it, the more I come to see that there is nothing more beautiful than a sister being natural.

Palante, vol. 3, no. 12, July 4-16, 1971

CHANGING DIRECTIONS

Call for Demonstration in Ponce

Ofensiva Rompe Cadenas Illustration
Palante, vol. 3, no. 3, February 1971 (Defense Supplement), back cover.

Ponce, March 21, 1971

INFORMATION MINISTRY

The Young Lords Party is calling for a demonstration on March 21, 1971 to be held in NYC, Philadelphia, Bridgeport, and Ponce, Puerto Rico. We are calling it on March 21 along with the Nationalist Party of Puerto Rico in commemoration of the Ponce Massacre. After the demonstration, we will announce the opening of our first branch in Puerto Rico. . . . After the demonstration, the YLP is not going to pack up and come back to work only in the Puerto Rican communities in the usa. We are going to stay. After March 21st, the YLP will have branches in the following cities—National Headquarters in NYC, El Barrio branch (East Harlem, NY), Bronx, Lower East Side, (Manhattan, NY), Philadelphia, Bridgeport, and Ponce, Puerto Rico.

We are going to have Lords here on the mainland, and on the island, to make that link, that connection between our people in the usa and in Puerto Rico. This is because the Puerto Rican Nation is divided—⅓ of us are here, and ⅔ of us in Puerto Rico. We have to fight wherever we are.

Never before has a Puerto Rican revolutionary political party worked to make that connection between the mainland and the island. Because the Young Lords Party is doing this, we expected heavy repression. . . .

Although we know that the government is mobilizing to try to stop the uniting of our nation, we will go ahead as planned. . . .

As things develop, we will let you know through *Palante*, and also through our radio show every other Monday night at 11 p.m. on WBAI, 99.7 FM. The Young Lords Party belongs to the people, to you.

In order to succeed in establishing the branch in Ponce, we need your help. Decide now where you stand: National Liberation or continued exploitation by the yanquis. If you believe in the right of Puerto Ricans to determine their own future, send us whatever you can: money, food, typewriters, paper, etc. We need everything in order to break off the chains of slavery. Unidos Venceremos!

Palante, vol. 3, no. 4, March 5–19, 1971

Editorial: 1ˢᵗ Party Congress

CENTRAL COMMITTEE

The time is coming near for the first Congress of the Puerto Rican Revolutionary Party. From June 20 to July 3 members of the Young Lords Party along with delegates of the Puerto Rican Workers Federation, the Committee to Defend the Community, the Puerto Rican Student Union, the Third World Students League, and the Women's Union, will meet in New York City.

During these four days we will discuss and plan the work of the new Puerto Rican Revolutionary Party. Before this time, all the people in Puerto Rico and the United States will participate in Peoples Assemblies, on the 18 of June in Aguadilla, Santurce, Philadelphia, Bridgeport, and New York.

In all these meetings the discussions will be the same. Why a Puerto Rican Revolutionary Party? What are the Young Lords doing? What is the purpose of this new party?

In the past the government has called us a gang, a bunch of criminals, hoodlums, extremists, etc. They have called us everything but what we are – a political party, a party of a new type – not a PNP or PPD, the parties of the rich, of the Yankees who dominate the people. Not like other political parties composed of lawyers and professor of the well off, comfortable rich.

We are a party built by the people, with the same sweat of the working people. We are a party of the workers, the sons and daughters of workers, the unemployed, the poor students, the inmates, the housewives of Puerto Rico and the United States.

We are a party determined to end this system of oppression, of suffering, of the misery under which we have lived since the first division of people into rich and poor, especially since the United States invaded Puerto Rico and made us slaves.

Many people say that things can never change, that there will always be the rich and the poor. But we do not believe this. The poor produce all that there is in the world and everything belongs to us. The dirty lazy rich have robbed us for years, and this will change.

Our people have always struggled against oppression.

Palante, vol. 4, no. 10, May 12-26, 1972.

215

Report From the Y.L.P Congress

PUERTO RICAN REVOLUTIONARY WORKERS ORGANIZATION

From Friday, June 30 to Monday, July 3, 1972, the Young Lords Party held a Congress of all its members.

This Congress took place in the South Bronx. The comrade organizations of our organization participated. . . .

The Congress approved a three-part resolution. The first part, on the present world situation, declared firmly our commitment to fight all forms of imperialism and to unite with broad numbers of people to defeat U.S. imperialism in particular.

The second part covered the history of the Young Lords Party. The successes and contribution to the struggle, as well as the errors and weaknesses of the Lords were sharply analyzed. . . .

The third part dealt with the tasks of our organization. Since we recognized the error of trying to build one organization for Puerto Ricans in both Puerto Rico and the United States, we set ourselves to the task of laying groundwork for the future division of our organization into two. One, with its primary task being the National Liberation of Puerto Rico (and working in Puerto Rico), the other having as its primary task the bringing of the multi-national proletariat into power (working in the U.S.). The secondary task of both organizations is building unity with the other country (from Puerto Rico to the U.S. or vice versa). . . .

The Congress voted on changing the organization's name. We are no longer the Young Lords Party, but the PUERTO RICAN REVOLUTIONARY WORKERS ORGANIZATION (PRRWO). In addition, the new central committee was elected. . . .

The Congress closed with presentations by the comrade organization on the present situation and the growing proletariat revolution. . . . Finally the session ended with much unity of will and spirit as the entire assembly first sang the Puerto Rican National Anthem "La Borinqueña" and the Internationale in English and Chinese.

Palante, vol. 4, no. 15, July 21, 1971–August 4 (Front page)

Resolutions of the
Puerto Rican Revolutionary Workers Organization

OUR TASKS

[...] The Puerto Rican nation is not divided; it is in Puerto Rico. Once Puerto Ricans come to the States, we became an oppressed national minority. But we became something more: most of us, the workers, became part of the multi-national U.S. proletariat, a proletariat that is Black, White, Chicano, other Latin nationalities, Asian, and Native American (Indian), as well as Puerto Rican. Out of a particular set of conditions a proletariat faces, it builds a struggle that, in order to succeed, must be led by a party. In Puerto Rico, the proletariat faces one set of conditions; it the United States, it faces another. . . .

In the United States our primary task is to create the conditions for the formation of the multi-national party. One aspect of this is to fight against the national oppression of Puerto Ricans in the U.S. . . .

The secondary task of this organization in the United States is to give direct and resolute aid to the national liberation struggle of Puerto Rico.

In the past, when we believed one party could be built for both Puerto Rico and the United States, we tried to establish branches in Puerto Rico in the same way as our branches in the U.S. We realize this was incorrect. We therefore conclude that revolutionaries who feel their work is primarily the national liberation of Puerto Rico should be there, living among the people, working, raising families, learning the conditions there as they unite with other revolutionaries to build the party of the proletariat in Puerto Rico. . . . The group in Puerto Rico will be autonomous, with its own decision-making apparatus and chain of command. . . .

The general strategy for this stage of struggle, in the United States and Puerto Rico, is building a united front of all popular classes against imperialism under proletarian leadership. This united front will unite all progressive forces against an isolated enemy, U.S. imperialism. [...]

Resolutions and Speeches, First Congress,
November 1972, 31–33

AFTERWORD

Berets and Barrettes

LENINA NADAL

There are women who wear berets.
There are women who wear barrettes.
To be a woman is to carry life at all points
A heavy pink toolbox with no wheels
Wearing pantalones or falditas
With strong legs and sturdy spirit
The berets and barrettes, feel heavy in tasks yet
find power in empathy
And have nervios and attacks openly,
without a macho shame

BERETS, Barrettes
Spicy ladies squinting in granny glasses clipping newspaper articles of
everyday daughters and mothers
in Iraq, China, Cuba, Grenada, India and Nicaragua, Chicago, NY,
Ferguson and Baltimore, and on...
circling together
igniting human energy
birthing new ideas and strategic power plans
teaching their daughters to draw maps of countries
feeling Earth's texture in blue and brown crayon
Yet strength lies not only under the red star beret
but also under the rainbow-colored barrette

BARETTES, Berets
Women who take great care in decorating the thickness of their hair
forming braids and crowns above powdered faces
Women who sew and make dolls from bottle caps, aluminum foil,
pipe cleaners and left over fabric

Women who need barrettes to keep from getting their hair in the restaurant food or sweat from their foreheads on the machines,
Women who do not stress over writing a thesis
or the best and catchiest phrase for a picket sign

But who take time to pray for their daughters and sisters
on the frontlines,
make them something to munch on so that the berets can continue to
fight with their words.

barrette, beret
To direct an army and put on some lip-gloss
To feel the universe in a child's smile or an Internet image
balancing magic with routine
noticing
when the tools of rebellion change
when the stories once relegated to the kitchen table
Are being sent in a text message of a rhinestone mobile

And that those that wear berets
and those that wear barrettes are both questioning
Their perceived strength
Are both attempting to reconcile their rebellions
Are both locking arms in streets together

Barrettes, berets,
Have no fear of blood or the men who don't understand them
Both See
Ugliness
As small blossoms and
Glamour as a crime
Both see that men and markets
Have kept them from realizing the unity-
fabulous and furious
beautiful,
fierce rebellion on the outside and
within.

July 2008

Lenina Nadal is a community activist, poet, filmmaker, and mother currently living and working in New York City.

On the 40th Anniversary
of the Young Lords in Chicago

IRIS MORALES

Speech delivered in Chicago, Illinois
September 2009

Good afternoon. *Buenas tardes. Mi nombre es Iris Morales,* and I was a member of the Young Lords in New York City. I am truly pleased, *es un gran placer,* to see so many of you here, *para celebrar* the Young Lords Organization and this important chapter in our history. It is an honor to be with you here in Humboldt Park, and I thank Cha Cha Jiménez *por la invitación.*

Forty years ago, the Young Lords stepped to the forefront. They organized, advocated, took militant action to let the world know about the deplorable living conditions of Puerto Ricans and Latinos, and they inspired Puerto Ricans and Latinos to organize and take to the streets in communities across the United States.

A lot has happened since then, some wins, and many losses—and the situation for poor people, for brown and black people are worse than ever.

I don't have to tell you—no jobs, terrible schools, HIV/AIDS killing our community, police killing our young men and women.

I don't have to tell you about high incarceration rates, mass deportation of immigrants, and long prison terms for political prisoners.

I don't have to tell you about new FBI assaults on Puerto Ricans—in the United States and Puerto Rico—about the Patriot Act, mass government-sanctioned surveillance, and the suspension of civil liberties.

I don't have to tell you about the horrors of Vieques or Katrina, or environmental racism or climate change.

I don't have to tell you about political distractions, lies, corruption, and bailouts for the wealthy and super rich.

I appreciate that we are here today to *look back, so that we may look forward.* My neighbor, Pat, who just returned from Ghana, reminded me of the principle of *sankofa*, which means "taking what is good from the past and bringing it into the present to make positive progress." We must study and reclaim our past so that we can move forward; so we understand why and how we came to be who we are, and where we are going.

Cha Cha Jiménez asked me to say a few words so I'd like to share some of my reflections about the Young Lords. I first met Cha Cha in March 1969 at the National Chicano Youth Conference in Denver. A busload of young Puerto Rican, Latino, Latina, and African American activists from New York City traveled several days through middle America to participate in the historic gathering of brown and black activists from around the country, an important moment in the Chicano Power movement. The Young Lords Organization was only six-months old then. When I met Cha Cha and other Young Lords, I was impressed with their political ideals and militancy—with their sense of urgency and need for action. The Young Lords chapter in New York had not formed yet, and I did not anticipate that, within a short time, I too would be a proud member of the organization.

I was a student at the City College of New York at the time—the first person in my family to attend college. My father worked as an elevator operator in a downtown hotel and had been a sugarcane cutter in Sabana Grande, Puerto Rico. My mother worked as a sewing machine operator in a sweatshop and had been a seamstress and domestic worker in Aguadilla, Puerto Rico. My parents both arrived in New York City after World War II, at different times but for the same reason—the search for work. They left a country they loved, but where they could not make a living. About half a million Puerto Ricans made the same journey fleeing economic despair, the result of the US colonization of the island. Government officials blamed the people for the disastrous economic situation claiming that the problem was "overpopulation." They promoted the mass exodus of Puerto Ricans and implemented policies that sterilized thousands of poor and working-women. The Young Lords are the sons and daughters of this Great Migration. As young people growing up in the United States, we witnessed how our parents were exploited, degraded, and humiliated. We felt their suffering, and we too had experiences with poverty and racism. All of this propelled us into action to fight for justice.

The Chicago Young Lords gave a militant and compassionate voice to our experiences and inspired other young Puerto Ricans and Latinos across the country with clear ideas and vision. "Serve the People," they said, believing that every person should have his/her basic needs met—jobs, food, housing, shelter, health, and education—and that the streets should be clean, our homes safe from lead-based paint, and our neighborhoods free from drugs and toxic waste. Not surprising, one of the first acts of the Young Lords in Chicago was to join the Rainbow Coalition—uniting with our allies, our brothers and sisters, in the Black Panther Party, the Brown Berets, the Young Patriots, and Rising Up Angry. The Young Lords understood the importance of collaboration and of building a broad people's movement in order to transform society.

The Young Lords attracted organizers—young people in their teens and twenties—who carried out the day-to-day programs, working collectively in low-income neighborhoods. We ran service programs, did door-to-door health testing, and sold newspapers on street corners. When needed, we moved to different cities to organize in other communities and workplaces. We strategized and employed all tactics. We agitated, advocated, demonstrated, and mobilized.

The rich and powerful were ruthless about maintaining the status quo. The FBI's COINTELPRO, counterintelligence program, and local police departments, combined resources to destroy the people's movement, the Black Panther Party, the Young Lords, and all progressive organizations and individuals. The police beat, arrested, sent to prison, and killed activists. The government and police succeeded in destroying organizations, but they could not destroy the peoples' love of freedom.

Looking back to look forward, we had internal weaknesses—shifting ideologies, individuals promoting themselves instead of the movement, and the exclusion of women from decision making. Our biggest success was our organizing, our community work—we engaged with people in our neighborhoods on a daily basis, provided information and education about national and international issues, and built strong bases of people engaged in collective action for social justice and human rights.

I revisit the past to arrive at the present. We are again in an important historical moment, a time to mobilize masses of people in order to transform society for the benefit of poor and working people, for the advancement of all humanity.

It is key that we learn from our past successes and failures.

I don't have to tell you. We must train and support another generation of organizers, put forth clear ideals and raise consciousness, go among the people and build organizations, and networks of organizations, coalitions, and take action.

I don't have to tell you. We must do the day-to-day work that educates and builds unity.

In the spirit of the Young Lords and all of our ancestors who have fought oppression and injustice, we must continue to fight for human liberation.

So I close with the words of Ella Baker, "We who believe in freedom cannot rest until it's won!"

All Power to the People!

¡Qué Viva Puerto Rico Libre!

APPENDIX

As part of *Handschu* consent decree in 1985, the New York City Police Department (NYPD) was to preserve its surveillance files of political activists and organizations. Despite this court mandate, when Professor Johanna Fernández, in connection with her academic research, requested the files on the Young Lords, the NYPD claimed they could not be found. Dr. Fernández sued. Still the NYPD insisted the files were "lost." Then suddenly in June 2016, the City's Municipal Archive announced that more than 520 boxes of records were found in a Queens's warehouse. The press release below outlines the details of "the surprising discovery."

CITY OF NEW YORK DISCOVERS TROVE OF "LOST" NYPD "HANDSCHU RECORDS" OF NYPD SPYING ON 60'S AND 70'S ACTIVISTS -- 520+ boxes found just after dismissal of CUNY Professor's lawsuit seeking the records.

FOR IMMEDIATE RELEASE - JUNE 16, 2016

New York. A month after a professor lost her lawsuit seeking disclosure by New York City records of NYPD surveillance of the Young Lords Party ("YLP") in the 1960s and 1970s, the City of New York announced a "surprise" discovery of the records. Many more like them were also uncovered in what the City called a "routine inventory" of a Queens's warehouse.

In a June 14, 2016 letter, the Law Department revealed that the City's Municipal Archive ("DORIS") had found more than 520 boxes, or around an estimated 1,100,000 pages, apparently containing the complete remaining records documenting the NYPD's political surveillance activities in the 1960s and 1970s – including, it seems, the YLP records she had sued for access to under the New York State Freedom of Information Law.

Working with attorney Gideon Oliver, Dr. Johanna Fernandez, CUNY Baruch Professor of History, had sued in 2014 to force the City to locate and make records of YLP surveillance and infiltration public after the NYPD claimed it had looked and could not find any.

Exceeding documents related to the YLP, the newly found records located appear to be the entire remaining trove of so-called "Handschu Documents" – all records of the NYPD's surveillance operations of political activists between 1955 and 1972. The documents were segregated by the NYPD from active police intelligence files as a result of requirements to preserve and make them available for disclosure in the Handschu class action lawsuit, brought in 1971 to challenge NYPD surveillance and infiltration of political activists.

After both the NYPD and DORIS provided sworn affidavits in Dr. Fernandez's lawsuit saying they could not find the "lost" Handschu records despite more than 100 hours of searches, New York State Supreme Court Justice Alice Schlesinger reluctantly dismissed the lawsuit in a May 15, 2016 decision, calling the case "unique" and the result "frustrating."

This week's revelation surprised Dr. Fernandez and her lawyer because an affidavit stated that DORIS had searched for and could not find "any documentation concerning the disposition of the requested records, which would include transfer to DORIS." The City represented to the Court that there was "no basis whatsoever for speculating that" DORIS had the records. Fernandez's lawyer, Gideon Oliver, called the City's prior representations "troubling" but praised DORIS for locating the records and promising to make them available to the public.

On June 15, 2016, Dr. Fernandez met with DORIS Commissioner Pauline Toole and Municipal Archives Director Sylvia Kollar and reviewed a fifteen-page summary of the found records. A summary index matched an index of "missing" Handschu documents provided by Dr. Fernandez's lawyer to the City's lawyer.

Fernandez observed: "This is an epic win for civil liberties and historians seeking to understand the history of New York. The records open a window to the efforts of hundreds of civic organizations and thousands of New York City residents, surveilled and obstructed by the police, in their work to make our city and our nation more just and democratic."

DORIS has offered Dr. Fernandez immediate access to the records she requested access to, over a decade ago, for a book she has been writing about the YLP. She will also assist in developing an inventory of the Handschu records to make them available to the public.

ACKNOWLEDGEMENTS

Through the Eyes of Rebel Women began with the demands for justice in the late 1960s and is the result of many experiences, inspirations, and influences. So many years later, I appreciated the opportunity to revisit the ideas, events, and work of the Young Lords and other organizations that contributed to the Puerto Rican revolutionary movement in the United States. I'm especially grateful for the chance to pay tribute to the rebel women in the Young Lords who risked their lives with loving hearts determined to end the exploitation of all people and the particular oppression of women.

Many persons supported my efforts to make this book a reality. My mother, Almida Roldán Reices, was my first teacher, an independent woman whose hardships and struggles from rural Puerto Rico to the factories of New York City inspired my yearning for justice and compassion.

My son, Adrien, was the first person to express unshakable confidence in the importance of writing this *herstory*. I would not have embarked on the project without his support and youthful wisdom. His initial steps doing research, typing articles, reading early drafts, and offering feedback encouraged me to get started.

My compañero, José Angel Figueroa, helped me complete the book. His reassuring and loving support was there to challenge my doubts and catch me when I wavered. I'm deeply grateful for his probing questions, editorial advice, and structural suggestions, which greatly enhanced the manuscript and got me to the finish line.

Denise Oliver-Vélez, my life-long friend, whom I first met in the East Harlem branch, was the first Young Lord to support the project, sharing notes and memories I had long forgotten. Thanks also to my Young Lord sisters: Martha Arguello for writing an essay for the book, and Diana Caballero, Gloria Rodríguez, and Minerva Solla for their *testimonios* bringing to life the intensity and passions of those years, and to my Black Panther sister, Ericka Huggins, for her notes and comments supporting the book.

As a long-time admirer of Dr. Edna Acosta-Belén's scholarship, I am sincerely grateful for her insightful and comprehensive introduction to *Through the Eyes of Rebel Women*. She beautifully expresses the idea that women's voices in collective historical memory are necessary to inspire "present and future spheres of activism and resistance."

I thank Edgardo Miranda-Rodriguez of Somos Arte for our collaboration and for the creativity and joy he brought to the book cover design and to Francesca Ciregia, the illustrator, for her artistry.

I'm indebted to Lori Salmon for her early support and recovering copies of *La Luchadora*, and for reading drafts and taking meticulous care of technical details.

Martha Arguello shared her research, and I'm extremely thankful for her detailed and insightful notes to the manuscript. Thanks also goes to several readers for reviewing specific chapters or sections, specifically Kathleen Cleaver, Chong Chon Smith, Kathe Sandler, Carlos Aponte, Sofia Quintero, Suzanne Oboler, and Andrés Torres, and to Norman Ware for his excellent editorial work.

I extend a special thank you to Michael Abramson who without any hesitation allowed his beautiful and iconic photographs to be part of this book, and to Lenina Nadal for the gift of her poem, "Berets and Barrettes."

Darrel Wanzer-Serrano deserves credit for reviving interest in the history of the Young Lords with the thoroughness of his research and books. I'm especially thankful to him for the CD compilation of primary source documents that he generously gave to former members, which proved an invaluable resource in writing this book. I thank Johanna Fernández for keeping alive the stories of our liberation struggles and for bringing a lawsuit against the New York City police department compelling them to open their surveillance files.

I also acknowledge and thank special friends and colleagues who offered advice, encouragement, and support at critical crossroads moments, especially: Francia Castro, Vernon Douglas, Anna Gyorgy, Hector Soto, Maria Lebrón, Charlie Hey-Maestre, Patricia Leonard, Vanessa Roman, José Santiago, Candy Taffee, Amy Shore, Alvin Starks, Arva Rice, Irini Neofotistos, Cynthia Wong, Carmen Rivera, Magdalena Gómez, Betsy Salas, and Karina Hurtado-Ocampo.

I thank them all for joining me on this political and personal journey.

NOTES

INTRODUCTION

1. For the construction of feminist decolonial imaginaries, see the work of Latina scholar Emma Pérez in *The Decolonial Imaginary: Writing Chicanas into History* (Bloomington: Indiana University Press, 1999). For more information on discussions of coloniality and decolonial thinking as critical theory, see the special issue of Cultural Studies entitled "Globalization and the De-Colonial Option," 21: 2-3 (2007).

2. A comprehensive view of different aspects of the Puerto Rican civil rights struggles is offered by Andrés Torres and José E. Velázquez in the edited volume, *The Puerto Rican Movement: Voices from the Diaspora* (Philadelphia: Temple University Press, 1998).

3. A synthesis of some of the revolutionary pro-independence activism of this period is provided in Juan Angel Silén, *La nueva lucha de independencia* (Río Piedras, PR: Editorial Edil, 1973) and Luis Nieves Falcón, *Puerto Rico: Grito y mordaza* (Río Piedras, Ediciones Librería Internacional, 1971).

4. See Eric R. Wolf, *Europe and the People without History* (Berkeley: University of California Press, 1982) and Lydia Milagros González and Angel Quintero Rivera, *La otra cara de la historia: La otra historia de Puerto Rico desde su cara obrera, 1800-1925* (Río Piedras, PR: Centro de Estudios de la Realidad Puertorriqueña , 1970).

5. See the special issue of *Latino(a) Research Review* 7:1-2 (2012) on "The Legacies of Puerto Rican Social, Cultural, and Political Activism," edited by Edna Acosta-Belén.

6. The Young Lords created a button that popularized the slogan "Tengo Puerto Rico en Mi Corazón" [I have Puerto Rico in my heart], signaling their commitment to a free Puerto Rico. The patriotic sentiment was later adopted by pro-independence *nueva trova* singers Pepe y Flora for the title of a 1971 LP recording. Although the correct Spanish would be "Tengo a Puerto Rico en mi corazón," the Young Lords version came to be widely accepted by both stateside and island Puerto Ricans.

7. Occupy Wall Street, Black Lives Matter, environmental movements, and the growing activism to denounce campus violence against women, institutionalized racism, and the lack of diversity at US colleges and universities are a few of the most recent examples of youth mobilizing around specific concerns. Among these concerns are the unfettered corporate power and capitalist excesses of US banks and financial markets responsible for the Great Recession; police brutality and underlying racism toward African Americans and other groups of color in law enforcement and the prison system; the obliteration of gun control laws and the violence that it unleashes throughout the country; and the role of corporations in impeding or derailing badly needed government policies and reforms to protect the environment and deal with the catastrophic local and global effects and human toll of climate change.

PART 1.
YOUNG LORDS EARLY YEARS, 1969-1971, AN OVERVIEW

1. Andrés Torres, "Introduction: Political Radicalism in the Diaspora: The Puerto Rican Experience," in *The Puerto Rican Movement: Voices from the Diaspora,* ed. Andrés Torres and José E. Velázquez (Philadelphia: Temple University Press, 1998), 3.

2. Mao Tse-tung, "Chapter 17: Serving the People," Mao Tse Tung Internet Archive, at https://www.marxists.org/reference/archive/mao/works/red-book/ch17.htm, accessed January 27, 2015.

3. Frank Browning, "From Rumble to Revolution: The Young Lords," *Ramparts* (October 1970), 23.

4. "Trial is ordered for Young Lords," *New York Times,* January 17, 1970.

5. "Young Lords Defy Take-Over Order," *New York Times*, January 3, 1970.

6. Gloria Rodríguez (Santiago), Interview by Iris Morales in documentary, *¡Palante, Siempre Palante! The Young Lords,* (1996).

7. In 2009, East Harlem residents petitioned the community board to name 111th Street and Lexington Avenue "Young Lords Way." The announcement was made on August 23, 2009, at the fortieth anniversary reunion of the New York Young Lords at the People's Church. Former women members addressed the gathering: Connie Cruz (Morales), Mar-

tha Arguello (Duarte), Sonia Ivany, Doleza Miah, Denise Oliver-Vélez, Olguie Robles, Gloria Rodríguez (Santiago), Marlin Segarra, Cleo Silvers, Minerva Solla, and myself.

8. Young Lords Party Central Committee, "Evaluation and Retreat Report," December 1970, 9.

9. Michael Robert Gonzales. "Ruffians and Revolutionaries: the Development of the Young Lords Organization in Chicago" (PhD dissertation, University of Wisconsin-Milwaukee, 2015), 19.

10. Rosalyn Baxandall and Linda Gordon, eds. *Dear Sisters: Dispatches from the Women's Liberation Movement* (New York: Basic Books, 2000), 64.

11. Lucille Banta, "Editor's Foreword," *WE: A Magazine of the Arts in Revolt*, circa 1971.

12. Alfonso R. Narvaez, "The Young Lords Seize X-Ray Unit," *New York Times*, June 18, 1970. 17.

13. Ibid.

14. Carl Pastor, "Socialism at Lincoln," *Palante* 2:8 (1970): 5.

15. Huey Jung, "Pigs Attack Health Rally." *Palante* 2:7 (1970): 2.

16. Ibid.

17. Alfonso A. Narvaez, "Young Lords Seize Lincoln Hospital Building," *New York Times*, July 15, 1970. 34.

18. Juan González, "The Beginnings." Rough Draft #3 (1988): 27. Center for Puerto Rican Studies at Hunter College of New York: Archives.

19. "Young Lords Council Removes Luciano as National Chairman," *New York Times*, September 5, 1970.

20. Young Lords Party Central Committee, "On Felipe Luciano," *Palante* 2:11 (1970): 2.

21. Young Lords Party Central Committee, "Press Release on Felipe," *Palante* 2:12 (1970): 17.

22. "On Felipe Luciano," *Palante*, 2:11 (1970): 2.

23. Paul L. Montgomery. "2 Inmates Found Hanged in Cells," *New York Times*, October 17, 1970, 60.

24. Young Lords Party Ministry of Information, "Seize the Jails," *Palante* 2:10 (1970): 7.

25. "Inmates Front." *Village Voice*, January 7, 1971, 36

26. The Movement Pro Independence (*Movimiento Pro-Independen cia*) or MPI was founded in 1959 in the city of Mayagüez, Puerto Rico by former members of the Puerto Rican Independence Party (PIP), Nationalist Party, Communist Party, and university students, some of them members of the Federación de Universitarios Pro Independencia (FUPI). In 1971, MPI changed its name to the Puerto Rican Socialist Party (*Partido Socialista Puertorriqueño*) or the PSP.

27. Young Asians in New York City formed I Wor Kuen in 1969, and they opened a storefront in Chinatown. The name translates as "Fist of Harmony" and originates from the Chinese fight to overthrow imperialism and colonialism during the Boxer Rebellion of 1900.

28. "Los Siete de la Raza" were seven young Latinos from San Francisco's Mission District accused of murdering a policeman in 1969. The community organized, and the men were acquitted in 1970.

29. Michael T. Kaufman, "200 Armed Young Lords Seize Church After Taking Body There," *New York Times*, October 19, 1970. 26.

30. "Juran Vengar Muerte Julio Roldán," *Palante* 2:15 (1970): 16.

31. William J. vanden Heuvel, interviewed by Jeffrey A. Kroessler, February 2, 2011, Justice in New York: Oral History no. 12, at http://dc.lib.jjay.cuny.edu/index.php/Detail/Object/Show/object_id/657, accessed September 29, 2014.

32. Joshua Bloom and Waldo E. Martin. Jr., *Black against Empire: The History and Politics of the Black Panther Party* (Berkeley: University of California Press, 2013), 295-296.

33. Richie Pérez, "Julio Roldán Center Opens," *Palante* 2:14 (1970): 4.

WOMEN ORGANIZING WOMEN

1. Judy Klemesrud, "Young Women Find a Place in High Command of Young Lords," *New York Times*, November 11, 1970, 78.

2. The Last Poets was the name of several groups of poets and musicians who arose out of the black nationalist movement in the late 1960s. Their combination of spoken word, music, and politics is credited with influencing rap and hip-hop. Felipe Luciano was a member of the group.

3. Young Lords Party and Michael Abramson. *PALANTE: Voices and Photographs of the Young Lords, 1969-1971* (Chicago: Haymarket Books, 2011), 41. The book was originally published in 1971 as *Palante: Young Lords Party* (New York: McGraw-Hill). It is out of print.

4. In the 1960s and 1970s, black nationalism generally pursued the idea of reclaiming African American history and identity, and organizing for black power collectively.

5. Johnnetta Betsch Cole and Beverly Guy-Sheftall, *Gender Talk: The Struggle for Women's Equality in African American Communities* (New York: Ballentine Books, 2003), 80.

6. Baxandall and Gordon, *Dear Sisters*, 10.

7. Felipe Luciano, "On Revolutionary Nationalism," *Palante* 2:2 (1970): Centerfold. The Young Lords defined revolutionary nationalism as a left-wing form of nationalism that sought to replace the capitalist-imperialist social order with socialism.

8. In 1969, twenty-one Black Panther Party members in New York City were indicted on charges that included conspiring to kill police officers and bomb police stations, department stores, and other public buildings. Bail was set at $100,000 for each person, and the trial ran for eight months. On May 13, 1971, after deliberating for ninety minutes, the jury acquitted the defendants on all counts.

9. Chicanos/Chicanas formed the Brown Berets in 1967 to fight for social justice in East Los Angeles, California, and they organized chapters in Arizona, Texas, Colorado, New Mexico, Wisconsin, Illinois, Michigan, Minnesota, Ohio, Oregon, and Indiana.

10. As noted in the previous chapter, Young Asians in New York City formed I Wor Kuen in 1969 and opened a storefront in Chinatown. The name translates as "Fist of Harmony" and originates from the Chinese fight to overthrow imperialism and colonialism during the Boxer Rebellion of 1900.

11. As noted in the previous chapter, the MPI, Movement Pro Independence (*Movimiento Pro Independencia*) was founded in 1959 in Mayagüez, Puerto Rico by former members of the Puerto Rican Independence Party (PIP), Nationalist Party, Communist Party, and university students. In 1971, the MPI changed its name to the Puerto Rican Socialist Party (*Partido Socialista Puertorriqueño*) or the PSP.

12. Formed in 1970, El Comité initially organized against urban renewal's displacement of low-income residents on the West Side of Manhattan in New York City and evolved into a revolutionary nationalist organization like the Young Lords.

13. Winifred Breines, "Hope and Anger: Black Women and Black Power" in *The Trouble Between US: An Uneasy History of White and Black Women in the Feminist Movement* (Oxford: Oxford University Press, 2006), 55.

14. Mary Uyematsu Kao, "Stirrin' Waters 'n Buildin' Bridges: A Conversation with Ericka Huggins and Yuri Kochiyama," *Amerasia Journal* 35:1 (2009): 147.

15. Mary Phillips, "The Feminist Leadership of Ericka Huggins in the Black Panther Party," *Black Diaspora Review* Vol. 4, no. 1, Winter 2014: 200, at https://scholarworks.iu.edu/journals/index.php/bdr/article/view/4241/3849, accessed July 7, 2016.

16. The Black Women's Alliance originated out of the Student Nonviolent Coordinating Committee (SNCC), a civil rights organization that led sit-ins and freedom rides in the South. Among its leaders were Ella Baker, Stokely Carmichael, and Jamil Abdullah Al-Amin (H. Rap Brown).

17. Baxandall and Gordon. *Dear Sisters,* 65.

18. Frances M. Beal, "Double Jeopardy: To Be Black and Female," in *Black Women's Manifesto* (New York: Third World Women's Alliance, 1969), 21-22.

19. Beal. "Double Jeopardy," 30.

20. "History of Chicana Feminism," at www.umich.edu/~ac 213/student_projects05/cf/history.html, accessed May 21, 2015.

21. Mirta Vidal, *Chicanas Speak Out: Women, New Voice of La Raza* (New York: Pathfinder Press, 1971); available at Duke University Libraries Digital Collections at, library.duke.edu/digitalcollections/wlmpc_wlmms01005/, accessed April 26, 2015.

22. Beal. "Double Jeopardy," 23.

23. Erica González, "La Mujeres de Los Young Lords," *El Diario La Prensa,* June 14, 2009.

24. Pablo "Yoruba" Guzmán, "Why the Young Lords Party?," *Palante* 2:17 (1970): 13.

25. Chana Gazit, *The Pill*, Public Broadcasting Service, 2007, at http://www.pbs.org/wgbh/amex/pill/index.html.

26. Lourdes Miranda King, "Puertorriqueñas In the United States: The Impact of Double Discrimination." *Civil Rights Digest*, 6:3 (Spring 1974): 27.

27. Laura Briggs, *Reproducing Empire: Race, Sex, Science, and US Imperialism in Puerto Rico* (Berkeley: University of California Press, 2002), 83-87.

28. M. Jacqui Alexander, Lisa Albrecht, Sharon Day, and Mab Segrest, eds., *Sing, Whisper, Shout, Pray! Feminist Visions for a Just World* (Fort Bragg, CA: EdgeWork Publishing, 2003), 128.

29. Committee to End Sterilization Abuse, "Sterilization Abuse of Women: The Facts," at www.freedomarchives.org/Documents/Finder/DOC46_scans/46.SterilizationAbuseWomenTheFacts.pdf, accessed April 26, 2015.

30. Jennifer Nelson, *Women of Color and the Reproductive Rights Movement.* (New York: New York University Press, 2003)

31. Iris Morales, "Puerto Rican Genocide." *Palante* 2:2 (1970): 8.

32. "¡Somos Puertorriqueños y Estamos Despertando!/We Are Puerto Ricans, and We Are Waking Up," Puerto Rican Student Union, 1970.

33. In 1982, filmmaker Ana María García produced *La Operación*, a forty-minute documentary about population control politics and the mass sterilization of women in Puerto Rico.

34. Dr. Helen Rodríguez-Trías, interview dated October 9, 1974. Published in the newsletter of the Committee to End Sterilization Abuse (CESA).

35. Sue Davis, "A Doctor Who Fought Sterilization Abuse," *Workers World*, at http://www.workers.org/2005/us/ rakow-0428, accessed April 20, 2005.

36. Charlayne Hunter, "Community Dispute Cuts Service at City Hospital, *The New York Times*, August 26, 1970: 1.

37. Jennifer Nelson, "Abortions under Community Control: Feminism, Nationalism, and the Politics of Reproduction among New York City's Young Lords," *Journal of Women's History* 13:1 (2001): 171.

38. Young Lords Party Health Ministry, "Lincoln Hospital Must Serve the People," *Palante* 2:11 (1970).

39. Fitzhugh Mullan, "Seize the Hospital to Serve the People," *Social Medicine Journal* 2:2 (2007), 112.

40. Theresa Horvath, "The Health Initiatives of the Young Lords Party: How a Group of 1960s Radicals Made Health a Revolutionary Concern," at http://www.hofstra.edu/pdf/community/culctr/culctr_events_healthcare0310_%20horvath_paper.pdf, accessed October 15, 2014.

41. Gloria Colón, "Abortions," *Palante* 3:5 (1971): 12.

42. Young Lords Party Central Committee, "Young Lords Party Position On Women," *Palante* 2:12 (1970): 11.

43. Young Lords Party and Abramson, *Palante: Voices and Photographs* (2011), 48.

44. González, "La Mujeres de Los Young Lords."

45. Ibid.

46. Young Lords Party and Abramson, *Palante: Voices and Photographs,* 50.

47. Sylvia Rivera, "I'm Glad I Was in the Stonewall Riot," interview by Leslie Feinberg, *Workers World*, at www.workers.org/ww/1998/sylvia 0702.php, accessed September 7, 2009.

48. For a history of the squatters movement, see Gregory Heller, "Self Help Housing: An Historical Overview of Squatting in New York City," at http://home.gregoryheller.com/node/35, accessed August 14, 2009.

49. Young Lords Party and Abramson, *Palante: Voices and Photographs,* 41.

50. Young Lords Party Central Committee, "Young Lords Party Position On Women," *Palante* 2:12 (1970): 12.

51. For a contemporary analysis of women's oppression, struggle and equality, see Fred Ho's article, "Matriarchy: The First and Final Communism" in *Wicked Theory, Naked Practice*. Minneapolis: University of Minnesota Press, 2009.

52. "Young Lords Council Removes Luciano as National Chairman," *New York Times*, September 5, 1970.

53. Young Lords Party Central Committee, "On Felipe Luciano," *Palante* 2:11 (1970): 2.

54. Nydia Mercado. "Revolutionary Wedding," *Palante* 2:9 (1970): 9.

55. Young Lords Party Central Committee, "Evaluation and Retreat Report," December 1970, 2.

56. Ibid., 5.

57. Ibid.

58. The term, "Third World Women" referred to women in Africa, Asia and Latin America and their descendants in the United States and throughout the world.

59. Clara Colón, *Enter Fighting: Today's Woman, A Marxist-Leninist View* (New York: New Outlook Publishers, 1970).

60. Young Lords Party Women's Union, "Why a Women's Union?," *La Luchadora,* 1:1 (June 7-20, 1971), centerfold.

61. Andrés Torres and José E. Velázquez, eds., *The Puerto Rican Movement: Voices from the Diaspora,* (Philadelphia: Temple University Press, 1998), 205.

62. Che Guevara, *Man and Socialism in Cuba* (Havana: Guairas Book Institute, 1967).

63. bell hooks, *Feminist Theory: From Margin to Center* (Cambridge: South End Press, 1984), 73.

64. Alma M. García, ed., *Chicana Feminist Thought: The Basic Historical Writings* (London: Routledge, 1997), 151.

65. Max Elbaum, "History Is a Weapon: What Legacy from the Radical Internationalism of 1968?," at www.historyisaweapon.com/defcon1/ elbaum.html, accessed July 11, 2015.

66. "Journeys towards Peace: Internationalism and Radical Orientalism during the US War in Vietnam," Indochinese Women's Conference, Toronto, April 1971, at http://historyandcurrentcontext.blogspot.com/2014/08/journeys-towards-peace-internationalism.html/[http://digitaluni on.osu.edu/r2/summer09/caldwell/Pages/indochinesewomen.html], accessed May 21, 2015.

67. Iris Morales, "US Orders Asian Sisters Tortured," *Palante* 3:8 (1971): 15.

68. The Young Lords Party, "Position on Women's Liberation," *Palante* 3:8 (1971): 17.

69. Ibid.

70. Young Lords Party Central Committee, July 1971 Retreat Report, 33.

71. Ibid., 5.

72. Young Lords Party Central Committee, "Young Lords Party Position On Women." *Palante,* 2:12 (1970): 11.

73. Bonnie G. Smith. *Women's History in Global Perspective,* vol. 1, (Urbana: University of Illinois Press, 2004), 264.

74. Lina Sunseri. "Moving Beyond the Feminism Versus Nationalism Dichotomy; An Anti-Colonial Feminist Perspective on Aboriginal Liberation Struggles." *Canadian Woman Studies/Les Cahiers De La Femme.* 20: 2 (2000): 146.

75. Maria I. Bryant, "Puerto Rican Women's Roles in Independence Nationalism: Unwavering Women," (PhD dissertation, American University, 2011), 82.

76. Vanessa Pérez Rosario. *Becoming Julia de Burgos: The Making of a Puerto Rican Icon* (Urbana: University of Illinois Press, 2014), 29.

77. Bryant, "Puerto Rican Women's Roles in Independence Nationalism: Unwavering Women," 77.

78. Elizabeth Crespo-Kebler, "Feminist Activism and Women's Studies in Puerto Rico," in *Women's Studies: Research, Conceptual Developments, and Action* (Kampala: Women and Gender Studies, Makerere University, 2005), 128.

79. Torres and Velázquez, *The Puerto Rican Movement,* 205.

80. Crespo-Kebler, "Feminist Activism and Women's Studies in Puerto Rico," 128.

81. Young Lords Party Central Committee, July 1971 Retreat Report, 4-6.

82. Ibid.

83. Ibid., 6

84. Brenda Ortiz-Loyola, "En busca de la solidaridad: feminismo y nación en el Caribe hispano, 1880-1940," (PhD dissertation, University of California, 2013), 241.

85. Pablo "Yoruba" Guzmán, "Our Present Situation, Statement, Analysis, Suggestions," Report to the Central Committee, December 7, 1971. 17-18.

86. Ibid.

87. Norma Valle-Ferrer, *Luisa Capetillo, Pioneer Puerto Rican Feminist* (New York: Peter Lang, 2006), 6.

88. Ibid., 45.

89. Torres and Velázquez, *The Puerto Rican Movement*, 184.

90. The Yellow Seeds was a radical student group that joined the fight to "Save Chinatown" in Philadelphia in the early 1970s from encroachment by proposed highway development. Their slogan, "Same Struggle, Same Fight," expressed the link with the struggles of African Americans, Latino/Latinas, and other "minority and working people."

91. For background, watch *The Thin Blue Lie*, a made-for-television film released in 2000 about two reporters who exposed the corruption of Mayor Rizzo and the Philadelphia police department. The file depicts how police beat and tortured suspects to meet the high quotas that had been established for cases to be solved by detectives.

NEW DIRECTIONS TO SHATTERED DREAMS

1. Victor Villanueva, "Colonial Memory and the Crime of Rhetoric: Pedro Albizu Campos," College English, Special Topic: Writing, Rhetoric, and Latinidad, 71:6 (July 2009): 630–38, at http://www.jstor.org/stable /25653000, accessed April 13, 2015.

2. "Tet Offensive: Turning Point in Vietnam War," *New York Times*, January 31, 1988, at http://www.nytimes.com/1988/01/31/world/tet-offensive-turning-point-in-vietnam-war.html, accessed July 3, 2015.

3. "Tet Offensive," History, at http://www.history.com/topics/ vietnam-war/tet-offensive, accessed July 3, 2015.

4. Dr. Martin Luther King Jr., "Beyond Vietnam: A Time to Break Silence; Declaration of Independence from the War in Vietnam," speech delivered on April 4, 1967 at the Riverside Church, New York, at http://www.commondreams.org/views04/0115-13.htm, accessed July 3, 2015.

5. Robert T. Chase, "Class Resurrection: The Poor People's Campaign of 1968 and Resurrection City," *Essays in History* (Department of History, University of Virginia), at http://www.essaysinhistory.com /articles/2012 /116, accessed July 3, 2015.

6. Komozi Woodward, "Rethinking the Black Power Movement," Africana Age, Schomburg Center for Research in Black Culture, The New York Public Library at http://exhibitions.nypl.org/africanaage/essay-black-power.html, accessed April 8, 2015.

7. "Achieving the Dream: Death of a Panther," WTTW Digital Archives, at http://www.wttw.com/main.taf?p=76,4,6,1, accessed July 3, 2015.

8. "Cosmoe Speaks," *Y.L.O.*, newspaper of the Chicago Young Lords Organization, 1:4 (1969).

9. Edna Acosta-Belén and Carlos E. Santiago, *Puerto Ricans in the United States: A Contemporary Portrait* (Boulder, CO: Lynne Rienner Publishers, 2006), 81.

10. Ibid.

11. Gabriel Haslip-Viera and Angelo Falcón, *Boricuas in Gotham: Puerto Ricans in the Making of New York City* (Princeton, NJ: Markus Wiener, 2005), 8.

12. Ibid., 89.

13. William H. Tucker. *Princeton Radicals of the 1960s: Then and Now.* (Jefferson, NC: McFarland, 2015), 204. The phrase, "in the belly of the beast," is attributed to Che Guevara as a reference to the United States as the world's major imperialist power.

14. Felipe Luciano, "On Revolutionary Nationalism," *Palante* 2:2 (1970): 10-11.

15. Lillian Guerra, *Popular Expression and National Identity in Puerto Rico: The Struggle for Self, Community, and Nation.* (Gainesville: University Press of Florida, 1998), 22.

16. Nelson A. Denis, *War Against All Puerto Ricans, Revolution and Terror in America's Colony* (New York: Nation Books, 2015), 44-48.

17. Ibid., 191-204.

18. Pedro A. Malavet, *America's Colony: The Political and Cultural Conflict between the United States and Puerto Rico* (New York: New York University Press, 2004), 92.

19. Gary L. Anderson and Kathryn G. Herr, eds. *Encyclopedia of Activism and Social Justice,* 3 vols. (Thousand Oaks, CA: Sage Publications, 2007), 54.

20. Malavet, *America's Colony*, 92.

21. Nydia Mercado, "Revolutionary Wedding," *Palante* 2:9 (1970): 9.

22. Young Lords Party Central Committee, "Evaluation and Retreat Report," December 1970, 13–15.

23. Ibid., 15.

24. Ibid., 14.

25. The Young Lords defined the "lumpen" or lumpenproletariat as the unemployable—people on drugs or in jail, prostitutes, and welfare mothers. A jíbaro was an agricultural worker.

26. Gloria González, "Ofensiva Rompe Cadenas," *Palante* 3:2 (1971): 12-13.

27. Richie Pérez, "¡Palante, Siempre Palante!," interview by Iris Morales, *Centro Journal* 21:2 (Fall 2009): 155–56.

28. Young Lords Party Ministry of Defense, "Police Agents," *Palante* 3:3 (1971): 14.

29. Young Lords Party Central Committee, "Carlos Aponte," *Palante* 3:5 (1971): 23.

30. Young Lords Party Central Committee, "Statement on Denise," *Palante* 3:5 (1971): 19.

31. Nicole Waller. *Contradictory Violence: Revolution and Subversion in the Caribbean,* (Heidelberg: Universitätsverlag Winter, 2005), 208.

32. Young Lords Party Central Committee, "Evaluation and Retreat Report," December 1970, 18.

33. Young Lords Party Central Committee, "Two Years of Struggle." *Palante* 3:13 (1971): 10.

34. Members of the Puerto Rican Student Union cleaned and renovated a garbage-filled lot in the South Bronx and painted the faces of Puerto Rican patriots on the side of the building overlooking it. Named *La Plaza Borinqueña,* it became a popular community space for rallies, political education classes, and film screenings.

35. Eddie Díaz, "NY: March 21," *Palante* 3:6 (1971): 8.

36. Richie Pérez, "¡Qué Viva Puerto Rico Libre!" *Palante* 3:6 (1971): 3.

37. Richie Pérez, "¡Palante, Siempre Palante!," interview by Iris Morales, *Centro Journal,* 155–56.

38. Torres and Velázquez, The *Puerto Rican Movement,* 262.

39. Iris Morales, *¡Palante, Siempre Palante! The Young Lords,* 1996. Documentary distributed by Third World Newsreel.

40. Mireya Navarro, "New Light on Old F.B.I. Fight: Decades of Surveillance of Puerto Rican Groups," *New York Times,* November 23, 2003, at http://www.nytimes.com/2003/11/28/nyregion/new-light-on-old-fbi-fight-decades-of-surveillance-of-puerto-rican-groups.html?pagewanted= all, accessed October 25, 2015.

41. Ward Churchill and Jim Vander Wall, *The COINTELPRO Papers: Documents from the FBI's Secret Wars against Domestic Dissent* (Cambridge, MA: South End Press: 1990), 69.

42. Ibid., preface by Brian Glick. x.

43. FBI memo dated May 12, 1970 in File "NY 157-4479:" 14.

44. An FBI memo dated March 11, 1971 states: "The booklets entitled 'The History of the Puerto Rican Student Union' and 'The Puerto Rican Student in New York and His Contribution to the Fight for Independence and National Liberation of Puerto Rico' were translated from Spanish by the Translation Unit of the NYO."

45. Various Freedom of Information Act files from December 1968 through December 20, 1972.

46. Kristian Williams, *Our Enemies in Blue: Police and Power in America* (Oakland, California: AK Press: 2015).

47. Stacy k. McGoldrick and Andrea McArdle, *Uniform Behavior: Police Localism and National Politics* (New York: Palgrave Macmillan: 2006), 86.

48. Professor Johanna Fernández of Baruch College filed a Freedom of Information request with the New York Police Department in 2010 seeking its records about the Young Lords. On June 16, 2016, New York City announced that it had made a "surprise" discovery of the records in a "routine inventory" of a Queens' warehouse. See Appendix.

49. Juan González, "The Young Lords Party," in *The Young Lords: A Reader,* ed., Darrel Enck-Wanzer (New York: New York University Press, 2010), 61.

50. Ten-Point Health Program in *The Young Lords: A Reader*, ed., Darrel Enck-Wanzer (New York: New York University Press, 2010), 188.

51. "Somos Puertorriqueños y Estamos Despertando / We Are Puerto Ricans, and We Are Walking Up," Puerto Rican Student Union Pamphlet, 1970.

52. Young Lords Party Central Committee, July 1971 Retreat Report, 4.

53. Ibid., 2.

54. Ibid., 7.

55. Ibid.

56. Richie Pérez, "¡Palante, Siempre Palante!," interview by Iris Morales, 150.

57. Young Lords Party Central Committee, "Evaluation and Retreat Report," December 1970, 9.

58. Young Lords Party Central Committee, July 1971 Retreat Report, 6.

59. Young Lords Party Central Committee, communiqué, meeting of December 7-28, 1971, 1.

60. Young Lords Party and Abramson, *Palante: Young Lords Party* (1971); reprinted as *Palante: Voices and Photographs of the Young Lords, 1969–1971* (2011).

61. Juan González, "*On Our Errors*," *Palante* 4:4 (1972): 12.

62. Pablo Guzmán. "La Vida Pura: A Lord of the Barrio" in *The Norton Anthology of Latino Literature*, ed. Ilan Stavans (New York: W.W. Norton & Company, 2011), 1456.

63. Pablo "Yoruba" Guzmán, "Our Present Situation: Statement, Analysis, Suggestions," November 10, 1971.

64. Ibid., See also, Pablo "Yoruba" Guzmán, Report to the Central Committee, December 7, 1971.

65. Guzmán. "La Vida Pura," 1456.

66. Young Lords Party Central Committee, communiqué, meeting of December 7-28, 1971. "Introduction: Deviations in Party Line."

67. Torres and Velázquez, *The Puerto Rican Movement*, 118.

68. Young Lords Party Central Committee, "Faction leaves Young Lords Party," *Palante,* 4:2 (1972): special edition.

69. Puerto Rican Revolutionary Workers Organization, "Resolutions and Speeches," First Party Congress, November 1972, New York: 31-32.

70. Young Lords Party Central Committee, Elections Report, (Recommendations of persons to be appointed to the Central Committee of the Puerto Rican Revolutionary Workers Organization) July 1972. Cruz is described as a cadre-in-training. 5.

71. Puerto Rican Revolutionary Workers Organization, "Resolutions and Speeches." First Party Congress. November 1972, New York City, 31.

72. Ibid., 10.

73. Guzmán. "La Vida Pura," 1458.

74. Richie Pérez, "¡Palante, Siempre Palante!," interview by Iris Morales, Centro Journal 21:2 (Fall 2009): 155–56.

75. Ibid., 153.

76. Guzmán. "La Vida Pura," 1459.

77. Anonymous Former PRRWO cadre, "The Degeneration of PRRWO: From Revolutionary Organization to Neo-Trotskyite Sect," 1976.

78. Puerto Rican Forum, *A Study of Poverty Conditions in the New York Puerto Rican Community* (New York: Puerto Rican Forum, 1970).

79. Acosta-Belén and Santiago, *Puerto Ricans in the United States,* 115.

80. Carmen Teresa Whalen and Victor Vásquez-Hernández, eds., *The Puerto Rican Diaspora: Historical Perspectives* (Philadelphia: Temple University Press, 2005), 35.

81. Min Hyoung Song. *Strange Future: Pessimism and the 1992 Los Angeles Riots.* (Durham, NC: Duke University Press, 2005), 45-58.

82. Matthew Gandy. *Concrete and Clay, Reworking Nature in New York City,* (Cambridge, MA: MIT Press, 2002), 181

83. Anonymous Former PRRWO cadre, "The Degeneration of PRRWO: From Revolutionary Organization to Neo-Trotskyite Sect," 1976.

84. Gandy, *Concrete and Clay,* 181.

85. Barbara Ransby, "Ella Taught Me: Shattering the Myth of the Leaderless Movement," *Portside,* June 12, 2015, at http://portside.org

/2015-06-15/ella-taught-me-shattering-myth-leaderless-movement, accessed June 30, 2015.

86. Ibid.

87. Lolita Lebrón, Rafael Cancel Miranda, Irving Flores Rodríguez, and Oscar Collazo had been in prison since the 1950s for the attack on Congress and the Blair house. Their sentences were commuted in 1979. Andrés Figueroa Cordero, the fifth Nationalist pardoned by President Carter, had been released earlier because he was dying from cancer.

88. The political prisoners released in 1999 included Edwin Cortés arrested in 1983 and sentenced to 35 years; Elizam Escobar arrested in 1980 and sentenced to 68 years; Ricardo Jiménez arrested in 1980 and sentenced to 98 years; Adolfo Matos arrested in 1980 and sentenced to 78 years; Dylcia Pagán arrested in 1980 and sentenced to 63 years; Alberto Rodríguez arrested in 1983 and sentenced to 35 years; Alicia Rodríguez arrested in 1980 and sentenced to 85 years; Ida Luz Rodríguez arrested in 1980 and sentenced to 83 years; Luis Rosa arrested in 1980 and sentenced to 105 years; Alejandrina Torres arrested in 1983 and sentenced to 35 years; and Carmen Valentín arrested in 1980 and sentenced to 98 years.

PART 2.
PALANTE SIEMPRE REFLECTIONS

"The Excitement Was in the Streets!"

1. The Deacons for Defense and Justice formed in 1964 to protect members of the Congress of Racial Equality against Ku Klux Klan violence. Most members were World War II or Korean War veterans. Their confrontation with the Klan in Bogalusa, Louisiana, forced the federal government to intervene on behalf of the African American community. The Deacons emerged as one of the first visible self-defense forces in the South. They effectively provided protection for African Americans who sought to register to vote and for white and black civil rights workers.

2. Comandos Armados de Liberación (CAL, the Armed Commandos of Liberation) and Movimiento Independentista Revolucionario Armado (MIRA, the Armed Revolutionary Independence Movement) were clandestine groups active in Puerto Rico in the late sixties through the mid-seventies. They targeted property: US military installations, police sta-

tions, federal agencies, US banks, and department stores seeking to end US colonial control and domination.

3. The SS *Marine Tiger* passenger ship brought thousands of Puerto Ricans from San Juan to Brooklyn from June 1946 through 1947.

"Woman, Dominican, and Young Lord"

1. The Mirabal sisters (Minerva, Mate, Patria, and Dedé) were activists opposed to the regime of Rafael Leonidas Trujillo in the Dominican Republic. Trujillo ordered three of the women assassinated, and they became heroines in the fight against his dictatorship. One sister, Dedé Mirabal, survived to tell the story.

2. The Fort Hood Three—James Johnson, David Samas, and Dennis Mora—US Army soldiers stationed at Fort Hood, Texas, refused to be deployed to Vietnam in 1966, saying they would not participate in "a war of extermination." They were court-martialed and jailed for two years.

"The Final Days and The Struggle Continues"

1. "English Only" refers to efforts to make English the only official language in the United States. Attempts seek Anglo-conformity by terminating services in other languages. See Sandra Del Valle, *Language Rights and the Law in the United States: Finding Our Voices (Bilingual Education and Bilingualism)* (Clevedon, England: Multilingual Matters, 2003).

CONTRIBUTORS

PALANTE SIEMPRE REFLECTIONS

The interviews were conducted for the documentary ¡Palante, Siempre Palante! The Young Lords in 1995 and were edited for Through the Eyes of Rebel Women, The Young Lords: 1969-1976.

Martha Arguello (Duarte) was an early member of the Young Lords Organization in East Harlem, one of the first women in the Defense Ministry, later transferred to the Lower East Side branch. Ms. Arguello wrote "Women, Dominican, and Young Lord" in 2015 for inclusion in this book. Currently, she is a college professor of history in southern California.

Diana Caballero was a member of Puerto Rican Revolutionary Workers Organization. She was an educator and an organizer for the release of Puerto Rican political prisoners. Ms. Caballero was the first woman president of the National Congress for Puerto Rican Rights. Currently, she is a clinical associate professor in New York City specializing in curriculum and teaching.

Denise Oliver-Vélez was the first woman on the Central Committee of the Young Lords Party and a founding leader of the Women's Caucus. In addition to her interview, the book includes Ms. Oliver-Vélez's essay, "Colonized Mentality and Non-Conscious Ideology (1969)." Currently, she is a college professor in New York specializing in cultural anthropology and a writer for the blog, Daily Kos.

Gloria Rodríguez (Santiago) joined the Young Lords Party in the Lower East Side branch and subsequently transferred to Philadelphia where she was a coleader of the branch. Currently, Ms. Rodríguez is a college professor of psychology in New York City and the founder of DeAlmas Women's Institute.

Minerva Solla joined the Young Lords Party in the Lower East Side branch and was among the first women in the Defense Ministry. Currently, Ms. Solla is a union organizer in the health care industry and has participated in workers' campaigns across the United States.

PALANTE ARTICLES

Copies of *Palante,* the Young Lords' newspaper, are archived at the Center for Puerto Rican Studies at Hunter College of the City University of New York and at The Tamiment Library and Robert F. Wagner Archives at New York University.

Mecca Adai was a member of Young Lords in the Information Ministry in the Bronx branch. Ms. Adai was a leading member of the team that produced *Palante.*

Blanca Canales (1906-1996) submitted "Message from Blanca Canales" to *Palante* to express solidarity with the 1970 march to the United Nations demanding the decolonization of Puerto Rico. Ms. Canales was a leader of the Nationalist Party of Puerto Rico and spent seventeen years in prison for her political beliefs and activities.

Gloria Colón was a member of the Young Lords Party in the Education Ministry in New York. She was assigned to Puerto Rico in 1971 and was a leading member of the YLP branch in El Caño, Santurce.

Connie Cruz (Morales) joined the Young Lords during the first People's Church and was one of the first women in the Defense Ministry. She worked out of both the East Harlem and the Bronx branches.

Jenny Figueroa joined the Lower East Side branch of the Young Lords Party and was a leading member of the Information Ministry.

Lulu Rovira was a member of the YLP Ministry of Economic Development and an initial member of the Central Committee of the Puerto Rican Revolutionary Workers Organization.

Other women in the Young Lords wrote for *Palante,* among them: Micky Agrait, Bernadette Baken, Iris Benítez, Lulu Carreras, Aida Cruset, Mirta González, Beverly Kruset, Elsie López, Iris López, Letty Lozano, Myrna Martínez, Nydia Mercado, Carmen Mercado, Raquel Merced, Luisa Ramírez, Isa Ríos, Olguie Robles, Heidy Ruiz, Lydia Silva, Cleo Silvers, Becky Serrano, and Miriam Rodríguez.

INDEX

Bold page numbers refer to illustrations.

ABOUT THE AUTHOR AND EDITOR

IRIS MORALES is an educator and longtime activist. She brings her legacy of social justice activism to her work with young people, teachers, and media producers on projects promoting human rights and the decolonization of Puerto Rico. For thirty years, Ms. Morales has built organizations dedicated to grassroots organizing, community empowerment, and media education. As the founder and executive editor of Red Sugarcane Press, she publishes books about the Puerto Rican and Latino/a diasporas in the Americas.

Ms. Morales was a member of the Young Lords for five years serving as the organization's deputy minister of education, cofounder of its Women's Caucus and Women's Union, and coleader of the Philadelphia chapter. Her interviews and writings about the Young Lords have appeared in numerous books and magazines. She is also the producer, writer, and codirector of the award-winning documentary, *¡Palante, Siempre Palante! The Young Lords,* which premiered on national public television and has screened across the United States and the Caribbean.

Ms. Morales travels nationally as a public speaker at colleges, universities, and community venues. She is an attorney, a graduate of New York University School of Law, and earned an MFA in Integrated Media Arts from Hunter College in New York.

ABOUT RED SUGARCANE PRESS, INC.

RED SUGARCANE PRESS, INC., established in 2012, is an independent press dedicated to presenting the history and culture of the Puerto Rican, Latino/Latina, and African diasporas in the Americas. Its mission is to publish authors whose distinct voices and artistic styles deepen and broaden our knowledge about history and contemporary social, political, and cultural issues, and introduce forgotten or unknown stories from the journey of indigenous and African people in the Americas who from enslavement to the present have triumphed through the courage and tenacity of many generations.

RED SUGARCANE PRESS is dedicated to the exchange of ideas and perspectives toward advancing a more humane and just world.

www.RedSugarcanePress.com
facebook.com/redsugarcanepress

Printed in the USA
CPSIA information can be obtained
at www.ICGtesting.com
LVHW010550191223
766839LV00003B/17